The Tragic Middle

THE TRAGIC MIDDLE

Racine, Aristotle, Euripides

Richard E. Goodkin

The University of Wisconsin Press

The University of Wisconsin Press
114 North Murray Street
Madison, Wisconsin 53715

3 Henrietta Street
London WC2E 8LU, England

5 4 3 2 1

Printed in the United States of America

Library of Congress Cataloging-in-Publication Data
Goodkin, Richard E.
    The tragic middle : Racine, Aristotle, Euripides /
  Richard E. Goodkin.
    222 pp.   cm.
    Includes bibliographical references and index.
    ISBN 0-299-13080-0
    1. Racine, Jean, 1639–1699–Sources. 2. Racine, Jean,
  1639–1699–Knowledge–Literature.
  3. French drama (Tragedy)–Greek influences.
  4. Mythology, Greek, in literature. 5. Euripides–Influence.
  6. Aristotle–Influence.   I. Title.
  PQ1907.G66   1991
  842'.4–dc20   91-3595
                          CIP

For my mother, with love

Contents

Acknowledgments

The research for this book was completed thanks to two grants from the National Endowment for the Humanities, a summer stipend in 1983 and a year-long fellowship in 1984–85. The book was finished during the course of a Yale University Senior Faculty Fellowship which I held in 1988–89. My thanks to the French Department at Yale for their support.

A version of chapter 10 appeared in *Poétique* 67 (September 1986): 349–70 under the title "Racine en marge d'Aristote: *Phèdre* et le milieu exclu." A shorter version of chapter 8, on Racine's *Iphigénie,* forms a section of an article entitled *"Killing Order(s):* Iphigenia and the Detection of Tragic Intertextuality," *Yale French Studies* 76 (1989): 81–107. The theoretical framework based on Racine's reading of Aristotle is also used in an article entitled "Racine and the Excluded Third (Person): *Britannicus, Bérénice, Bajazet,* and the Tragic 'Milieu,' " which was published in *Continuum* 2 (1990): 107–49.

I would like to thank various teachers, students, and colleagues. Froma Zeitlin of Princeton University taught me how to read tragedy in several remarkable seminars on Greek tragedy in 1976–78. I taught several seminars on tragedy at Yale, and among the many students, both graduate and undergraduate, who made that experience a particularly rewarding one, I think of Karen Erickson, John Gallucci, Lisa Gosselin, Erec Koch, Jay Lutz, Karen McPherson, and Jonathan Towers. Teaching in the Directed Studies program at Yale helped to focus my ideas about tragedy, and I thank Tom Gould, Sheila Murnaghan, Greg Thalmann, and Susanne Wofford for innumerable discussions about works ranging from the tragedies of Aeschylus to those of Goethe. Among the many colleagues whose support and encouragement have been a godsend are: Ora Avni, Faith Beasley, Claudia Brodsky, Peter Brooks, Joan DeJean, Ned Duval, Shoshana Felman, Liliane Greene, Tom Greene, Jacques Guicharnaud, Philippe Hamon, Elizabeth MacArthur, Elaine Marks, Georges May, Michael Metteer, Yvonne Ozzello, Charles Porter, David Lee Rubin, and Domna Stanton.

I would like to give special thanks to William Levitan of Princeton University and to Barbara Fowler of the University of Wisconsin–Madison for their extraordinarily careful reading of the manuscript and their invaluable suggestions for improvement.

Finally, thanks to Charlie and to my family for their boundless support over the years.

The Tragic Middle

Introduction

It is difficult not to begin *in medias res* when the *medium* is the *res*. If tragedy is the genre which, more than any other, begins in the middle of things, during a crisis which has been building since some undefined cause or "beginning" and which will subsequently demand some sort of resolution or "ending," it is nonetheless a genre which takes place in a middle time of irresolution, caught between a backward-looking exploration of the causes of its crisis and a forward-directed search for a solution. And if tragedy takes place in a sort of zero point of human time—the clocks stopped and the heartbeat postponed in the anticipation and the uncertainty of what is to come—it is also a unified, concentrated representation of something that has been going on for years, decades, even centuries, a crystallization of a situation that typifies the way in which irresolvable human problems can be and must be put off from generation to generation, and yet must also periodically come to a head.

It is my belief that tragedy is in fact a genre, that across the centuries and across national, linguistic, and cultural boundaries there are important elements shared by the works of tragedians as varied as Aeschylus, Shakespeare, Corneille, and Goethe—to mention only a very few names—even when they are not conscious of working within a single, strictly defined tradition. Meaningful links may undoubtedly exist even between writers who are not at all aware of each other's work, although as it happens, very direct and obvious connections do exist between the two playwrights I have chosen to study in this book: Racine was an avid reader and imitator of Euripides, whose works he read in the original Greek and to whom he turned more often as a source of inspiration than to any other playwright, ancient or modern. But it is not my goal here to emphasize these direct connections between Racine and Euripides. My aim is not to do the sort of comparative study which might point out surface resemblances or differences. Rather, I would like to use the "shared" works of Racine and Euripides—the four pairs of plays in which the two tragedians deal with the same myth—in the elaboration of a tragic discourse, a discourse centered on the problem of the middle.

The source of this problem is not a tragedian, nor even a playwright, but rather a philosopher, Aristotle. Now Aristotle has for centuries been linked with the study of tragedy, but almost exclusively through his famous *Poetics*. And yet many critics have felt that Aristotle's attempt at classifying tragedies using the kinds of clear, stable categories which form the foundation of his general method of philosophical inquiry is not always

3

satisfactory. The spirit of tragedy is not as compatible with a self-consciously systematic thinker like Aristotle as it is to someone like Plato, whose need to ban tragedy from his ideal state is an incredibly perceptive reading of the power of tragedy—even if it is, fortunately, not the only conceivable reaction one might have to that power. By contrast Aristotle appears to shrink from any conscious recognition of the full power of tragedy: for example, he claims that contradiction in tragedy is merely a criterion by which the critic can condemn the tragedian (*Poetics,* XXV), whereas the contradictory and paradoxical nature of human experience is, I believe, one of tragedy's most fundamental premises. Thus the *Poetics* is for my purposes not a central text; I find it an interesting text and a useful one to read, and I have certainly tried not to overlook Racine's interest in it, but it is not an integral part of the theoretical formulation I am trying to elaborate here.

In what context, then, can one link the works of a systematic, abstract thinker like Aristotle with the tragedies of Euripides and Racine? An important current in recent literary criticism has been the reemphasis on contextualization in the study of works of literature. I say "reemphasis" because in fact before the advent of new criticism, structuralism, and poststructuralism, it was quite usual for literary studies in general—and studies of Classical and Neoclassical tragedy in particular—to highlight the ways in which a given work of literature reflected its historical, cultural, and political setting, that is, to use the work of literature essentially as a historical artifact. There was certainly something to be gained from this way of approaching literature: every work of literature undoubtedly bears a complex and interesting relation to the society which gave rise to it. But this kind of historical approach also had severe limitations. It implicitly subordinated literary texts to various nonliterary domains, and suggested that texts were valuable only insofar as they reflected a reality outside of themselves.

What the criticism of the past few decades has stressed is the autonomy of the text and its workings, independently of its context. A book like Roland Barthes' *Sur Racine* (1963) is exemplary in this, as it analyzes recurrent structures in Racine's plays without extensive reference to the historical and cultural context in which Racine was working. And in fact critics like Barthes have run up against tremendous resistance in the fields of Classical and Neoclassical literature—one has only to think of the polemic set off by *Sur Racine* and Raymond Picard's response to it, *Nouvelle Critique ou nouvelle imposture?* (1965). One of the reasons for this resistance is precisely that these are fields which have traditionally drawn attention to the links between works of literature and their historical context, so that any attempt at reading works independently of their context has been seen by some as failing to do justice to the works.

Is the current reemphasis on contextualization nothing more than a turning back of the clocks? Does the criticism of contextualization suggest that structuralism and poststructuralism were merely regrettable errors, and that it is now time to get back to serious (i.e., historically based) study of literature and to leave behind fanciful (i.e., analytical) approaches to literary works?

Perhaps a few critics might believe this is so, but I would warrant most do not, and I would certainly count myself among the ranks of those who find the methods of reading set forth by structuralist and poststructuralist criticism invaluable. Contextualization need not be—and should not be—a simple return to earlier approaches to literature. Rather, it should take advantage of the methods and techniques pioneered by structuralism even as it examines works of literature in their contexts. Traditional historical criticism essentially came to literature asking what the historical context of a work could tell us about it—that is, how its setting could provide a key to its meaning, could "explain" the work. The criticism of contextualization should reverse this procedure—and, more important, the prioritization it implies—by asking what a text can tell us about its context through its very literariness, its functioning as a literary artifact and nothing else. What this approach incorporates from structuralism and poststructuralism is the basic autonomy of the text, and consequently the specificity of literature: even though the text is related to a context, the workings of the text stand on their own. What the text says, it says as only a work of literature could say it. And it is only once we have established what we believe the text to be saying—and, at least as important, how it is saying it—that we can make fruitful connections to the extraliterary domain.

Another difference between contextualization and traditional historical approaches to literature is the nature of the contexts in question. Historical approaches to literature generally assumed that a given work could be situated in a particular historical context without problematizing the question of the context itself, without recognizing the fact that establishing a context is already a way of taking a position. For example, how do we as twentieth-century readers define the context of Euripides' or Racine's work? Do we look at Euripides' relation to the social and political institutions of the Athenian polis, and if so, which ones? Or do we examine his relation to his fellow tragedians, Aeschylus and Sophocles? Do we consider Racine's close ties to the court of Louis XIV as primordial, or his affiliation with the Jansenists? Or, in fact, his relation to Euripides?

It is one of my premises in this book that contextualization studies need not be limited to the historical, that writers work in a cultural, aesthetic, and philosophical context as well as a historical and political one. It is clear that studying Racine in relation to Jansenism or Louis XIV—as critics like Lucien Goldmann and Jean-Marie Apostolidès have done—can be rewarding. In the realm of the history of aesthetics, it is also clear that Racine's works bear a close relation to those of contemporaries like Corneille and Molière, just as a number of Euripides' plays can be understood as responses to Aeschylus or Sophocles. But are Racine's intellectual and aesthetic "others" limited to an immediate historical context, France in the 1660s and 1670s? Or can the thinkers of antiquity whose works he read and commented upon not also be said to form the context within which he wrote his tragedies?

Now Racine apparently did own a copy of the complete works of Aristotle (in Greek and Latin), and, as we shall see, he wrote marginal comments on certain key passages from the *Nicomachean Ethics* which speak about the middle. But here once again, I would like to go beyond this immediate context: my discussion of Aristotle will include texts with which Racine very possibly was not familiar. In any case the section on Aristotle which establishes the terms of the subsequent analyses of the plays, chapter 2, is meant to stand on its own, even though it takes Racine's reading of Aristotle as a starting point. In some sense what for me ultimately justifies using certain elements from the Greek philosopher's work in a study of tragedy is less Racine's familiarity with Aristotle than the applicability of those elements to a discussion of tragedy. And it is, of course, only insofar as the readings of the plays teach us something about tragedy—as well as about the plays themselves—that that applicability can be judged.

The context that is thus formed is not only a cultural, aesthetic, and intellectual context, but also a critical context. For given the subjectivity of any contextualization—since each reader will perceive different connections between a given text and its various possible contexts—all literary contexts are established (perhaps "hypothesized" would be a more accurate term here) by the critic. In the end the validity of a given contextualization ought to be judged as a function of the validity of the analyses which result from it.

Thus contextualization studies have the potential to reverse the priorities of traditional historical approaches to literature by asking what the text can tell us about the context rather than asking how the context can account for the text. Analogously, I have tried to approach Aristotle with the lessons of tragedy in mind rather than simply approaching tragedy through the lessons of Aristotle. It is perhaps partly for this reason that I have found in Aristotle the sort of conflict which I believe fundamentally characterizes tragedy. Before proceeding to a closer examination of Racine's relation to Aristotle in chapter 1, I would like to discuss briefly the ways in which my use of Aristotle is determined by the tragic context in which I am studying his works.

The conflict which defines the tragic middle is created by two distinct visions of the middle in Aristotle: the virtuous middle of moderation in the *Nicomachean Ethics* and the logical middle (the law of excluded middle) in the *Metaphysics*. Aristotle himself never put these two texts together. Indeed, he is very largely responsible for the subsequent separation in philosophy between ethics and metaphysics. I want to make clear at the outset that the conflict between these two conceptions of the middle is a conflict which Aristotle does not directly address, indeed, a conflict which he very likely did not even recognize. Certainly, as I will try to make clear in my discussion of Aristotle, I am not speaking of a logical contradiction or even of a thoroughgoing inconsistency in Aristotle's thought, but rather of a hesitation in the relation between ethics and metaphysics. Although there is value in separating philosophical thought and speculation into discrete domains of inquiry, I believe there may also be value in questioning the relation between these domains, and even in doing so in ways that philosophers might not use. In fact many philosophers—among them Aristotle—certainly do address questions dealing with the articulations between the separate domains into which they have compartmentalized their thought. Aristotle himself would probably not recognize the relation between the ethical middle and the excluded middle as a conflictual one, or, more precisely, would not recognize that there might be a relation between them at all. And yet it is my conviction that considering these two parts of Aristotle's philosophy in light of each other may help to show us something which considering them separately would not show us: the very separation of ethics and metaphysics itself demands—or at the very least allows—interpretation.

The conjunction of these two texts, even though it is artificial to the extent that it is a conjunction which Aristotle himself did not make, may help us to reexamine one of the central conflicts in Aristotle's work: the conflict between theory and praxis, or between the contemplative life and the practical life, two equally central human activities. This is a conflict which, although it too is one which Aristotle avoids addressing explicitly, has drawn a good deal of critical attention. Indeed, this potential conflict may well be one of the reasons Aristotle so rigorously attempts to separate ethical questions from metaphysical questions, something which Plato, for example, does not do to the same extent. As a student of literature, I have relied heavily on the work of philosophers writing about Aristotle, and I am grateful to them for showing me the issues involved in the often problematic relation between the contemplative and the practical life. As a student of literature I also beg their indulgence as I attempt what is essentially a literary rather than a philosophical treatment of certain passages of Aristotle. When I speak of Aristotle's thought and its articulations, I am not, in many cases, speaking of the philosopher's explicit intentions. Rather, since my goal is to speculate about the elements of a theory of tragedy and to read a certain number of tragedies in the light of—or, rather, as a part of—that speculation, I have tried to look at Aristotle from a tragic perspective, for it seems to me that the difficulty of the articulation between the contemplative life and the practical life as two possible elements in a definition of the human condition has something fundamentally tragic about it.

Critically I owe a debt to the work of René Girard. I have not referred to Girard's work extensively, nor do I consider my analyses to be applications of it, but the idea of the middle as a structuring element of tragedy is undoubtedly influenced to some extent by Girard's depiction of the scapegoat, described at length in *La Violence et le sacré*. The scapegoat is a focus for a certain kind of collective energy and at the same time (and by the same token) must be excluded from the very community of which he or she is the center. As such the scapegoat, as Girard points out, bears a close relation to Attic tragedy: tragedy epitomizes certain unresolved conflicts felt by the spectators as social beings and yet in some sense also aims to relieve them (if only temporarily) of those conflicts. Moreover, Girard is to my knowledge one of the only writers about tragedy whose work not only avoids the trap of discussing this genre in unexamined moral terms, but also actively addresses the uneasy question of tragedy's moral component—uneasy partly because of the conclusions tragedy leads us to about the limitations of morality, as Girard has so convincingly demonstrated.

I would also like to acknowledge a very different kind of debt to the work of Georges Poulet. Poulet has provided me with an invaluable methodological (rather than conceptual) model: his use of the circle, in its various literary metamorphoses, has helped me to see the possibilities of using what is to some extent an extraliterary structure to define a literary problem. The very power of Poulet's circle is that in different literary contexts it can take on a tremendous variety of forms and values. I have tried to follow Poulet in allowing the concept of the tragic middle the flexibility, the power of metamorphosis, which is to my mind one of the central attributes of literature.

I would like to speak briefly of the organization of this study. The first section, "The Problem of the Middle," is principally concerned with the theoretical formulation of the problem and the setting out of the terms of the analyses that follow. In this section I do not wish to draw or even look ahead to any conclusions, but rather simply to establish the terms and the "stakes—what the French would call *l'enjeu*—of the analyses. I have tried to use the Aristotle texts to define a problem whose principal value for me resides in its power to provide a complex and flexible framework for discussing the tragedies, rather than in any possibility of an easy solution.

I have chosen this rather open-ended structure partly to avoid the impression of overdetermination which I find is given by much criticism about tragedy in general, and Racine in particular. Perhaps this frequent "fatality" of readings of tragedy in turn stems from the feeling of overdetermination which many believe essentially characterizes the tragic universe, especially in the case of a writer like Racine, who was undoubtedly influenced by the fatalism of the Jansenists.

Although I would agree that tragedy generally presents the human condition as one of impingement, constraint, and conflicting demands, I do not believe that its most fundamental impression is one of futility or predetermination. Rather, what I will be emphasizing in my analyses is the necessity—and at some level even the value—of conflict in tragedy. Even though there is almost always a feeling in tragedy that no adequate solution to the conflicts at hand can be imagined, the tragic hero or heroine does everything possible to avoid giving in even to irreconcilable conflicts. Analogously, what I would like to bring out in the analyses themselves is the clash of conflicting forces whose outcome cannot be known ahead of time and often remains basically unresolved even retrospectively.

The middle section, "Readings in the Tragic Middle," is the elaboration of the conflict set forth in the first section, the combination and recombination of the terms that make up that conflict as they apply to the plays in question. I have made only minimal direct reference to Euripides in the Racine chapters and vice versa. Each chapter is meant to stand on its own as a reading of the play in question, and at the same time to contribute to developing patterns which will eventually become discernible.

I have refrained from calling the last section the "Conclusion" because, as I hope will become clear by the end of my analysis of Racine's *Phèdre,* one of the lessons of the tragic middle is that once one has seen it for what it is, one can never fully escape from it. The tragic "milieu" is just that, an environment, a unity (or rather disunity) of place which one can enter but not leave; the tragic middle allows of no true end.

The concept of the tragic middle will thus not be that of a *milieu* in any historical or sociological sense, for example in the sense that Taine speaks of "milieu" and "moment" as factors which largely predetermine the work of art. Rather it will be a reflection about tragedy as an environment, a *medium* of communication which endlessly absorbs and deflects the irreconcilable demands of the tragic universe without ever letting its inhabitants fully escape.

Finally, a word is in order about my general approach to all of the texts examined here. I have tried to respect the split between ancient and modern texts insofar as the analyses of Euripides are geared to an audience of Hellenists and those of Racine to students of French literature, although it is my hope that all of the analyses will be accessible to nonspecialists as well. It seems to me that very few studies which attempt to link ancient and modern texts do so in an even-handed way, without "taking sides." In studies of Racine and Euripides this usually entails either making Euripides into a figure whose principal purpose at times seems to be to lead to Racine or exposing Racine as a pallid imitator of Euripides. I have tried to avoid doing either of these things, and rather to treat Euripides and Racine as aesthetic equals.

Another of my goals is to draw attention to the tragedies' particular and marvelous use of language, not through specifically stylistic analyses of the plays, but rather through a sensitivity to the recurrence of certain key terms which because of their strategic repetition take on a peculiar resonance. This is undoubtedly the case with Euripides' drama as well, but I believe that it is especially true of Racine's plays. The very form which Racine uses, the rigorously regular alexandrine, with its unfailing twelve-syllable line alternating, without exception, between masculine and feminine rhymes, does a great deal to train the ear as well as the eye to listen or look for recurring patterns. Moreover Racine's extraordinarily restrained vocabulary throws these patterns into relief: anyone knowing Racine's works well who consults Freeman and Batson's extremely useful concordance to Racine has probably had the experience of feeling as if he or she recognized with an almost uncanny familiarity each occurrence of a particular term listed, as if the lines were still ringing in the ears. Racine uses few words, and unlike Shakespeare, whose elaborate and inventive language spans many registers, he limits himself almost exclusively to quite common words, repeating them in endlessly varying combinations, like a kind of kaleidoscope made up of few colors which become all the more striking as they appear to take on different qualities in different contexts.

All of this is simply to say that one of the ways I have tried to focus attention on this peculiar linguistic quality of the tragedies, by which a single word uttered in a particular context can crystallize the conflicts of many previous lines, is by trying to use language as a kind of network in my own analyses. This involves repeating key terms in different combinations; it also means aiming for a self-consciousness of language which I believe is very much in the spirit of tragedy. Such an approach inevitably leads, at times, to a playfulness which may at first seem at odds with the serious matters at hand. But quite apart from the fact that Euripides, and even at times Racine, can actually be quite funny—is there a more hilarious scene in European drama than the parody of Aeschylus' recognition scene between Electra and Orestes in Euripides' *Electra?*—this is meant, once again, to foster a certain awareness of linguistic patterns, a willingness to look at a single term backwards, or upside-down, or inside-out in order to view it from a number of different perspectives.

For if there is a single lesson that tragedy can teach us—and it will be precisely the lesson of Aristotle's two incompatible theories of middles—it is the impossibility, or at least the danger, of going through life with a single perspective.

Part 1
The Problem of the Middle

Thou hast pared thy wit o' both sides and left nothing in the middle.
— Shakespeare, *King Lear*

1

Racine and the Classical Middle

> A virtue has been made of moderation in order to limit great men's ambi-
> tions, and to console mediocre people over their paltry fortune and their
> paltry worth.
>
> La Rochefoucauld, Maximes

Numerous are those who have divided the life and career of Jean Racine
into three elegant, almost geometrical parts.[1] The first period, from the poet's
birth until his break with Port-Royal (1639–63), covers Racine's youth and
education, the main influence during this time being the Jansenists, with
whom his family was closely linked. After Racine's falling out with his
spiritual masters, he spent the next fourteen years (1663–77) leading the
life of a theatrical writer in Paris. This middle period includes nearly all
of Racine's tragedies, nine out of eleven, or all of the "profane" plays. Finally, in 1677, immediately after presenting *Phèdre,* Racine accepts the
position of historiographer royal to Louis XIV, obeys Louis's request that
he stop writing tragedies and is thereby (ironically) also reconciled with
Port-Royal, and marries a pious young woman, thus initiating by this triply concerted gesture of order the third phase of his life, going from 1677
up to his death in 1699. In the case of Racine, then, the theatrical "milieu"
carries a mathematical as well as a social meaning: this is a theater which
is the product of a biographical "milieu" or middle.

   Even if we don't go so far as to see the symmetry of Racine's biography —
and more specifically the position of his theater in the very middle of his
life — as an example of Classical measure and equilibrium,[2] in many ways
Racine appears to offer a model of Classical moderation. Karl Vossler speaks
of the man's respect for moderation in all things: "He was a fundamentally
modest person. . . . It was Racine's way and his destiny to hope and try,
again and again, by dint of his own pliability and his capacity for compromise and renunciation, to escape collision with public opinion and

powers. . . . Racine was not a man of violent resolutions; it was his habit to avoid everything radical."[3] Vossler's portrait, although it lacks the detail and *piquant* of one of La Bruyère's *Caractères,* puts one in mind of an *honnête homme* of the sort described at length by such seventeenth-century writers as Nicolas Faret and the Chevalier de Méré. The central tenet of the *honnête homme* is the avoidance of any extreme position, the espousal of moderation and adaptability as the necessary tools for virtually all social interaction. Perhaps it is not surprising that Racine, who wrote during a period which saw a considerable reaction against the artistic excesses of the early part of the seventeenth century, should present this sort of image of moderation.

Racine's seeming moderation is also apparent in his aesthetic theory. His commentaries and translations of Aristotle's *Poetics*—which along with the prefaces to his plays are virtually the only indications we have of what might be called an *ars poetica* of Racine—emphasize the importance of moderation: "La tragédie est l'imitation d'une action grave et complète, et qui a sa (juste) grandeur."[4] The word which Racine adds here is "juste," since Aristotle's text merely says that tragedy has "magnitude" [megethos]. "La juste grandeur" of tragedy is an heir to "le juste milieu," the golden mean, the Classical doctrine of moderation in all things. Is this not an indication that Racine approaches tragedy with an eminently Classical respect for moderation?

When Racine does recognize the need for excess in tragedy, he does so in order to negate it: "Il faut donc que [le héros tragique] soit un homme qui soit entre les deux, c'est-à-dire qui ne soit point extrêmement juste et vertueux, et qui ne mérite point aussi son malheur par (un excès de) méchanceté" (2:925). What Racine emphasizes in his translation is extremity: the "excess" of badness is his addition, and even the phrase "*extrêmement* juste et vertueux" is a very loose translation of Aristotle's text, "mete arete diapheron kai dikaiosyne," which merely means "not standing out [etymologically, not "differing"] in virtue and justice." Extremity and excess, Racine's interpolations here, are called forth only to be denied: the tragic hero, who is in a middle position ("entre les deux"), must mediate between "extreme" virtue and "excessive" evil, thus affirming the middle by refusing the two extremes.

It is not only the tragic hero but also tragedy itself which must be "moderate": "([La tragédie] ne se fait) point par un récit, mais par une représentation vive qui, excitant la pitié et la terreur, purge (et tempère) ces sortes de passions. (C'est-à-dire qu'en émouvant ces passions, elle leur ôte ce qu'elles ont d'excessif et de vicieux, et les ramène à un état modéré et conforme à la raison)" (2:923). Racine's first insertion here, "tempère," once again points to tragedy's moderating function, and his commentary makes this explicit. The goal of tragedy would appear to be to use the excesses of pity and terror in order to rid the audience of these very excesses, "to bring them back to a moderate state in conformance with reason." That moderation is implicitly synonymous with virtue here is clear in the pairing of "excessif" and "vicieux"; if excess is a vice, surely moderation is a virtue. Can this, then, be the value of Racine's theatrical "milieu" or middle? Is the keystone of his theory of tragedy the simple purgation of excess and the reaching of a state of virtuous moderation, a kind of moralizing catharsis? Is the theatrical middle a virtuous middle?

In order to begin to answer these questions, let us turn to another of Aristotle's texts with which Racine was familiar: the *Nicomachean Ethics*. Racine's marginalia in his copy of the *Ethics* draw our attention to a small but extremely interesting selection of translated and annotated passages,[5] beginning with what might be called a definition of the virtuous middle of moderation:

Strength is destroyed both by excessive and by deficient exercises, and similarly health is destroyed both by too much and by too little food and drink; while they are produced, increased and preserved by suitable quantities. (*Nicomachean Ethics*, II, ii, 6, 1104a16–18)[6]

There are then three dispositions—two vices, one of excess and one of defect, and one virtue which is the observance of the mean [mesotes, "middle"]. (II, viii, 1, 1108b14–15; Rackham, p. 107)

The goals of strength and health are here representative of the larger ethical goals of virtue: the virtuous middle is based upon the principle of avoiding the extremes of deficiency and excess.

But if the Classical middle is to some extent based on an ethical (as well as an aesthetic) middle of moderation, tragedy severely challenges that ethical middle. As Jean-François Marmontel puts it, "The first rule [of tragedy] is that the alternatives have no middle-point."[7] Racine's further translations of Aristotle's text suggest that using moderation as a guiding principle may mean having to choose the less objectionable of two extremes, as a sort of *pis-aller:*

For of the two extremes one is a more serious error [hamartoloteron] than the other. Hence, inasmuch as to hit the mean extremely well is difficult, the second best way to sail . . . is to take the least of the evils. . . . (*Nicomachean Ethics*, II, ix, 4, 1109a33–35; Rackham, p. 111)

Il faut d'abord fuir les extrémités les plus vicieuses. — Et surtout celles auxquelles nous penchons le plus. (2:933)

If each of the extremes is an "error" — "hamartoloteron" recalling tragic "hamartia" — then it is not surprising that tragedy is based on this kind of "error": the doctrine of the virtuous middle is at least implicitly dependent on the concept of choice (*Nicomachean Ethics,* III, ii), and insofar as tragic choice precludes any idea of a compromise, of a mediation between two alternatives which are both experienced as unacceptable extremes by the character who must choose between them, it is precisely in the domain of *tragic* choice that the doctrine of the virtuous middle becomes insufficient. Another of Racine's notes to the *Ethics* in fact comments on the limitations of choice: "[Le] choix ne convient pas à tout. Mais il (*ce choix*) est des choses qui dépendent de nous" (2:933).

Tragedy tells us, as no other genre does, that even though not everything depends on us, even though we are acted upon and constrained by forces beyond our control, nonetheless we must *make unmakable choices.* And indeed, Racine's translations of the doctrine of the virtuous middle come to resemble proverbs drawn from the sufferings of a tragic hero forced to choose between two incompatible extremes:[8]

[M]oral virtue is a mean . . . because it aims at hitting the middle point in feelings and in actions [tou mesou . . . tou en tois pathesi kai tais praxesin]. This is why it is a hard task to be good, for it is hard to find the middle point in anything. (*Nicomachean Ethics,* II, ix, 1–2, 1109a20–26; Rackham, p. 111)

Il est bien difficile d'être vertueux et de choisir le milieu. (2:933)

One should lean sometimes to the side of excess and sometimes to that of deficiency, since this is the easiest way of hitting the mean and the right course. (*Nicomachean Ethics,* II, ix, 9, 1109b24–26, p. 115)

Il faut tantôt prendre une extrémité et tantôt l'autre. (2:933)

It may be a "hard task" to find the middle point in anything, but tragedy shows us that it is particularly difficult to hit the middle precisely in the domains mentioned here — in feeling [pathos] and in action [praxis], which Aristotle names as two indispensable elements of tragedy.[9] Feelings, as is shown by Racine's translation of Aristotle's discussion of fear and pity in the *Poetics,* have a persistent tendency toward extremity ("ce qu'elles [ces passions, "pathematon"] ont d'excessifs et de vicieux"), and action — in tragedy at least—consists of going one way or the other, of weighing the opposing alternatives and then being forced to come down on one side.

Racine's association with Jansenism brought him into contact with various philosophical and theological formulations which problematize the middle, not least Pascal's depiction of the middle as the unbearable locus of the human condition:

> For what is man in nature? Nothingness in relation to the infinite, everything in relation to nothingness, a middle between nothing and everything, infinitely separated from any understanding of the extremes; the end of things and their principles are for him inevitably hidden in an impenetrable secret. . . .
>
> Limited, as we are, in every way, this state which holds the middle between two extremes is perceptible in all of our powers. . . .
>
> That is our true state. It is what makes us incapable of certain knowledge and of absolute ignorance. We drift along on a vast middle, always uncertain and floating, pushed from one end toward the other; whatever is the end to which we think we can attach ourselves and anchor ourselves, it shakes free and gets away from us. ("Disproportion de l'homme")[10]

Leaving the middle means leaving humanity.[11]

"Incapable of certain knowledge and of absolute ignorance," we in the middle nonetheless carry the curse of knowing one thing at least: that we are in the middle. And not only do we know that we are in the middle, but also we can never quite forget that something in us strives for the purity of the extremes. Any effort to "attach ourselves" to a stable position— the very goal of the law of excluded middle—is spoiled by our inhabiting of the middle, our being partially—although never completely—defined by its hybrid nature.

The Jansenists are in themselves extremists of a sort; in spite of humanity's median position, they see no possible mediation between the human and the divine. As Paul Bénichou puts it:

> [Jansenism wished] to cut the bridges between man and God without giving up the possibility of making them exist for each other. On the contrary, optimistic Christianity linked the natural order to the divine order by an ascending and continuous scale of perfections. Undoubtedly dogma imposed distinct levels: grace; excellent nature, virtue and knowledge; and brute nature; that is, God, Eden, fallen man. . . . But about the middle term, the heritage of Eden, there was disagreement. . . . The rehabilitation of man was expressed [according to optimistic Christianity] . . . by a tendency to erase or smooth out the heterogeneity of the orders. On the contrary, Pascal, whose point of departure is also the distinctness of the three orders, essentially views them in the perspec-

> tive of heterogeneity and discontinuity. . . . But this absolute heterogeneity is made possible only by a peculiar conception of the middle term: the separation of the orders is linked to the destruction of the intermediary order, the one which Pascals calls the order of spirits or of man's greatness. . . . All that is left is the contrast between the two opposite terms, and what has managed to persist in man's original, transitional state, far from smoothing out this contrast, presently only exaggerates it. Pascal goes even further than denying human greatness; he forces it to deny itself, to hollow out its own abyss.[12]

The Jansenist middle, the unbearable feeling of being in a middle state as unacceptable as it is irremediable, forces humanity to feel the existence of the two extremes, but allows it to do nothing to reconcile them. Humanity becomes poised above a treacherous void, a situation which the Jansenists exacerbate by reducing the mediating capabilities of the clergy and placing man, unprotected, at the mercy of a severe and judging divinity. The middle position between fallen humanity and God, the position which might potentially define humanity's greatness, the position of heroism, straddling the mortal and the divine, is reduced to the pure perception of a problem, a break, a fundamental discontinuity. Jansenist man is made to inhabit a kind of vacuum, or rather a whirlwind: it is no more possible to regulate the middle than to escape from it.

Yet Jansenist man, acutely aware of his middle position, is also ignorant of what is at the center of his being: "In the end all these [Jansenist] criticisms finally cast doubt on the value of the feeling each person may have, even if it is sincere, of his own states. . . . The result is that man becomes a being obscure to himself, ignorant of his true motives and acting without self-knowledge. The knowledge we have of ourselves reaches only the outside of our being."[13]

No one more dramatically sums up this utterly paradoxical position of humanity than the Jansenist writer Pierre Nicole, one of Racine's teachers at Port-Royal. In his famous attack on theater, *Les Visionnaires,* which Racine took as being directed against himself personally,[14] Nicole does indeed go to the "root" of mortal man's—and more specifically Racine's—problem:

> And although it is our duty to purify ourselves incessantly of all pride and self-interest, nevertheless we do not know if this very desire to be purified of self-interest does not itself come from another self-interest, albeit a more spiritual and delicate one. For one may desire out of pride to be saved from pride. An infinite and imperceptible circle is formed, a circle of endless returns and reflections in these actions of the soul, and there is always in us a certain underlying element, a certain root [une certaine racine] which remains unknown and impenetrable to us all of our lives. (Letter 27, 10 April 1666)[15]

Is this unknown "racine" not at the root of Racine's tragic middle? If the outside cannot successfully communicate with the inside, how can the middle ever be knowable? And where, in that case, is there room for the middle, or theatrical period of Racine's life to be defined as a place of virtuous moderation? Is Racine not perhaps thinking of himself and of his own attempt at forging a theory of tragedy and of tragic heroism when in another commentary on Aristotle's text he muses over the paradox of trying to reach the middle by a movement of opposition?

> [T]hen we must drag ourselves away in the opposite direction, for by steering wide of our besetting error [tou hamartanein] we shall make a middle course. This is the method adopted by carpenters to straighten warped timber. (*Nicomachean Ethics,* II, ix, 5, 1109b5–7; Rackham, p. 113)

> Comme on redresse un arbre en lui faisant prendre un pli contraire au sien. (2: 933)

One can hardly imagine a more extreme lesson in what is purportedly a treatise on moderation: whatever we are inclined to do, whichever extremity tempts us, we can be sure that we should oppose ourselves and move to the opposite extreme, for our inclination is our error ("hamartanein," again related to "hamartia").

The "radicality" of this lesson, in an etymological sense, is precisely the subject of Racine's commentary on it: if you "straighten" ("redresse") a tree — surely an image of moral uprightness and virtue — by making it oppose its natural bent, have you really got to the root ("racine") of the problem?[16] Can a tree which perpetually takes "un pli contraire au sien" bear fruit, or will it inevitably come to resemble perhaps the most moving image in all of Racine's theater, and one that seems at some level to refer to its weary author: "cet arbre séché jusque dans ses racines"?[17]

Confronted with the tension in Racine's theater between what George Steiner calls "the cool severity of the technique and the passionate drive of the material,"[18] we may well begin to wonder whether Racine's tragedy is in fact based on Classical moderation or whether, within a framework which appears to impose moderation, it is not one of the most radical expressions in the history of literature. The two possible responses to this question, each opposing the other, once again bring us to the very essence of Racine:

> Feeling pity for the misfortune of someone similar to ourselves leads us to fear a similar misfortune; this fear leads us to desire avoiding such a misfortune, and this desire leads us to purge, moderate, rectify, and even root out within

ourselves [déraciner en nous] the passion which plunges the people we pity into misfortune in front of our very eyes. (Corneille, "Discours de la tragédie")[19]

Tragic error [for Racine] will be neither a moral blemish which "deserves to be punished" [La Mesnardière], nor an unthought-out action or word, but rather a loss of direction inherent to the character which comes from an "irradicable" [irradicable] and murderous passion. (Eugène Vinaver)[20]

Even though Corneille's essay is slightly too early (1660) to provide an intentional — or even subconscious — word play on the name of Racine ("déraciner en nous"), Corneille's comments provide a brief and yet remarkably accurate description of one fundamental difference between the two rival tragedians: for Corneille, unwanted, extreme passions can be "rooted out" by tragedy through the mechanism of catharsis; in Racine, who indeed recognizes the extremity of such passions and even their "unvirtuous" nature, this is ultimately not so certain. Even if Racine aims to rid his audience of such extreme emotions, would a Racine character be a Racine character if a viable sense of moderation inhabited his or her center, if the passions within, which oppose the needs of moderate virtue, could be extricated? Or, as seems more likely, are such passions, to borrow Vinaver's term, "irradicable"?[21] Is there not something "indéracinable" at the heart of Racinian tragedy?

The problem is that the Racinian hero is at pains to empty out the secret contents of his inner being and to make what he experiences as an unmakable choice, to put an end to the ambivalence which characterizes his inner self. Georges Poulet puts it in these terms: "Instead of living in relative security, here we find Racinian man surrounded 'by arms and enemies.' But his hostile world is not simply the world of the outside. Carried by the magic of passion into an uninhabited region of their beings, Racine's characters are forced to recognize themselves literally lost within their own depths."[22] If the problem could be externalized, relegated to an outside, however hostile, it would cease to be the sort of problem that it is. What the Racinian hero is at pains to do is to break out of himself, to create himself as a being without ambivalence, a creature of a single value, the supreme heroic gesture.

There is an Aristotelian doctrine which establishes the sort of univalence which Racine's heroes — like many tragic heroes — are after: the law of excluded middle or excluded third. When one is faced with two contradictory extremes, the law of excluded middle requires us to choose one extreme or the other; there is no third solution possible that might mediate between them: "There cannot be anything between contradictory statements, but of one thing we must either assert or deny one thing, whatever it may be" (*Metaphysics*, IV, vii, 1, 1011b24–25 [trans. mine]). Although it is uncertain whether Racine knew this passage of the *Metaphysics*,[23] I would like to suggest that the issues raised by the law of excluded middle are at least as central to his tragedy as the doctrine of the virtuous middle, with its close relation to traditional definitions of Classicism.

In the tragic cosmos of Racine's plays, the failure of mediation is not simply an imposition on the hero vainly trying to evade the demands of choice; rather, the excluded middle itself expresses the hero's most profound desire, that of reaching an absolute, of finding simple answers to complex questions. But in the radicalized tragic universe, simple answers, choices of one out of two, of one extreme over the other, are not necessarily forthcoming. Here is Lucien Goldmann's description of the tragic condition: "[In tragedy] it is not a question of carrying out responsibilities 'well' in the world or using resources 'well' on the one hand, or of turning one's back on them and abandoning them on the other. Here, as everywhere, tragedy knows only one valid form of thought or attitude, the *yes and no,* paradox."[24] Where the law of excluded middle demands a yes or a no, a yes given to one contradictory extreme and a no to the other, tragedy responds "yes and no," neither affirming nor denying one thing but affirming only ambivalence itself.

If the law of excluded middle is one of the principles of Racine's tragedy, this does not mean that the middle can ever be *successfully* excluded. The excluded middle is both a problem and the appearance of a solution: since no mediation between two contradictory alternatives can be found, a single one of the two must be selected; this is what the law of excluded middle prescribes. But Racine's is a universe in which no resolution is possible between contradictory extremes. Roland Barthes puts it in this way: "[T]he world is made of pure opposites that nothing can ever mediate. . . . The absolute division of the universe . . . excludes all mediation; the Racinian world is a world with two terms, its status paradoxical rather than dialectical: the third term is lacking."[25] The absence of a salutary third term, of a middle-as-resolution, does not necessarily lead to the stability of an excluded middle. Racinian tragedy is based upon a struggle between opposites which cannot be mediated, but what this proves is not only the absence of a middle of virtuous moderation, but also the need for an application of the law of excluded middle: as we shall see, that law exists precisely in order to be used as a source of artificial stability where no authentic stability exists.

We have reached the point at which a closer examination of the Aristotelian concepts of the virtuous middle and the excluded middle is necessary. It is clear that the middle—whether Pascal's metaphysical "milieu" of the human condition or the aesthetic and ethical "juste milieu" of Classicism—creates a conflict in Racine; indeed it poses a problem for much of the French seventeenth century. But before we can approach the question of how that conflict operates in Racine's tragedy—and even how it plays a role in motivating his repeated choice of Euripides as a model for his own tragic milieu—we must understand the nature and the extent of the problem. Let us turn, then, to the relationship within Aristotle's thought between the virtuous middle and the excluded middle.

2
The Virtuous Middle and the Excluded Middle in Aristotle

> You'll never be happy if the pros and cons give you equal concern. You must take a side, and stick with it.
>
> —Diderot, *Le Neveu de Rameau*

The doctrine of virtuous moderation is the keystone of the *Nicomachean Ethics:* "First of all then we have to observe, that moral qualities are so constituted as to be destroyed by excess and by deficiency. . . . Thus Temperance and Courage are destroyed by excess and deficiency, and preserved by the observance of the mean [mesotes]" II, ii, 6–7, 1104a12–27).[1] This doctrine is representative of a very widespread belief: "Aristotle's view that moderation is good, and excess to be avoided, had been anticipated by popular morality and by poets as well as by Plato."[2] Moderation in all things is presented as a virtual panacea; exceptions may be made for domains or actions for which no moderation is possible, like murder, adultery, and other crimes which are "blamed as being bad in themselves" (II, vi, 18, 1107a13; Rackham, p. 97), but for the vast majority of life's moral choices, a human being armed with the principle of moderation is formidably armed.

Perhaps the most remarkable characteristic of this moral system is its reliance on context and position in defining moral terms, its thoroughgoing relativity. There is something eminently comforting about this moral vision. In its filtered, moderate light—the antithesis of the uncompromising glare of the investigators' lamp made familiar by that most moralizing of all modern genres, the detective novel—errors are viewed as misguided attempts, merely aimed either too high (excess) or too low (deficiency) to hit virtue, and the whole of human moral endeavor as a series of arrows trying to strike the golden bull's eye in the middle of the target of possible human actions.[3]

We thus first get the impression that reaching virtue is almost as simple

25

as calculating a mathematical mean: "By the mean [meson] of the thing I denote a point equally distant from either extreme, which is one and the same for everybody; by the mean relative to us, that amount which is neither too much nor too little, and this is not one and the same for everybody" (II, vi, 5, 1106a30–32; Rackham, p. 91). Aristotle even provides us with an example: "let 10 be many and 2 few; then one takes the mean with respect to the thing if one takes 6; since $6 - 2 = 10 - 6$, and this is the mean" (II, vi, 6–7, 1106a33–35; Rackham, p. 91). What easier arithmetical operation could be asked for as a formula for the infinitely complex issue of moral action?

And yet, problems arise even in this preliminary sketching out of virtue, as Aristotle himself recognizes: the mathematical mean may be simple, but it is not necessarily "the mean relative to us," the point of the middle-as-virtue which distinguishes and differentiates each individual:

> But we cannot arrive by this method at the mean relative to us. Suppose that 10 lb. of food is a large ration for anybody and 2 lb. a small one: it does not follow that a trainer will prescribe 6 lb., for perhaps even this will be a large ration, or a small one, for the particular athlete who is to receive it; it is a small ration for a Milo, but a large one for a man just beginning to go in for athletics. (II, vi, 7, 1106a35–1106b5; Rackham, pp. 91–93)

The virtuous middle is not merely a midpoint, an average between two extremes. The relativity of the doctrine of the middle-as-virtue, while it brings adaptability and comfort, also brings uncertainty: the ration of one athlete will not do for another, nor, indeed, will it necessarily do even for the same athlete at a later point in time. Virtue as a mean requires not only individual adjustment for each case, but also continual adjustment for any given case considered across time.

Thus the first qualification which Aristotle places on his doctrine of the middle-as-virtue is its need to be defined in the context of human temporality. Virtue is not a synchronic, purely conceptual, mathematical midpoint equally dividing excess and deficiency. Rather, it is a mobile, adjustable point whose extremes are merely the limits of its range of movements: "Moreover this activity [virtue] must occupy a complete life-time; . . . one day or a brief period of happiness does not make a man supremely blessed and happy" (I, vii, 16, 1098a18–20; Rackham, p. 33). As Kathleen Wilkes puts it, "A good or happy life becomes, in part at least, one that works . . . over time."[4]

Indeed, humans as Aristotle describes them are possessed of an irrepressible second impulse, a kind of inbred alterity that always pulls them in two directions at once, and this too is a proof of their fundamentally temporal nature:

> Nothing however can continue to give us pleasure always, because our nature is not simple, but contains a second element (which is what makes us perishable beings), and consequently, whenever one of these two elements is active, its activity runs counter to the nature of the other, while when the two are balanced, their action feels neither painful nor pleasant. . . . Hence God enjoys a single simple pleasure perpetually. . . . But change in all things is sweet, as the poet [Euripides] says, owing to some badness in us; since just as a changeable man is bad, so also is a nature that needs change; for it is not simple nor good. (VII, xiv, 8, 1154b21–31; Rackham, pp. 447–49)

According to a common Greek belief, second thoughts are better.[5] This bit of conventional wisdom, which might well be said to characterize many of Euripides' and Racine's vacillating and impetuous protagonists, is reflected in the temporal element of Aristotle's doctrine, the need for constant revision and modification which is one of the key features of his definition of moderate virtue.

The need for "second thoughts" also suggests a possible limitation of Aristotle's doctrine of moderation: the difficulty of quantifying ethical questions may well be the very reason people frequently do have second thoughts. Aristotle places the "good" into the categories of both quality and quantity (I, vi, 3, 1096a24–26; Rackham, p. 19), and this, as W. F. R. Hardie points out, is a potential trouble spot in this ethical system:

> Now in at least one obvious respect this statement of the doctrine does indeed lack detail and precision. A quantitative ideal is applied to virtue and to vice with only a vague indication of how it can be applicable. Quantities of food and drink can be weighed and measured; exercise can be timed. But the quantities involved in virtuous and vicious action . . . must at least be roughly measurable if the analogy with athletic training is to hold.[6]

We might go a long way toward defining the limitations of the middle-as-virtue if we begin to think of this ethical system as having two axes:

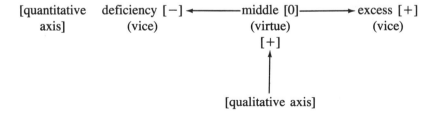

[quantitative axis]   deficiency [−] ←———— middle [0] ———→ excess [+]
                      (vice)   (virtue)   (vice)
                                          [+]

[qualitative axis]

Virtue is a zero—neither deficiency nor excess—on the scale of quantity, but a plus—the very sign of moral value—on the scale of quality, as Aristotle himself recognizes: "Hence while in respect of its substance and the definition that states what it really is in essence virtue is the observance of the mean, in point of excellence and rightness it is an extreme [akrotes]" (II, vi, 17, 1107a6–8; Rackham, p. 95). Though virtue is to be found as a mean between two quantitative extremes, it is the endpoint, or *telos,* on the axis of quality, the superlative of human moral endeavor.

The real issue here is time and its conflict with the irrepressible human impulse to find an absolute which resists the movements and relativities imposed by it. The axis of quantity is in fact the axis of time, an axis which has no real endpoints, not because human life doesn't come to an end, but because so long as one is defining (and redefining) virtue as a mean, one is being carried along by time. It is only the qualitative axis which has a terminus; on this axis, virtue may be conceived as an extreme which stands out from the passage of time and remains a fixed, timeless goal.

This conflict between the temporal and the immobile leads us to one of the most important tensions in Aristotle's ethical system: "Now of everything that is continuous and divisible, it is possible to take the larger part, or the smaller part, or an equal part, and these parts may be larger, smaller, and equal either with respect to the thing itself or relatively to us; the equal part being a mean between excess and deficiency" (II, vi, 4, 1106a27–29; Rackham, p. 91). The doctrine of the mean works only if it is applied to a moral universe which is "continuous and divisible." A continuum of moral actions is scrutinized, a point of moderation is distinguished and "pulled out" of the continuum, which then presumably regroups into two new continua, labeled "excess" and "deficiency." W. F. R. Hardie comments on this passage by giving a further clarification of the sense of the word "continuous": "Note first the precise meaning of the phrase 'continuous and divisible.' Quantity which is continuous is not merely divisible, but divisible *ad infinitum:* it has no indivisible, atomic parts. This is the definition of continuous (*suneches*) in *De Caelo* 268a6 and *Physics* 231b16. Thus the sense conveyed by the whole phrase is that of continuous, i.e. divisible ad infinitum."[7]

A conflict arises from this definition of "continuity," the *sine qua non* of moderate virtue. If the spectrum of choices is *infinitely* divisible, no given division, or choice, has any stability, for it can always be further subdivided and perfected. It is conceptually impossible in this system to arrive at a *point* of moderation, because a point is a nondimensional space, one which cannot be further subdivided. Indeed, if this sort of endpoint or goal of moral perfection could be reached, then the domain of choices and possible actions would not be continuous, i.e., infinitely divisible.

We have reached the double bind of the system, the point at which it cannot have it both ways, for the moral universe can be considered to be continuous or discontinuous, but not both. If it is continuous, the point of virtue can never be reached, since a point has no storage capacity and cannot contain anything. If it is discontinuous, there is the *possibility* of a unit of virtue with some sort of holding power, but the moral universe then becomes a series of contiguities, and the unit of virtue is separated from its generating poles or extremes by a quantum leap and is thus unreachable.

It is for this reason that the movement of virtue toward its purported goal, the middle, is unstable:

Aristotle will go on to add that virtue . . . tends toward the middle.

Virtue . . . reaches the middle.[8]

Does virtue actually hit the middle which it is aiming for? Or does it merely tend toward a middle which it reaches only conceptually, that is, after an infinite number of infinitesimal divisions and subdivisions along the spectrum of moral action?

The problem here is essentially that of Zeno's paradoxes, the ancient source for which is Aristotle's *Physics,* and particularly the paradox of the dichotomy: "The first is the one about the impossibility of motion, since the moving body must get to the halfway point before the endpoint [telos] (*Physics,* VI, 239b).[9] The paradox about the impossibility of motion replicates the pattern of the movement of virtue which always stops in the middle, halfway between the extremes of deficiency and excess. Even though motion is attempting to reach an endpoint [telos] but is repeatedly "stopped" midway, whereas virtue actually aims for the middle, the paradox is the same: that of being prevented from reaching a goal by the process one has to use to reach it, by the series of discontinuous steps or contiguous units which, however finely they are divided and subdivided, never appear to add up to the distance to be covered if the endpoint is to be reached.

Thus Aristotle's version of the paradox of the dichotomy can be seen in the light of the paradox of his own moral system. In order to constitute a moral continuum, human actions must be infinite; but if they are infinite, if even the different possible quantities involved in a moral decision—how many grains of wheat to give to the beggar, how angry to become during an argument—are to all intents and purposes infinite, how can one reach the "goal" of virtue? Can every provisional reaching of a goal not itself be further subdivided and moderated, halved and halved again? If, as Henri Bergson claims, "quantity is quality in a nascent state . . . , the limiting case of quality,"[10] does quality not "reach" quantity only in the sense that an asymptotic curve tending toward a limit touches it "at" infinity?

Zeno's paradoxes essentially pose the question of the relation of the middle—the halfway point, the point of being on the way, or in the process, or in the instant of change—to the ends.[11] The search for the middle term is the search for the moment of change in itself, and reflects the desire to seize becoming and process in their essence. The attempt at quantifying or representing movement and process may continue endlessly to circumscribe them, but it never even becomes contiguous to them, since a process, insofar as it is a continuum, is infinitely divisible and cannot support being "next" to anything: "If it is said that a pleasure or pain is becoming continuously more intense, this means that the change does not occur in jumps from one degree of intensity to the next; there is no next, any more than, if an extensive quantity is continuous, there is a next size."[12]

Henri Bergson, whose disagreement with Bertrand Russell over Zeno's paradoxes is like a latter-day version of the conflict between Heraclitus and Parmenides which partially motivated Plato's theory of Forms,[13] perfectly captures the uncapturable nature of the middle:

> As the letter x designates a certain unknown quantity, whatever it may be, so my "becoming in general," always the same, symbolizes here a certain transition of which I have taken some snapshots; of the transition itself it teaches me nothing. Let me then concentrate myself wholly on the transition, and, between any two snapshots, endeavor to realize what is going on. As I apply the same method, I obtain the same result; a third view merely slips in between the two others. I may begin again as often as I will, I may set views alongside of views forever, I shall obtain nothing else. . . . The movement slips through the interval . . . because every attempt to reconstitute change out of states implies the absurd proposition, that movement is made up of immobilities.[14]

The desire to seize the instant of change implies eliminating the third, intermediate term between two hypothetically "adjacent" points, and this is impossible because the "third view" always slips in between any two views, however close they may be. "The movement slips through the interval": we may know the boundaries of the interval, the extremes which delimit a domain of change, but while the outside of this interval may *represent* motion and change, we will never know motion and change in themselves, the inside of the interval. For the inside of the interval, as Bergson points out in his *Introduction to Metaphysics,* is the domain of the gods: "It is more than human to grasp what is happening in the interval. But philosophy can only be an effort to transcend the human condition" (77). Let us then take a step outside of the human condition as it is embodied in the virtuous middle and into the realm of metaphysics, the domain of the excluded middle.

We have come to the point of reversal in our discussion of the Aristotelian middle, the point that requires us to go back briefly to our starting point to see where we have gone. According to the doctrine of the middle-as-virtue, the human condition means being defined by a temporally bound search for moderation. And yet this virtuous middle shows the limitations of the human condition as well as its advantages: the virtuous middle is an unending process which reveals the inherent element of imprecision involved in searching for virtue through moderation.

Thus the doctrine of the virtuous middle, which is predicated on the possibility of change and adaptability, nonetheless cannot—any more than Zeno's paradoxes—resolve the difficult problem of quantifying change and the approximate nature of attempts at doing so. Bergson characterizes Aristotle's effort to define the concept of movement as unsuccessful, "seeking its principle in the concepts of *high* and *low,* two immobilities by which Aristotle believed he could adequately explain the mobility."[15]

Indeed, even though his ethical theory is based upon change and movement, Aristotle, as Bergson points out, will come to favor immobility as a necessary element in any *systematic* view of reality. And in this he will be following in the (immobile) footsteps of Zeno: "Metaphysics dates back to the day Zeno of Elea pointed out the contradictions inherent to movement and change, or at least to the way our intelligence represents them. . . . Metaphysics was thus led to search for the reality of things in a realm superior to temporality, beyond what moves and changes. . . . From that time on metaphysics could be nothing but a more or less artificial arrangement of concepts, a hypothetical construction."[16]

As we have seen in chapter 1, there is in fact an Aristotelian axiom which might be defined as an attempt at circumventing these "contradictions inherent to movement and change": the law of excluded middle. A passage from Aristotle's *Physics* which, like Zeno's paradoxes, discusses a potential barrier to the possibility of change looks ahead to that axiom:

Nor need we be troubled by any attack on the possibility of change based on the axiom that a thing "must either be or not be" but cannot "both be and not be" this or that at the same time. For, it is argued, if a thing is changing, for instance, from being not-white to being white, and is on its way from one to the other, you can truly assert at the same time that it is neither white nor not-white. But this is not true, for we sometimes call a thing "white" even if it is not entirely white, and we sometimes call a thing "not-white" even if there is some trace of white in it; we speak of it according to its prevailing condition or the conditions of its most significant parts or aspects. For to say that a thing is not in a certain condition "at all" and to say that it is not "altogether" in it are two different things. And so, too, in the case of being or not being or any other pair of contradictory opposites. For during the whole process of changing it must be prevailingly one or the other and can never be exclusively either. (*Physics*, VI, 240a; Wicksteed and Cornford, 2:189–91)

A thing "must either be or not be" but cannot "both be and not be." This is a succinct statement of what will become in Aristotle's *Metaphysics*, respectively, the law of excluded middle (IV, vii, 1, 1011b23–25) and the law of contradiction (IV, iii, 9, 1005b19–20), restated with clarity by John Neville Keynes in his *Formal Logic:* "Everything is x or not-x" (law of excluded middle or excluded third); "Nothing is at the same time both x and not-x" (law of contradiction).[17] If we apply these laws to theories of the process of change and movement and to the attempt at "capturing" or stopping movement—parallel to the desire to find a truly stable and permanent point of moderate virtue resistant to the vagaries of continuous time—they emphasize the impossibility of seizing the middle, indeed, sound a prohibition against even trying to do so.

We may more easily conceive of the difference between the inclusive middle-as-virtue and the excluded middle if we analyze the example given by Aristotle above, the change from white to not-white (or to black), in terms of each kind of middle. The middle-as-virtue deals with contrary opposites ("enantiotes," "opposition") and not contradictory opposites ("antiphasis," "contradiction"), two terms which Keynes distinguishes in this way:

A pair of terms are called contradictories if they are so related that between them they exhaust the entire universe to which reference is made. . . . The contrary of a term is usually defined as the term denoting that which, in some particular universe, is furthest removed from that which is denoted by the original term; e.g., black and white, wise and foolish. Contraries differ from contradictories in that they admit of a mean, and therefore do not between them exhaust the entire universe of discourse.

Generalizing the relation between [contraries], we should naturally characterize the contrary of a given proposition by saying that it goes beyond mere denial, and sets up a further assertion as far as possible removed from the original assertion, declaring not merely the falsity of the given proposition taken as a whole, but the falsity of every part of it; so that, whilst the contradictory of a proposition denies its entire truth, its contrary may be said to assert its entire falsehood.[18]

Thus, "white" and "black" are contraries, between which a middle is possible (gray). "White" and "not-white" or "black" and "not-black" are contradictories, between which no middle is possible (a thing is either white or not-white, either black or not-black). The middle-as-virtue conforms to the model white-black: it aims for the best-chosen point between black and white, the extremes to be avoided by mediating between them.

It is in this sense that the extremes involved in the doctrine of the middle-as-virtue are not simple negations of each other, white and not-white or black and not-black, for as we have seen, the virtuous middle essentially functions without a negative pole, a principle of complete exclusion. Rather, each extreme provides a counterforce, a principle as far removed from its opposite as is possible, not the mere absence of its opposite but a counter-principle to it. But if we now return to the passage in the *Physics* quoted above, we discover that "we sometimes call a thing 'white' even if it is not entirely white, and we sometimes call a thing 'not-white' even if there is some trace of white in it; we speak of it according to its prevailing condition." One of the times we do this is in fact when we are obeying the law of excluded middle, since according to its dictates, no distinction can be made between the true extremes on the one hand, altogether white or altogether black, and the "predominant" approximations of each extreme on the other, represented as "white" and "black" but in fact a mixture in which one or the other simply predominates; no point can be allowed to be classified as being "between" white and not-white, between black and not-black; each point must be called one or the other, even if this involves an element of approximation and representation as well: "And so, too, in the case of being or not being or any other pair of contradictory opposites. For during the whole process of changing it must be prevailingly one or the other and can never be exclusively either."

Aristotle is here recognizing what he will not recognize when he presents the law of excluded middle in the *Metaphysics:* that this law deals more with the necessity of unalloyed identification of entities than with the truth of any such existing purity. We may thus represent the law of excluded middle in this way:

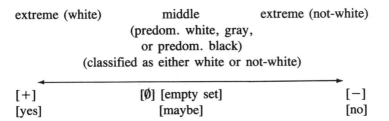

This is a system which cannot recognize degrees of any sort: "not altogether white" or "predominantly white" may be in its eyes the equivalent of "not white at all," or they may be assimilated to the category of "white" in certain circumstances, but they cannot remain in the middle; "maybe" white and "maybe" not-white is not a possible classification here.

Thus, the two middles which are at the center of Aristotle's ethical and logical theories[19] provide us with two opposite advantages or abilities: the doctrine of the middle-as-virtue attempts to be inclusive of the spectrum of moral actions, infinitely adjustable, temporally defined, and compromising in a comforting sort of way; it defines virtue as an average, and human identity as an unremarkable mean. It is centripetal: everything is drawn to the middle, assimilated to it. The law of excluded middle is extreme, exclusive, and uncompromising, and generally incompatible with any change of position or revision once it has ruled upon a question. As a strictly binary operation, it is completely disinterested in the process by which one extreme is chosen over the other; it throws away the tally sheets and represents results pure and simple. It is centrifugal: according to its terms, the middle itself becomes a pure boundary, that is, something which is not meant to be reached as a goal but rather has a simple separating function; which pushes any two points on either side of it toward the extremes.

It is undoubtedly the desire to create a stabilizing milieu, a middle which will erase the equivocation and ambiguity of recognizing the artificial nature of representation, that leads Aristotle to exclude the middle in establishing his logical system. Indeed, insofar as the law of excluded middle may be considered an act of foundation, it shows that logic itself has an inextricable ethical value, if only because of what that law tries to ignore. As the logician Jan Lukasiewicz remarks in comments which might apply equally to the law of contradiction and the law of excluded middle:

> The Law of Contradiction has no *logical* value, since it only has the status of an assumption; but it does have a *practical and ethical* value, which is all the more important for that. *The Law of Contradiction is our only weapon against error and falsehood.* . . . . [T]he need to recognise the Law of Contradiction is *a sign of the intellectual and moral imperfection of man.* . . . At a time when Greece was in a political decline, Aristotle founded and developed the systematic study of man and the world. . . . He must have been anxious to stress the value of scientific and philosophical studies. . . . Aristotle attacked the opponents of the Law . . . and against them he fought for a theoretical principle with all the ardour of a man fighting for his personal possessions. He may himself have felt the weakness of his arguments; and that may have led him to present his Law as an ultimate *axiom* — an unassailable *dogma*.[20]

The excluded middle is a sort of zero, a placeholder that is necessary for the creation of stable units. It is a kind of unmoved mover, perhaps a conceptual example of the godlike; immobile itself where the middle is always in motion, it moves the extremes to either side and, more important, advances any investigation concluded under its auspices. Its aim is not unity, but units: well-defined, exclusive entities upon which further well-defined entities can be built. Like the very principle of affirmation and negation which is the basis of systems as diverse as the disciplining of children ("yes, you may," "no, you may not") and the programming of computers ("bit," or "binary digit," requiring the choice between two alternatives to define a unit of information), it is a model of clarity: "Nor indeed can there be any intermediate [metaxy] between contradictory statements, but of one thing we must either assert or deny one thing, whatever it may be" (*Metaphysics,* IV, vii, 1, 1011b24–25; Tredennick, pp. 199–201 [modified trans.]). The excluded middle is the point of detachment at the center of any incremental binary system. Unlike the middle-as-virtue, this middle, by allowing us the luxury of believing that some problems have been solved once and for all, leads us always forward to the next question, for in this system there is in fact a next; it is a system made up of contiguities. And it is only by accepting the zero at the heart of the system that we may confer upon the system its power of attachment, the capacity of remembrance, of storing the "solutions" which it has produced up to any given present and of composing those solutions into a coherent, consistent whole.

That the law of excluded middle denies unity only to create units allows it to refute Zeno's claim that there is no movement in the world and that all things are one, that is, are a continuous unity which is infinitely subdivisible if it is divisible at all, for this law denies the infinite divisibility of things at the same time as it affirms their divisibility. In this sense it is the law of the rational individual—the person "undivided"—caught between a seamless unity and an infinite divisibility. It defines an "atom" of thought—"a-tomos," that beyond which things may be cut no further—and, by extension, a unified thinking individual, a sort of philosophic Adam, or first human.

The law of excluded middle has as its ultimate enemy the indeterminate: whatever cannot be fit into the system it purports to create or undermines the unity (or rather the unit) of the individual. As John Stuart Mill observes, "Between the true and the false there is a third possibility, the Unmeaning,"[21] and the unmeaning need not be limited to the nonsensical, but may also include the category of everything that resists meaning as an act of quantification and simplification. The fact that numerous statements of the law of excluded middle dismiss the meaningless as a category unworthy of consideration is in itself meaningful: it may be true that "the meaningless has no right to recognition as judgment,"[22] but that does not necessarily mean it has no right to recognition at all. In fact the disclaimer that the law of excluded middle does not apply to the meaningless is revealed as tautological once it has been recognized that the law is itself the founder of a system of meaning. What escapes this law is what cannot be made to yield meaning.

Indeed, eliminating the indeterminate means eliminating the very process of mediation and compromise which defines the doctrine of the virtuous middle, and as the logician Friedrich Ueberweg points out, it is for this reason that justice is not always served by the law of excluded middle:

> Others refuse to acknowledge the validity of the axiom [the law of excluded middle] at all. The mean between the contradictory predicates, they say, is often the true predicate. All development rests on the union of opposites. Between "guilty" and "not-guilty," there is "not-proven." . . . It would be a dangerous error to exclude this third case. It would often give judges the painful alternative of unjust acquittal or unjust condemnation, and give effect to expression of only half truth in spite of better knowledge and desire. Absolute recognition or rejection, the simple division of the character into good and evil, leaving out of consideration all the intermediate grades, the partition of systems into true and false without making allowance for the gradual advance of knowledge, the separation of statements into credible or incredible and forged without including the myth or poetic truth, – all denote a certain crudeness of thought.[23]

Are "guilty or not guilty" not the ultimate test case of the law of excluded middle? "Not proven," which is, as Aristotle admits, the status of the laws of excluded middle and contradiction themselves,[24] falls somewhere between "guilty" and "not guilty." That the person standing trial should also be able to have some recognition of this liminary status, some sort of benefit of the doubt, might be suggested by a counterexample to the law of excluded middle, one which seems to be taken from a particularly unjust court of law: "To be quite fair, it should be said, it can be and has been doubted whether this law [of excluded middle] has universal application: for example, is it true that either you have stopped beating your wife or you have not?"[25]

"To be quite fair" about the law of excluded middle is to point out that the law itself is not quite fair. The law of excluded middle does not provide the questions and the issues brought to it; it simply processes them. When it is presented with a question which is beyond its capacity, it reacts much as a human searcher for the truth does when given the words of the Delphic oracle to interpret: it is not so much incorrect as it is at a loss to function as it normally does. The law of excluded middle imposes upon the world a set of criteria—decidability, determination, finitude; in short, a certain kind of boundedness—which are far-reaching but not universal in their application, and to this extent it cannot do the entire world—everything that is—justice.

Although Aristotle never discusses the relation between the virtuous middle and the excluded middle, I would like to suggest that in some sense the two doctrines complement each other and at the same time compete with each other: each satisfies a basic human need but also neglects a basic human need. The law of excluded middle has the advantage of uncompromising clarity, but it also has the disadvantage of uncompromising inflexibility; from a tool for the pursuit of knowledge and inquisitiveness (x or not-x?), it may become a tool of persecution and Inquisition (did you or did you not . . . ?). Once we have lived with its seeming certainty, clarity of thought, and simplicity of outlook for a time, we feel the need to turn back to the doctrine of the virtuous middle, believing that if only we didn't have to decide one way or the other, come down completely on one side of a scale that is barely tipping, there would be justice in the world.

And yet, no sooner have we arrived in the comforting domain of the doctrine of the middle-as-justice than we are once again struck by its own inadequacy, its lack of justice, in short, its need for the law of excluded middle. G. C. Field speaks about the articulation between ethics and metaphysics, or rather the slippage of the one into the other: "Whenever we make a moral judgment or adopt a moral attitude, we think or claim that we are asserting a real fact which is there to be discovered and about which it is possible to be right or wrong. Some people would express this by saying that we claim 'objective validity' for our moral judgments . . . [which] means . . . that if two people make contradictory assertions about the same object one, at least, must be wrong."[26] Contradictory assertions are made by two people who both believe they are right. According to the doctrine of the middle-as-virtue, some compromise must be worked out; whatever the actual decision made, it must be somehow a product of these two positions and their interaction. But, as Field observes, a different and opposite impulse in these two interactants makes each of them wish for a straightforward solution to their argument. Indeed, they are not making "contrary" assertions, which would be a case more nearly conforming to the doctrine of the middle-as-virtue, since a mean can exist between two contraries, but rather "contradictory" assertions, between which there is no middle. Each of them wishes for a clear-cut and unequivocal solution, but in the problem as it stands there is, theoretically, no middle possible.

It is therefore a "natural tendency of the mind," even as it is working in the realm of ethics, to feel "compelled to take a step into Metaphysics": "In moral experience we find ourselves claiming or assuming that something really is the case, besides our own immediate feelings and besides the observable features of the situation. We cannot intelligently discuss this claim without explicitly or implicitly having some general idea of . . . the kinds of thing there are in reality, which is a typically metaphysical question."[27] The circle is now complete, or rather, it has been set into motion, for it is a self-perpetuating circle. The openendedness of the doctrine of the middle-as-virtue—which is its very advantage over the inflexibility of the law of excluded middle—is inseparable from its inability to arrive at any kind of an endpoint, to seize the uninterruptable flow of time and to create the stability of a unit with a capacity for storage and memory.

Thus, not only do the doctrine of the virtuous middle and the law of excluded middle have distinct advantages and distinct limitations, but the limitations of each correspond more or less to the advantages of the other. Does this mean that ethics and metaphysics, the domains of the virtuous middle and the excluded middle, go together, like two pieces in a single puzzle? Or, as Aristotle himself seems to have ultimately believed, that they must be kept apart?

Werner Jaeger, whose work on the evolution of Aristotle's thought over the course of his lifetime has been extremely influential, hypothesizes that, at the outset, the domains of ethics and metaphysics seemed to Aristotle to converge. Aristotle's original conception of metaphysics—represented by book lambda of the *Metaphysics,* which Jaeger identifies as an early basis of the later work—"seeks for a transcendental entity such as Plato's Idea, combining absolute reality (ousia) with absolute value (agathon). According to lambda values and realities are two separate ascending series, converging toward the top. They meet at the point where the highest value (ariston) coincides with the purest reality (ousia)."[28] Perhaps the conception of moderate justice in the *Nicomachean Ethics* could be compatible with the categorical nature of the law of excluded middle if the search for the good (ethics) and the search for what is (metaphysics) were consonant, if they could converge upon a single point.

Jaeger concludes, however, that as Aristotle developed as a thinker, he came more and more to doubt the possibility that ethics and metaphysics could be included in a single domain:

The two main parts of Aristotle's ethics, the ethical doctrine of morality based on the good will and the metaphysical doctrine of the contemplation of God as our norm, evince a tendency to rid themselves of each other more and more in the course of his development. . . . This juxtaposition of the two "lives" has always been felt to be in some way personal and dependent on the philosopher's own experience. It does not possess the radical consistency either of Plato, who finds only the philosophic life worth living, or of Kant, who breaks once and for all with the primacy of theoretical reason and declares the moral will to be the highest thing in the world. Both in ethics and in metaphysics Aristotle goes a little way with Kant, but something in him makes him shrink from the final conclusion. Neither the self-sufficiency of pure natural science nor the self-confidence of the mere will to fulfil one's moral obligations satisfied his sense of reality and of life. . . . [H]is view of life [has] its peculiar modern tension and two-sidedness.[29]

The ethical and the metaphysical become ever more exclusive of one another as Aristotle's thought develops. But this exclusion leads to no conclusion: "something in him makes him shrink from the final conclusion." The conflict is thus not resolved; it is perpetuated in a vacillation between the two domains.

Tragedy is an expression of this vacillation, a conflict between two irreconcilable impulses. The ethical middle, with its valorization of the collective and the average, its avoidance of strife and its resistance to any fundamental change, provides inessential "solutions" to the conflicts of the extremes and ignores the logical underpinnings of the problems it processes in a purely practical way, in the interests of avoiding a cataclysm. On the contrary, the excluded middle is the doctrine of heroic individuation; it accepts negation as what is necessary to forge the unit of the individual. It recognizes the tragic hero's need for difference and purity as well as the inevitable element of radicalization in that desire.

It is in terms of this conflict that we may explain Aristotle's ambivalent attitude toward the tragic hero in the *Poetics*. Aristotle describes the tragic hero in these terms:

[O]ne should not show worthy men passing from good fortune to bad. . . . Nor again wicked people [mochtherous] passing from bad fortune to good. . . . Nor again the passing of a thoroughly bad man [poneron] from good fortune to bad fortune. . . . There remains then the mean between these [ho metaxy]. This is the sort of man who is not pre-eminently virtuous and just [ho mete arete diapheron kai dikaiosyne], and yet it is through no badness or villainy of his own that he falls into the misfortune, but rather through some flaw in him.[30]

The tragic hero is a middle case: neither purely good nor purely bad, he seems to be defined as an average taken between extremes, an example of the ethical middle, a being who is in no essential way distinguishable — "mete arete diapheron," "not differing"—from the collectivity.

Nonetheless, Aristotle uses the term "metaxy" and not "meson" to describe this middle case. It is "meson," the middle, which describes the doctrine of the ethical middle, and "metaxy," the intermediary, what is between, that characterizes the excluded middle. "Metaxy" would thus seem to be a middle which exists only in order to have its existence negated: "nor can there be any intermediate [metaxy] between contradictory statements" (*Metaphysics*, IV, vii, 1, 1011b23–24).[31] And indeed, in other comments in the *Poetics*, Aristotle undermines his hero's purportedly average state:

> Comedy . . . is a representation of inferior people [phauloteron], not indeed in the full sense of the word bad, but the laughable is a species of the base or ugly. (V, 1, 1449a; Fyfe, p. 19)

> Tragedy is, then, a representation of an action that is heroic [spoudaias] and complete and of a certain magnitude. (VI, 2, 1449b; Fyfe, p. 23)

"Spoudaios," the term used to describe the action of tragedy, can be used by opposition to both "mochtheros" and "poneros," the two terms used of the evil characters who supposedly provide one of the poles between which the hero is situated.[32] To this extent, "spoudaios" represents not the middle term between good and bad where the hero is purportedly to be found, but rather an extreme in itself, that of goodness. And Aristotle does in fact later recognize the "goodness" of the tragic hero, first as an alternative ("such a man as we have described, or . . . one who is better rather than worse" [XIII, 6, 1453a; Fyfe, p. 47]) and finally as an imperative ("tragedy is a representation of men better than ourselves" [XV, 11, 1454b; Fyfe, p. 57]).

Even if there might be ways of reconciling this apparent inconsistency — perhaps Aristotle means that the hero himself is average, though his action is good — such explanations do nothing to efface the ambiguity of Aristotle's attitude toward the tragic hero, who is simultaneously meant to be like us, that is, average, and better than us. This, indeed, is one of the central instabilities of tragic representation. In order to stand for the collectivity, heroes must be assimilable to it, and to this extent they must be average. But they must also be different from those they are representing in order to reach the status and stability of representations; as representations they must have a value that is unswerving and determinable. In short, they must be both the same (neither especially good nor especially bad, in between) and different (exceptional, apart from the average).

It is in this context that Hegel's definition of tragedy as a conflict not of good against evil but rather of good against good takes on its full implications. Hegel takes the unmediable moral schematization of tragedy into contradictory opposites—"good" and "not-good"—and changes it into two contrary opposites, one "good" fighting another and refusing to recognize that its adversary is also, according to its own perspective, "good": "The tragic destruction of figures whose ethical life is in the highest plane can interest and elevate us and reconcile us to its occurrence only in so far as they come on the scene in opposition to one another together with equally justified but different ethical powers which have come into collision" ("Philosophy of Right").[33] Hegel's model of tragedy attempts to bypass the problem of the excluded middle—that of choosing between two contradictory positions neither of which can be selected as preferable to the other—by avoiding any description of the opponents in the terms required by the law of excluded middle ("x" and "not-x," e.g., "good" and "not-good"). But in fact Hegel can no more avoid the problem of the middle by his schematization of the tragic conflict than the tragic hero can. The excluded middle is a structural element of tragic heroism: it is at the same time the greatness of heroes and their downfall, as A. C. Bradley, in his commentary on Hegel's theory of tragedy, points out: "It is the nature of the tragic hero, at once his greatness and his doom, that he knows no shrinking or half-heartedness, but identifies himself wholly with the power that moves him, and will admit the justification of no other power."[34] The purity and the intensity of the tragic hero lead him to refuse any halfway meeting point between his own position and another.

The tragic conflict described by Hegel is essentially that of the *lex talionis,* or "law of the such," the law of the vendetta which is perhaps most forcefully dramatized in Aeschylus' *Oresteia.* According to the *lex talionis,* if an individual has been wronged, he or she has a right to retribution that is equal to the wrong; the wrong must be righted. The *lex talionis* is thus a sort of figurative scale of justice: the wrong is weighed, a counterweight of retribution is decided upon, and the scale is theoretically balanced. If the *lex talionis* functioned successfully, it would conform to the model of compromise prescribed by the *Nicomachean Ethics;* it would provide a return to the virtuous middle.[35]

What in fact makes the *lex talionis* a form of tragic reversal is that the scale is never balanced by it: this reversal is by its very nature endless, the middle position aimed for but never reached. The previously wronged parties, once they have gotten their retribution, are satisfied, but the parties from whom they have exacted their retribution now consider themselves to be wronged and keep the entire process in motion. Thus in the *Oresteia* the chain of retributions goes back so far that it trails off into family legend, but at no point in its multigenerational history is a stopping point ever reached, because the *lex talionis* relies upon a separation of the world into perpetrators and victims.

The self-perpetuating nature of this cycle of violence, the constant regeneration of new plans for retaliation at the very instant that the old ones are carried out, is elegantly described by René Girard:

> [T]he only satisfactory revenge for spilt blood is spilling the blood of the killer. . . . The crime to which the act of vengeance addresses itself is almost never an unprecedented offense; in almost every case it has been committed in revenge for some prior crime.
>
> Vengeance, then, is an interminable, infinitely repetitive process. . . . [I]n tragedy each character passionately embraces or rejects vengeance depending on the position he occupies at any given moment in the scheme of the drama.[36]

The paradox of this system is that although it is based on a radical and unmediable difference between its opponents, that difference is swallowed up as soon as one recognizes the equivalence of perpetrator and victim across time. As Girard puts it:

> In a tragedy the reciprocal relationship between the characters is real, but it is the sum of non-reciprocal moments. The antagonists never occupy the same positions at the same time, to be sure; but they occupy these positions in succession. There is never anything on one side of the system that cannot be found on the other side, provided we wait long enough. . . . In the temporal plan of the system there is not a moment when those involved in the action do not see themselves separated form their rivals by formidable differences. . . . That explains why the antagonists only rarely perceive the reciprocal nature of their involvement.[37]

The only way of providing any kind of "solution" to the dilemmas provided by this system is to recognize the limitations of the system itself, that is, to realize that the system never will lead to a solution. Thus at the end of the *Oresteia,* when Orestes is tried by a jury for the murder of his mother, the most recent in the endless series of retributions that characterize his family, the votes of the jury are tied—a deadlock that is in the very nature of the *lex talionis* itself—and the stalemate must be broken by Athena. Recognition in this case transcends the human condition, for it requires the impartiality of looking at plaintiff and defendent from a third position, the position of tragic recognition which judges the law of excluded middle and finds it, like the virtuous middle, wanting: "The end of the tragic conflict is the denial of both the exclusive claims . . . that which is denied is not the rightful powers with which the combatants have identified themselves. On the contrary, those powers, and with them the only thing for which the combatants cared, are affirmed. What is denied is the exclusive and therefore wrongful assertion of their right."[38] In the eyes of tragic recognition, so long as the system of the *lex talionis* is operable, every perpetrator will soon be reversed into a new victim. It is the strict polarization demanded by the system itself which needs to be called into question.

And yet we must not take this coming to a tragic recognition as a solution to the problem of the middle, as a simple critique of the law of excluded middle. The *lex talionis,* like the law of excluded middle, is emblematic of a profoundly human need, that of establishing (and taking) sides, that of discerning, within the complexity of any given situation, a plus and a minus, a stable perspective which establishes the "meaning" of the situation for a given individual. Girard says it in this way: "In tragedy everything alternates. But we must also reckon with the irresistible tendency of the human spirit to suspend this oscillation, to fix attention on one extreme or the other. This tendency is . . . responsible for the pseudo-determination of the protagonists, which in turn transforms revolving oppositions into stable differences."[39] The *lex talionis,* like the law of excluded middle, dichotomizes the moral universe, and although that dichotomization is beyond any doubt a simplification and so leads to radically partial and even reductive viewpoints, it is in some sense difficult to imagine how the world (or at least the individual) could operate without it. If the laws of contradiction and excluded middle are called the laws of thought, the law of excluded middle might be called the law of the self, for it corresponds to the individual's need to establish his or her boundaries and territory, even if that requires the radicalization of external limits in order to create an inside within them.

The tragedy of the two middles consists of the following paradox. If the law of excluded middle is respected, and the partiality it depends upon assures a protective barrier for the individual, the inside thus constituted is *nothing;* the individual is a pure limit, an unalloyed need to choose a simple solution in an infinitely complex world. If on the other hand the ethical middle is taken as a single principle, an inside may be said to exist, and the partiality of seemingly opposite positions to be drawn toward a moral middle in a spirit of equanimity and equilibrium, but in that case no boundaries are present to allow that inside to persist: the "inside" becomes reduced to a point, a dimensionless phenomenon with no identity and no capacity for individuation. The tragic middle recognizes not only that, as has been said of the tragic hero, you can't have it both ways, but also that you must have it both ways. One needs to exclude the middle, to empty it out as a dangerous source of ambivalence, in order to protect the unit of the individual. But by the same token that unit finds itself so radically polarized by its constitution that it becomes more a separation from the knowledge and understanding which it is trying to protect and store than a guarantor of it. From the other direction, the tragic middle recognizes the need for compromise as a means of assuring continuity, an avoidance mechanism to keep away the dangers of a cataclysmic confrontation. But at the same time the utterly ad hoc nature of the virtuous middle means that a thorough-going reliance on it precludes any essential judgment.

Once we have understood—but not solved—the problem of the middle, we have reached the moment at which our theoretical definition of tragedy must give way to its working out as a praxis. If, as is undoubtedly the case, the theory has raised more questions than it has resolved, it can only be hoped that the "practice"—the analysis of the plays themselves—will finally explain the theory.

Part 2
Readings in the Tragic Middle

> In the middle of our lives' path
> I found myself within a dark wood
> For the straight way was lost.
>
> — Dante, *Inferno*

3
The End Is the Beginning
Euripides' *Phoenissae*

If Aristotle seems to have taught Racine something about the problem of the middle, Euripides, whose tragedy has excited controversy at least as far back as Aristotle's *Poetics,* first appears to represent a kind of extreme for Racine. Racine translates Aristotle's qualification of Euripides as "tragikotatos" ("the most tragic") with the phrase *extrêmement tragique.* [1] Racine's career as a tragedian, as we have seen, occupies the middle period of his life, but his use of Euripides' plays in fact forms the framework of that career, not its center but its two extremes: *La Thébaïde* (1664) and *Andromaque* (1667), the very nearly contiguous plays inspired by Euripides' *Phoenissae* and *Andromache,* are Racine's first and third plays; only *Alexandre le Grand* (1665) separates this doubly Euripidean birth of Racinian tragedy. At the other end of the theatrical period of Racine's life we find *Iphigénie* (1674), based on Euripides' *Iphigeneia in Aulis,* and *Phèdre* (1677), largely drawn form the *Hippolytus.* These final two plays of Racine's theatrical period complete the near symmetry of Racine's use of Euripidean material. Euripides is the single model, ancient or modern, to whom Racine turned most often in the course of his career as a tragedian, and his placement at the two ends of Racine's tragic itinerary—as a starting point and an endpoint—emphasizes his status as an extreme.

Racine begins his theatrical career with a reworking of one of Euripides' most extreme plays, the *Phoenissae:* "[Euripides' imagination] is no longer inventing new themes or effects within a familiar framework; rather, it is breaking the framework. . . . This drama may be considered the end product of Euripides' experiments outside of the domain of tragedy. . . . [His] investigations lead him to try something extreme." [2] The play's extremity is largely a function of its complication, its overuse of mythic material:

47

The "overfulness" of the play, its inorganic, even incoherent structure, must, of course, be intentional: far from being embarrassed by an abundance of material, Euripides has gone out of his way to include everything possible.[3]

Far from concentrating on a single issue, Euripides is at pains to include as much as he can fit in.[4]

Euripides is not developing a tragic theme, or he would need neither this amount nor this variety of material.[5]

It is the longest Greek tragedy in existence, and covers the greatest stretch of story. . . . The *Phoenissae* seems like an attempt to run the matter of a whole trilogy into one play.[6]

The *Phoenissae*'s principal flaw seems to be the desire to include too much, to exclude nothing. Even when faced with the (theoretical) necessity of choosing between two possible endings, the play refuses to choose: "Apparently unwilling to choose between the two ends that the tradition awarded Antigone, [Euripides] takes them both (if our text of the exodos is so far to be trusted) and, over the protest of an outraged scholiast, sends Antigone off to brave Kreon's wrath by burying Polyneikes, and to accompany her blind old father into exile."[7] Will Antigone bury Polyneices and, as Sophocles' *Antigone* has it, lose her life in the process? Or will she steer clear of the problem of the burial and go off to accompany her father into exile, as the *Oedipus at Colonus* will suggest? Of course the exodos may not be free of textual interpolations,[8] but in fact this blithe refusal to choose is very much in the spirit of Euripides' entire treatment of the mythic material here.

The excess of mythic material in the *Phoenissae* bursts the framework of tragedy, and therein consists the play's radicality. The drama that has too many characters, too many events, too much material is ultimately a drama about the emptying out of the city, for the constitution of that city as a unit of place—the saving of the city, which most critics seem to agree is the subject of the play—coincides with the moment at which the city can no longer be inhabited. As we shall see, excluding the middle in this drama first means questioning the viability of the virtuous middle to solve the individual conflicts within the city and ultimately comes to mean sending its inhabitants outside of the city in the very name of guaranteeing its stability. The rebirth of the city is its own death, or at least a profound challenge upon its adequacy. Conversely, Racine's seizing upon Euripidean tragedy *in extremis*—the *Phoenissae* is one of Euripides' last plays—is what will allow him to make his first attempt at giving birth to his own form of tragedy.

Let us turn, then, to the *Phoenissae* in the perspective of the conflict between the virtuous middle and the excluded middle.

In the *Phoenissae*, the conflict of opposites—that is, of the two brothers, Eteocles and Polyneices, and of the two cities, Thebes and Argos, with which they are presently allied—first searches for a resolution according to the dictates of the virtuous middle. The goal of their mother, Jocasta, is to bring the two adversaries together and find some sort of middle ground of compromise between them, thereby avoiding the cataclysmic confrontation which she fears will otherwise separate the two brothers irrevocably. In her eyes, the success or failure of their meeting is the success or failure of the doctrine of the middle-as-virtue.

Jocasta, who plays the role of potential mediator[9] between her two sons, is thus the representative of the virtuous middle in the drama. Her role is structurally analogous to that of the chorus, the perennial defenders of moderation, and so it is not surprising that René Girard's general description of the tragic chorus admirably applies to Jocasta here: "Thus we can easily understand the terrified response of the chorus, its frantic efforts to remain uninvolved and avoid the contamination of mimetic rivalry. The virtues of moderation and 'common sense,' so dear to ordinary mortals, are openly challenged by the constant shiftings of the tragic situation."[10] During the scene in which her role as a mediator reaches its climax and proves to be an utter failure, Jocasta's appeal to Eteocles and Polyneices is firmly grounded in the thinking and the vocabulary of the ethical code which was to be expressed in the century following Euripides' death by the *Nicomachean Ethics*. Jocasta justifies her position and draws any authority she might have from her maturity ("gera," 528) and experience ("empeiria," 529), which allow her to speak more wisely ("sophoteron," 530) than the young, a claim which is very much in keeping with Aristotle's depiction of the doctrine of moderation and the virtuous middle as the domain of the experienced.[11]

Jocasta's address to her sons (528–85) has a double function: it defends the ethic of moderation and equality ("isotes," 536) and attacks the ethic of excess and ambition ("philotimia," 532). Jocasta's defense of equality makes of it a principle as beneficial as it is made to seem in the *Ethics;* the equal, the compromise or mediating position between the less and the more, functions primarily as a joint or a bond ("sundei," 538, "links together"). It is what rules over change, a sort of natural regulator: "In her mediating argument Jocasta finds the principle of equality in nature as well as in cities or in the minds of different men (535–48). . . . The *isotês* (equality) for which she argues, as many scholars have shown, has its origins in pre-socratic concepts that equate the political and the natural."[12]

Indeed, when Jocasta laments her sons' inability to abide by their father's wish that they share power by an alternating yearly cycle, she uses a natural metaphor to constrast her sons' quarreling with the equable alternation of the sun and the moon. Unlike the two brothers, the two heavenly bodies replace each other in a spirit of mutual respect for their equal right to rule the sky, each in its turn:

> And the lackluster eyelid of night and the light of the sun
> equally go their yearly round,
> and neither of them has jealousy of the victor.
> So while the sun and night are enslaved by measures [metrois],
> you [Eteocles] will not stand for having a part in the house
> equal [ison] to your brother's?
>
> (543–48)[13]

The virtuous middle is precisely the mechanism which would govern the two brothers' claims to power if they were to conform to their agreement to share the throne in a regular yearly cycle; neither claim could then be mutually exclusive, and both would be fundamentally equal. The key to the role of equality in this description is its synonymy with the concept of measure, "metron"; as Jocasta points out, equality is what sets out measures ("metr'," 541) for humans, and this it does by being a guarantor of continuity. It is not so much the idea that things do not change which is assured by equality, but rather that all changes are of equal value, so long as they come in moderation, at the right time, and in the right degree. The sun "replaces" the moon as the moon has replaced and will again replace the sun, so that no extreme position—always moon or always sun—is ever reached. Equality is thus established at a level higher than that of individual variation: it is the order of things itself that never changes.

The real issue here is whether the fluctuations that make up human time can be fully regulated, whether the brothers' yearly cycle of power can touch the next in an orderly way. Since Jocasta is trying to occupy a mediating position, her speech is an attempt at constituting a mean time or transition, and this is made explicit by Eteocles' reaction to her speech: "Mother, the fight is no longer to be fought with words, and the time in the middle [chronos houn meso] is wasted in vain" (588–89).

Jocasta's description of the "yearly cycle" of the sun and moon is puzzling. Is the cycle in this case not a daily one? The orderliness of Jocasta's vision of temporal change is close in spirit to the famous "Ode to Man" in Sophocles' Antigone, and that ode, in its praise of man's power to regulate his actions across time, makes a veiled allusion to the relation between Eteocles and Polyneices which may suggest a reason for Jocasta's transformation of days into years:

> He [man] works the imperishable, tireless earth,
> the furrows being rolled out year upon year [etos eis etos]
> turning them over [poleuon] with the race of horses.
>
> *(Antigone,* 338–40)

The word used for year here, "etos," stem "eteo-," could be construed as the first element in Eteocles' name. Usually interpreted as meaning "true glory," the name in fact carries the same ambiguity as the brothers' alternating reign. It seems to pose the question, is true glory ("eteos-kleos") the glory of a year (also "eteos-kleos"), that is, glory which can adapt itself to fluctuation or vacillation because it admits of a middle ground (in this case the orderly transmission of power) between being in power and recognizing the right of the opposition to share in that power? Or is genuine glory perpetual glory, a glory established once and for all, excluding the middle or transition which might allow for a reversal of power and thus protected from the passage of time and the changes it brings?

The question of the value of Eteocles' name is echoed by an opposing element in the *Antigone* passage, the word "poleuon," "turning over" — related to "polos," "pole" or "pivot" — which may well contain a hint of the first element of Polyneices' name. The name Polyneices might be interpreted — by the ear if not etymologically — as meaning "the quarrel [neikos] about the turning over [poleuo]," that is, the image of turning over the soil[14] being parallel to that of turning over power in due season, covering up what was formerly the visible surface where power or growth seem to reside and giving the underside of the soil the chance to renew the process. The first element of the name "Polyneices," like that of the name "Eteocles," would then be based upon two conflicting elements: "polos," "pole," and "polys," "much," the latter being part of the usual interpretation of the name ("much-quarreled," i.e., contentious). Once again, this verbal echo from the *Antigone* suggests the conflict of the two middles: the "polarity" or pivoting between the two brothers would be regulated, its alternation assured if they did indeed agree to share power in an equal way according to the dictates of the virtuous middle. But what each of the brothers wants is to exclude his brother, to establish himself as the permanent possessor of the "more" [polys/pleon].

To be sure, "to pleon," "the more," the comparative of "polys," is precisely what Jocasta attacks Eteocles for coveting when she chides him about his excess and ambition. Opposed to equality and the ethic of the virtuous middle is the desire for more which motivates Eteocles' refusal to give up power:

> Why do you honor . . .
> tyranny so excessively? . . .
> . . . it is an empty thing.
> Or do you want to get a lot [polla] of trouble by having a lot [poll'] of possessions in your house? What is the more [to pleon]? It is only a name.
>
> (549–53)

Eteocles is unaware of the relative origin of wealth, and this is the very point of Jocasta's attack on "the more." Wealth, the collection of goods, is not a one-sided matter, for whatever one has beyond the measure ("ta arkounth'," "the sufficient," 554), that is, beyond moderation, is had at the expense either of others who don't have it[15] or of another period in one's life when it will be dramatically and disastrously taken away (the very mechanism of tragedy). Eteocles' heroic illusion is that the resources of the world are simply additive: wealth becomes a sort of absolute, not so much a pole to be measured against its opposite as a goal to be reached. Eteocles wishes merely to take advantage of the benefits of the excluded middle, the permanence which it seems to assure, without paying its price in exclusion and suffering, for if Eteocles considers wealth to be separated from poverty by an emptiness or a gap, it is a gap of protection, the protection assured by the law of excluded middle.

The relation between "polys," "much," and "polis," "city," is not simply an aural and visual resemblance; rather the notions of quantity and accumulation are among the founding tenets of the city. Along with the names of Eteocles and Polyneices, the word "polis" finds itself in a sort of hinge position, a polemic between the excluded middle, represented by the words "polys/pleon" ("much"/"more"), and the virtuous middle, represented by the word "palin" ("back"):

> Ambition . . .
> comes to many [pollous] houses and happy
> cities [poleis] . . .
>
> (532–34)

> The lesser always wages war [polemion] on
> the greater [pleoni] . . .
>
> (539–40)

The "polemic" [polemion] raging both inside and outside the city [polis] is a war for the city walls, which must provide a protective container for the city's wealth. To this extent it is appropriate that the letters of "pleoni," the greater or wealthier side which according to Jocasta is always suscepti- ble to attack from the weaker, are a subset of the letters of "polemion," "war," for it is the very principle of stable, unvarying wealth that invites, almost demands the attack of the lesser in an attempt at reestablishing the ethic of equality. In opposition to this view of the "polis" as unassailable and irreversible we find the term "palin," "back." Jocasta uses the two terms one after the other in her speech to Eteocles:

And when [the gods] wish, they take [their possessions] back [palin]. . . .
But let me ask you two questions at one time:
Do you want to be king or save the city [polin]?

(557–60)

The true owners of the city's "property," according to Jocasta, are the gods, and reversibility — taking back (palin) what has been given — is the gods' prerogative. The paradox is that the city (polin, the accusative form which is very close indeed to "palin") can be saved if only Eteocles will recognize the reversibility ("palin") of his own reign; but in his eyes the city exists precisely in order to resist reversibility and the gods' repossession of what he thinks of as his right to rule alone.

We have thus arrived at the double bind of the city in the *Phoenissae:* if the city is to be considered as an accumulator of wealth, it must exclude the very middle which it is trying to protect. Alternating the cycles of wealth and power according to the regulation of the virtuous middle quickly leads to the need to exclude the very transition (middle) of wealth and power upon which that regulation depends. It is a paradox worthy of Zeno: if Eteo- cles and Polyneices as rulers of the city want to have the *more,* they cannot get (or get to) the *equal* which would seem to be a necessary step in getting to the more. The two brothers are "equalized" only through the shared in- adequacy of their positions, their common hatred or resistance to any equali- zation, as Jean Bollack points out: "Eteocles' and Polyneices' interests are expressed in two opposing political languages which Jocasta refutes one after the other. . . . Jocasta shows the *equal inadequation* of both of these antithetical discourses in their relation to the object they are seeking, the city."[16]

The brothers' inability to find a middle of compromise between them within the city is highly reminiscent of Thucydides' description of the civil strife during the Peloponnesian War:

> And so the cities began to be disturbed by revolutions. . . . The ordinary acceptation of words in their relation to things was changed as men thought fit. Reckless audacity [tolma] came to be regarded as courageous loyalty [andreia] to a party, prudent hesitation [mellesis] as specious cowardice [deilia], moderation as a cloak for unmanly weakness. . . . The cause of all these evils was the desire to rule which greed and ambition [pleonexian kai philotimian] inspire. . . . And citizens who belonged to neither party [ta de mesa ton politon, lit., "the middle elements of the citizens"] were continually destroyed by both.[17]

The relation of this passage to the *Phoenissae,* which has been remarked upon,[18] is reinforced by the use of the term "philotimia," "ambition," the word which Jocasta uses to sum up Eteocles' attitude (532). What should develop as an alternating movement between two opposing parties—each side giving and each taking in a gradual movement of reconciliation—is instead described as a pure movement of radicalization. The valorization of the word "tolma," or "daring," and the devalorization of the term "prudence" ("mellesis," i.e., "hesitation") reflect this polarizing action of the war, a polarization which makes the extreme (daring) seem like moderate virtue ("andreia," "bravery") and pushes the moderate (prudence) to a position of extremity ("deilia," "cowardice") or, in Aristotelian terms, deficiency.[19] And yet through this polarization each side has the impression of having more ("pleonexia," literally "having the more"), or of not being equal: "the middle elements [ta mesa] perished," for it is only in this exclusion of the middle that each extreme—i.e., the two "opposite" camps, called by Thucydides "hoi enantioi" (III, 82.7)—can keep from slipping toward an undesirable position of compromise.

The irony of the law of excluded middle as a protector of "property" is that both Eteocles and Polyneices ultimately fall victim to the needs of the excluded middle more than they reap its benefits. If there is no possible middle between the brothers, they themselves become a potential middle between the two cities at war, and this second, larger struggle might well reach its most favorable resolution not by a compromise (avoiding fratricide at all costs), but by reaffirming the separation between the two cities and seeing one of them emerge clearly victorious. One possible solution to the question of how to save Thebes would thus be the destruction of Eteocles and Polyneices themselves. Moved into a hypothetical middle ground of virtue by their mother, they clear the final boundaries between the two cities by reversing the value of the middle in the play from one of incorporation and overfulness to one of redefinition through purgation, through the excluded middle.

The movement from virtuous middle to excluded middle in the play is expressed by a reversal in the value of the city from being a centripetal to being a centrifugal force, the city as a center or a nucleus with a power of attraction giving way to an accelerating flight that manages to flush out even the tottering old Oedipus. This evolution is apparent in the attitude of all three of Jocasta's and Oedipus' children that appear here. All of them first perceive the city as a center of attraction. Eteocles, as we have seen, believes he can enter the city, take possession of it, and never leave it again. Antigone's attitude is apparent in the famous *teichoscopia,* a scene of observation from the heights of the city, in which the virginal princess and her tutor watch the gathering of Argive forces about the walls of Thebes. The scene, which is essentially voyeuristic, presupposes an asymmetry in the value of the city walls: the two observers believe that they can see without being seen. Finally Polyneices, at the moment of stepping across the boundaries of the city, attributes to them a kind of asymmetry, but this time it is an unfavorable kind:

> The doorkeepers' locks let me
> get into the walls with ease.
> What I'm afraid of is that having caught me in their nets,
> they won't let me out without blood on my skin.
>
> (261-64)

The city lets in, but it might not let out; its power of gravity, of irresistible attraction toward the center, can be menacing as well as beneficial.

The reversal of the city's apparent function as nucleus, as a force pulling those near or within it toward its center, comes after Jocasta's unsuccessful attempt at imposing the doctrine of the virtuous middle upon her sons. When Polyneices leaves the city, even though he gets away without bloodshed, the charge of the city has gone from positive to negative, from one of attraction to one of repulsion: he does not escape, but rather is thrown out on his ear. The true value of his exit is not lost upon Polyneices ("exelaunomai," "I am driven out," at 627 and again at 630), and it is perhaps this awareness of negativity which partially accounts for the frequency in his final speech (625–35) not only of negatives,[20] but also of alpha privatives: "argesei," "will remain workless" (625), "atimos," "without honor" (627), and "akon," "unwilling" (630).

The climax of Polyneices' final speech comes in its middle line: "For not willingly [ouch hekon] did I come, but unwillingly [akon] am I driven out of the land" (630). What this statement indicates is that a change of valence has taken place: if Polyneices came home "not willingly," it is because he

was resisting the pull of his home seen as a trap, but if he is leaving it unwillingly, it is because his city is no longer a source of dangerous attraction but a source of pure rejection. What has happened to the negative here
is that it has become incorporated into the idea of the positive, the now-
negative, expelling force of the formerly positive city being echoed by the
incorporation of the separate negative "ou" ("ouch hekon") into the attached
negative "a-" ("akon"). This pairing—which more commonly takes the
reversed form "akon kouch hekon" ("unwillingly and not willingly") and
is an example, like Eteocles and Polyneices themselves, of a kind of hendi-
adys ("two [words] for one [concept]")—is a frequent one in tragedy. But
its use here is particularly rich for yet another reason: the ambiguity of
the word "akon," meaning both "involuntarily" ("a-hekon"), as here, and
"spear" ("akon," "akontos"), the latter being a Homeric word which, although
extremely rare in tragedy, does appear in the *Phoenissae,* as we shall see.
This second sense of "akon," related to the term "akros," "extreme," the
spear being described by its point, already suggests the radicalization of
Polyneices. For him, action has become defined purely as reaction, since
he does nothing but move (or attempt to move) toward the pole opposite
his brother; his *raison d'être* is now to be Eteocles' other extreme. The
brothers thus take on the status of two opposing poles, and rather than a
positive and a negative pole of attraction which might be discharged by
reaching a point of neutrality, they are two positive or two negative poles,
repulsed by their sameness; two poles that ask no more than to be finally
distinguished, a clear-cut choice to be made between them.

We may resume the evolution of the "charge" of the city of Thebes as
the change from the attraction of electrons circling a positively charged nucleus to simply a line or continuum going from positive (Thebes) to negative (not-Thebes), the two poles being separated by a zero point, the walls
of the city. This development coincides with the play's shift in geographical focus. It starts out in the middle of the city, with Jocasta's prologue,
recited with the aplomb of a pillar of stability; Antigone watching the troops
from above but inside the walls; and the brothers' confrontation within the
city. From there it moves to the walls themselves, as Menoeceus' spectacu-
lar self-sacrifice, the drama's structural center,[21] takes place "pyrgon ep'
akron," "on the top of the towers" (1091), and the walls are then defended.
And the drama climaxes in a vague, ill-defined area around the city, that
is, the brothers' duel situated between the two armies.

Three moments in the play, the three descriptions of the warriors and
the fighting, put this evolving status of the city into focus: the *teichoscopia;*
the messengers' account of the attackers waiting outside the seven gates;
and the report of the brothers' duel and the subsequent battle between the

two forces. Although not explicitly an inventory of the seven gates and their attackers, the *teichoscopia* is built around a series of questions posed by Antigone about the identity and whereabouts of the seven attacking soldiers and the answers to those questions given by her tutor. The structure of the scene is based on a division into beginning (gate 1), middle (gate 4), and end (gate 7), and depends largely on the alternation in Antigone's interrogation between questions of "who" and questions of "where":

(1) *Hippomedon:* Who is this? Who and from where? What is his name? (119–24)
(2) *Tydeus:* And who is this? (133)
(3) *Parthenopaios:* And who is this? (145)
(4) *Polyneices:* But where is the one who was born of one and the same mother as I? Where is Polyneices? (156–58)
(5) *Adrastos:* (No question asked, mentioned by *paidagogos* along with Polyneices, 160)
(6) *Amphiaraos:* And that one, who would he happen to be? (171)
(7) *Capaneus:* And where's the one who makes terrible, arrogant threats to this city, Capaneus? (179–80)

The bread-and-butter of Antigone's interrogation, as might be expected, is "tis," "Who?" As a naïve observer, she takes as a given the images of the warriors she sees at a distance, and asks only to attach those images to a series of names. The questions that provide exceptions to this rule are found at gates 1, 4, and 7; only here does the criterion of location ("Where?" or "From where?") enter into Antigone's questioning. At the first gate we find the most complete question of the series: "Who is he? Who and from where? What is his name?" At the last gate Antigone gives her most complete response (182–92) once her own initial question has been answered, a lengthy diatribe against the arrogant Capaneus. The other gate which is immediately distinguishable is the fourth, the middle gate of the seven, where Polyneices is to be found.

It is extremely important that Antigone does not recognize her brother here, either before questioning the tutor—otherwise would she ask about his whereabouts?—or after:

Yes, I see him, but not clearly, I see a sort of
profile [typoma] of his form and a physique that quite resembles [exekasmena] his.
(161–62)

The middle of this series of questions and answers is familial, but not familiar: nowhere else does one feel so strongly the city's inability to unite its own as in Antigone's poignant remarks about Polyneices. In fact what she criticizes is the external nature of her brother's image: the profile [typoma, related to "type"] of his form is all the more frustrating to her in that, as a member of his family, Antigone wants to know this warrior entirely, not only by his outline but also by what is inside. Whereas she is satisfied with her "recognition" of the other warriors by their "types" and their names, she expects something else from the warrior at the middle gate:

> If only I could run through the air
> like a wind-swift cloud and reach [exanysaimi]
> my brother. . . .
>
> (163–65)

The intimacy promised by the middle position cannot be reached, "exanysaimi" echoing "'exekasmene," "resembling" (162) by the repetition of the prefix "ex," "out." The externality ("ex") of this middle vision is already a prefiguration of the subsequent failure of mediation between the two brothers.

The messenger's account of the attack and defense of the seven gates of Thebes, a reworking of the most famous scene in Aeschylus' *Seven against Thebes*,[22] reenacts the entire drama's movement from potential moderation to excess. The scene features descriptions of the attacking warriors' shields, and the shields are more and more "decentered" as the account progresses, moving from relative moderation to increasing violence. Parthenopaios, the first attacker, has a familial emblem in the middle of his shield ("en meso sakei," 1107), its physical position reflecting its moral stance as well, for it makes no excessive claims. The second shield, that of the seer Amphiaraos, has no emblem; that this refusal to boast is a mark of eminent moderation is indicated by the adverb "sophronos," "moderately" (1112), often applied by Aristotle to the person of moderate virtue. The third shield, that of Hippomedon, bears an image of caution and surveillance, "Panops" ("All-Eyes"), the legendary Argos hired by Hera to watch over Io, and this emblem is also explicitly said to be "en meso sakei," "in the middle of his shield" (1114).

Thus terminates the first half of the sequence: this is the last emblem said to be "in the middle" of its shield, and the next gate constitutes a kind of reversal. Here we find Tydeus holding a shield which contains not only a lion's skin, the mane standing on end as if in anticipation of the scenes of violence to follow, but also Prometheus holding a torch in his right hand and threatening to burn the city (1120–22). It is as if the legendary giver of fire to mankind had suddenly reversed his valence and begun using his gift as a threat, as if he were showing the negative potential of the benefit he conferred.

Starting from this point, the progression toward violence in the scene accelerates almost immeasurably: one of the key terms here is "mainesthai" (1127), "to rage," applied to the horses on Polyneices' shield (the fifth) which are made to jump by a mechanism linking them to the inside of the shield. The movement of decentering is altogether three dimensional: the last three emblems fairly jump from their planes. After Polyneices', the sixth shield, belonging to Capaneus, is like a sort of bas-relief:

> And on his iron-backed shield was struck [typois]
> an earth-born giant bearing upon his shoulders a whole city,
> having pulled it from its foundation with a lever.
>
> (1130–32)

The verticality of the scene is reenacted by its depth: this emblem is struck [typois] upon the shield just as the Titan rips the city from its foundations.

The excess of the emblems reaches its height with the final shield, that of Adrastos, which bears the image of the hydra of Lerna, whose hundred heads, figured as snakes, pull the defending Thebans off the wall and devour them. This is another image of decentering, the removal of the defenders from the city walls being clearly one of moving toward the periphery and crossing the threshold dividing city from non-city. The term "mesos" is used once again:

> And out of the middle of the walls [ek de teicheon meson]
> the snakes bore the children of the Cadmeans in their jaws.
>
> (1137–38)

The phrase "ek de teicheon meson," "out of the middle of the walls," is a response to the "en meso sakei" ("in the middle of the shield") of the beginning of the scene. The struggle from this point on will be a struggle at the walls, or rather for the walls; a struggle to define a middle — a dividing line, a boundary — around a city which no longer knows what it is.

Although the battle takes place outside the walls, it is set off by the Thebans penetrating "into the middle" ("kas mes'," 1191) of the Argive camp. By a peculiarly Euripidean topology, the battle reaches its most intimate, its innermost moment in the confrontation of the two brothers, which takes place outside of the city, but nonetheless "in the middle": not only, like the pouring of libations which seals their decision to duel, in the space between the two armies ("kan metaichmiois," 1240, "meta," "in the midst of," "amongst," being etymologically related to "meson," "middle"),[23] but in the middle of that middle ("es meson metaichmion," 1361), the center of the space dividing Thebes from not-Thebes; the soon-to-be-excluded middle.

The duel, which as the ultimate failure of Jocasta's efforts at reconciliation represents the culmination of the play's centrifugal movement away from the middle of moderation, simultaneously embodies the increasing concentration upon the middle as the focus of the city's problems and the locus of any "solution" that might be offered. In fact, the brothers are depicted as trying to reduce their bodily mass to the dimensions of a middle, the shields they hold before them:

> And they crouched under their circles [i.e., shields],
> so that the spear slipped in vain.
> But if either one saw the other's eye appearing above the shield,
> he showed his spear with a flourish, wishing to warn him with the point.
>
> (1382–85)

So long as each brother is held within the dimensions of the circle of his shield, he is safe; but he is also indistinguishable from his brother.[24] The extremity peeking over the edge of the shield is not only a danger for the brother so exposed, it is also a prefiguration of the necessity to give up the safety, the nondifferentiation of the middle if the battle is to be decided.

In this battle scene the conflict between the virtuous middle and the excluded middle reaches its climax. During the first part of the duel, Eteocles breaks his spear as he wounds his brother with it, and to even the sides he then snaps his brother's spear in the middle:

> And he breaks the middle of the spear [meson d' akont'];
> and the fight was now equal [ex isou].
>
> (1402–3)

Eteocles accomplishes an action which seems to equalize the two brothers ("ex isou"), as if in response to Jocasta's prayers throughout the entire drama. Now at last the brothers both seem to be in a salutary middle, for each has lost his "point," the end of his spear, here called an "akon" and earlier named an "akron dory" (1399), both words suggesting an extreme.

But the form of the action by which Eteocles seems to eliminate the extremity of his brother's spear to match the absence of his own negates any suggestion of moderation, for Eteocles breaks the spear by excluding its middle ("meson d' akont' "), thus making of the spear two ends, a metaphor for the two brothers: essentially undistinguishable, but no longer "attachable." The term "akon," "spear," echoes the earlier use of the word "akon," "unwilling" (630), but here, rather than the idea of incorporating opposition, we are witness to the breaking of this incorporation, the "akon" or spear snapped in the middle in an act representing the final separation of the two brothers. This is the moment of "decision" of the duel, a moment which prefigures its outcome: two equal brothers who are nonetheless irreconcilably radicalized; who are of equal value, but who no longer "touch." The fratricide, although it does not ultimately provide any genuine difference between the brothers, does at last redefine the boundaries of the city.

The end of the play reestablishes an order that cannot be arrived at by either the two armies or the two brothers. Only in death are the two brothers at last "distinguished": Eteocles is in, Polyneices out (literally), expelled and condemned to remain unburied just as Creon is in and Oedipus out. Thus by a sort of boomerang effect, the dead Eteocles enjoys the "benefits" of the law of excluded middle which he has lost his life trying to enforce.

It is in this sense that we may complete the evolution of the role of the city by saying that if it starts out as a potential terrain of compromise between the two brothers and then, because it fails to realize that potential, moves outward in a search for some unshakable boundary that might define it, the city in the end reasserts its power. That the city chooses to accept one of the brothers at the expense of the other once they are both dead has infinitely less to do with any authentic distinctness of the brothers than with the city's need to select one of two, to include one and to exclude one, as an ultimate means of "correcting" its own failure to effect a successful compromise. And it is precisely by refusing us the satisfaction of an authentic choice that Euripides so baldly reveals the highest cost of tragic choice: the undeniable knowledge of its own inadequacy.

The city as middle—its return to a form of normalcy coinciding with the moment at which the members of the audience exit from the theater and make their way back to the apparent safety of their homes—is thus reconstructed on the other side of extremity. The fact that the "choice" arrived at by this drama provides little more than a vestigial gesture, a skeleton, a charade of choice operated upon two cadavers, emphasizes by its gratuitousness the need in tragedy to make choices. It is the tragedy of the city that it must exercise its power of exclusion in order for its mechanisms of inclusion—of protection, storage, continuity, and memory—to function. Let us now turn from the end of Euripides—for we must not forget that the *Phoenissae* is one of his very last plays—to the beginning of Racine: *Les Frères Ennemis,* or *La Thébaïde.*

4

The (Still) Birth of the Racinian Individual

La Thébaïde

Thus, in the *Phoenissae* Racine finds a play which has no *unity,* but which creates a *unit,* the unit constituted by the play's excluded middle, a choice of one out of two contradictory, opposing brothers. Racine himself criticizes Euripides' play for its lack of unity,[1] and his own version is immeasurably more concentrated. Here we have no time for a *teichoscopia* in the style of Euripides' play, that having already taken place before the play begins:

> Du haut de la muraille
> Je les ai vus déjà tous rangés en bataille;
> J'ai vu déjà le fer briller de toutes parts.
> (7–9)[2]

The repetition of "déjà" is perhaps a subconscious nod of apology to Euripides' leisurely and thus unacceptable opening. That this is the day, even perhaps the moment of confrontation of the two brothers is established by Jocaste's instant setting of the action which, unlike her rambling history of Thebes in the *Phoenissae,* delves no further into the past than her recent spell of fretful insomnia ("Mes yeux depuis six mois étaient ouverts aux larmes," 3), and comes almost immediately to the present: "Nous voici donc, hélas! à ce jour détestable" (19). But, as we shall see, what Racine makes up for in the realm of unity, he loses in the domain of units, for his play describes the impossibility of creating the unit of tragic individuation.

To say that *La Thébaïde* begins *in medias res* would be paradoxical, since from the very start Racine's play—although it begins in the middle of things whereas Euripides' began at the beginning, with Jocasta's lengthy prologue[3]—also undermines any notion of the middle as a possible locus

62

of reconciliation or virtue for the two brothers. Thus, while Euripides' Jocasta wishes to bring her two sons together (*Phoenissae,* 81–82), Racine's Jocaste asks only to keep them apart:

> Il les faut séparer, ou mourir par leurs mains.
>
> (18)

> Quand deux frères armés vont s'égorger entre eux,
> Ne les pas séparer, c'est les perdre tous deux.
>
> (197–98)

Jocaste, in fact, like her Euripidean counterpart, represents the play's initial attitude toward the middle, but here her position is neither that of the virtuous middle nor that of the excluded middle, but rather an uneasy rejection of both. Jocaste's mistrust of the middle—that is, the coming together of the two brothers on some hypothetical terrain of compromise—reflects her suspicious attitude toward virtue. Gone is the belief, so prominent in Euripides' character, in the power of moderation and of the virtuous middle. In its place we find a thoroughgoing doubt of the very existence of virtue:

> O toi, soleil, ô toi qui rends le jour au monde,
> Que ne l'as-tu laissé dans une nuit profonde!
>
> . . . .
>
> Tu ne t'étonnes pas si mes fils sont perfides,
> S'ils sont tous deux méchants, et s'ils sont parricides;
> Tu sais qu'ils sont sortis d'un sang incestueux,
> Et tu t'étonnerais s'ils étaient vertueux.
>
> (23–34)

Jocaste wishes time to stop passing—and in this she is expressing Racine's ambition of concentrating action as much as possible—because she does not believe in the regularity of alternating cycles to which Euripides' character alludes in her attempt at persuading Eteocles to give up his power. On the contrary, Jocaste's words suggest that virtue, were it to exist, would be not a mediation between extremes, but rather an oxymoron, an unresolved coinciding of extremes: the image of the sun's being "étonné" ("astonished"), which Jocaste repeats (31, 34), recalls the etymology of the verb, Latin *extonare,* "to strike with thunder" (the French "tonner," "to thunder," is at any rate very close to "étonner"), which is fully incompatible with its subject, the sun. Jocaste's definition of virtue, then, is one of violent, irreconcilable opposition: in order to become virtuous, the two sons would have to become as self-contradictory as a thundering sun.

Yet Jocaste, even though she has no faith in the virtuous middle, is also not a proponent of the excluded middle. This is first apparent in her opening speech, which has all the immediacy and impact that Racine wished for:

> Ils sont sortis, Olympe? Ah! mortelles douleurs!
> Qu'un moment de repos me va coûter de pleurs!
>
> (1–2)

Jocaste's terror at the two brothers' "exit" is her fear that the entire situation will be precipitated and decided, for the only outcome she can envision is a disastrous one. "Sortir," one of the play's key terms, here suggests Jocaste's desire to keep the brothers inside a sort of womb of maternal surveillance. So long as they don't "get out," they can do nothing extreme, nothing definitive or individual, the "mortelles douleurs" of the escape from their mother's control being figurative labor pains.

Indeed, Jocaste's repetition of "sortir" at the end of this first scene, "ils sont sortis d'un sang incestueux" (33), is indicative of the real meaning of the term in her eyes: one's relation to one's origins and not one's separation from them. In order for the brothers to "leave" the incestuous blood of which they were born, they would have to go beyond themselves and their origins, that is, to break the seemingly endless cycle of incest and kin murder which is renewed with every generation of their family. This they will never do so long as "sortir" has only the meaning "to come from" and not the meaning "to exit" or "to leave behind."

Thus Jocaste finds herself in the paradoxical situation of wishing her sons neither to integrate themselves into the dreadful family tradition—the gesture of incorporation normally being emblematic of the virtuous middle, in the terms of which any given individual is a mediation between his two parents—nor to "exit" from the present crisis by an excluded middle that would decide the situation unsatisfactorily.[4] Her ambivalence toward the middle is summed up in her double-edged use of the term "obstacle": the brothers' hatred is, of course, irremediable ("La haine de mes fils est un trop grand obstacle," 692), but in the absence of an acceptable definitive choice between the two, any postponement of their meeting is a benevolent obstacle ("Va voir si leur fureur n'a point trouvé d'obstacle," 580), a temporary barrier against the final cataclysmic spilling of blood.[5]

This nonacceptance of both the ethical middle and the excluded middle is expressed in larger terms by the utterly paradoxical nature of the words "dernier" and "sang."[6] In *La Thébaïde*, "dernier" refuses to be one of the two extremes normally defining a middle. The most prominent occurrence of the word comes in the oracle which leads to the death of Ménécée:

> Thébains, pour n'avoir plus de guerres,
> Il faut, par un ordre fatal,
> Que le dernier du sang royal
> Par son trépas ensanglante vos terres.
>
> (393–96)

"Le dernier" has at least two distinct temporal values here: the very last, and the most recent (latest). "The very last," which projects an end to the violence, is clearly the hoped-for meaning,[7] but the other alternative undermines this possibility; it means not only the youngest, i.e., the last-born, which is how Ménécée interprets it ("Je suis le dernier sang de vos rois descendu," 645), but also the latest in a series which is not yet complete. In this case the oracular statement takes on a wonderfully tautological meaning: the cycle of violence will end as soon as "dernier" no longer has the force of a middle (the most recent, neither first nor last) but that of an end; that is, as soon as its middle value is excluded. In order for there to be an end to the violence, the oracle says, one must find a way to make the blood shed by the royal family be the last blood shed; this amounts to saying simply that the end of the bloodshed will come when an end has been found.

The oracle's difficulty resides in the conflict between its two central terms: "dernier" and "sang." Whereas it is easy to imagine a complete depletion of blood—which in this case would mark the end of the royal line altogether—it is difficult to conceive of the process by which such an end could be reached, that is, to conceptualize the last drop of blood itself, for this is as difficult to seize upon as the moment at which Achilles overtakes the tortoise in Zeno's paradox. "Last," a term which establishes a rank or hierarchy, cannot be properly applied to "blood," which is what Grévisse calls a "nom de matière" and thus cannot be pluralized,[8] the capacity for pluralization being a necessary precondition for the application of the concept of lastness. The problem of seizing the final unit of blood reverses the question posed by the Megarian philosophers of the number of grains it takes to produce a pile; it, too, is the expression of an irresolvable conflict between units and what constitutes them. The stability of the individual within a given lineage (that is, a succession of supposedly individual manifestations of "sang") is in this drama fully called into question.

What "dernier" does belong with, in contrast to "sang" and rhyming with it, is "rang," "dernier" being an example of a "rang." The problematic nature of the contrast between "rang" and "sang" soon becomes apparent in Jocaste's advice to Etéocle following Ménécée's sacrifice:

> Vous pouvez, en cédant un peu de votre rang,
> Faire plus qu'il n'a fait en versant tout son sang.
>
> (721–22)

Here once again we come up against the problem of the lack of units. Jocaste's words echo the conceptual "error" that the oracle made earlier: the problem with the phrase "le dernier du sang," a rank ("dernier") being applied to a substance ("sang"), is reversed in "un peu de votre rang," a measure which normally applies to substances ("un peu") being here used to describe a rank. "Un peu de votre rang" makes sense only if "rang" is considered to be a continuum, like "sang" a substance based on mass and consistency (cf. English "much blood") and not on units or contiguity ("many ranks"). Jocaste's attempt at making "sang" and "rang" commensurable fails to take into account the fact that the two cannot be measured in the same terms: what is a "little" of "first" or "third"?

The issue underlying the conflict between "sang" and "rang" is the relation of the individual, the would-be unit in a family lineage, to the lineage taken as a whole, as is suggested by Antigone's words of entreaty to her brother:

> Seulement quelques jours souffrez que l'on vous voie,
> Et donnez-nous le temps de chercher quelque voie
> Qui puisse vous remettre au rang de vos aïeux,
> Sans que vous répandiez un sang si précieux.
>
> (539–42)

The internal rhyme "rang"/"sang" in two consecutive lines immediately following the hemistiche is once again paradoxical. Antigone imagines two alternatives: either Polynice will be put back into the ranks of his ancestors, but in the process will run the risk of shedding his own blood, or he will give up his quest for recognition in Thebes, thus not joining the ranks of his ancestors, but also presumably not putting himself in danger of meeting a violent end. And yet in either case the projected action leaves a gap. If Polynice is put back into the ranks of his ancestors, thus showing that he comes from ("sortir de") those ranks, he would seem at first to be closing the gap left by his absence from those ranks; but if this indeed comes to pass, he himself will fail to constitute the required unit or stopgap, since he will then be emptied of his "so precious blood." On the other hand, if Polynice gives up his claims to the throne, he might conserve his own integrity—in the physical and not the moral sense, simply the boundaries of his body—by not shedding his blood, but he will then leave a discontinuity in the ranks of his ancestors. Hémon's words accepting the family curse make the paradox of this nonunit explicit:

> Et du sang de ses rois il est beau d'être issu,
> Dût-on rendre ce sang sitôt qu'on l'a reçu.
>
> (417–18)

This zero point describing the passing on of blood and thus of life itself from one generation to the next suggests that being in one's rightful "rang" means that one "rend" or gives back immediately the very lifeblood which being in that rank provides.[9]

The Racinian "individual" described by Antigone's words here is thus either a product of the past and virtually inexistent in the present, a pure origin, a history of attachments to the past, or a pure desire for rejection of the past which leaves behind it an unstable vacuum and thus cannot persist. One of the central questions which Racinian tragedy poses is the nature of the individual and of his or her relation to the past, that is, the question of the individual's *originality*. Does individuation consist of conforming to one's heritage—and the past in Racine always brings an essentially moral heritage, be it good or bad—or of resisting it? If one is nothing more than what one is destined or programmed to be by one's background, is one an "individual"? Or does individuation require an element of creation *ex nihilo* with every new generation? Is one an individual to the extent that one *is* or *is not* what one's predecessors have been? Is individuation a virtuous middle, a reconciliation of the present and the past, or an excluded middle, a fundamental break?

If in Euripides' play the excluded middle is necessary for the individual to be constituted and to save the collectivity, in Racine's play it is only the unremitting tension between the virtuous middle and the excluded middle which allows even the possibility of individuation. Opposed to this tension is the moment—or rather the beginning of the endless series of moments, the nontime—in which individuals attempting to constitute themselves admit failure by putting a stop to all resistance of the obstacles to their own rest, their "repos":

> *Jocaste:*
> Ils sont sortis, Olympe? Ah! mortelles douleurs!
> Qu'un moment de repos me va coûter de pleurs!
>
> (1–2)

Jocaste:
Ainsi donc la discorde a pour vous tant de charmes?
Vous lassez-vous déjà d'avoir posé les armes?

(499–500)

Créon:
Je ressens à la fois mille tourments divers,
Et je m'en vais chercher du repos aux enfers.

(1515–16)

The true—and terrifying—sense of the middle for Jocaste is in fact "le repos," which is mentioned in her opening speech as well as in Créon's concluding one and thus, as Judd Hubert points out, frames the play.[10] "Le repos" may represent a kind of "goal" for all of the characters, but its sense is not simple, as the middle quotation above demonstrates. What is "tiring" in this case is the "pose" itself, the setting down of weapons demanded by the truce between the two brothers: this "pose," rather than being "reposant" or restful, is in fact the very thing which causes the need for rest ("Vous lassez-vous déjà?"). Posing their weapons requires an effort from the brothers, for their "relaxed" state, the action to which they would both naturally drift, would be to attack and kill each other. Resisting this temptation is a centrifugal action, running from their innermost urges, and the end of resistance means being pulled back into the dangerous center of their being, the only position at which, in Racine's tragedy, one can be "at rest."

It is for this reason that the middle takes on such fearful proportions for Jocaste: the middle for her, unlike her Euripidean counterpart, is not the locus of an equality, linking two opposed terms, it is rather the domain of utter self-equality, of giving up the struggle to be anything more than one's heritage would lead one to be. It is at the same time an indefinite, limitless domain—for the possibilities of crime in Racine are endless—and a virtual zero point, the practically dimensionless time to which all resistance to one's criminal nature is ultimately reduced. This middle is based upon the same paradox as Georges Poulet's definition of Racinian time: "The Racinian moment thus becomes enslaved to a past or future duration which sucks it into a vacuum and determines its extremity. The extreme point of a dying past, of a future, of a monster 'being born,' the Racinian moment is virtually stifled between two walls of events which join and already touch. It does not have the time to become time."[11]

The middle or meeting point between past and future is also an "extreme," a limit, a single last *chance* to constitute a unit of time in a present not yet fully hemmed in by the past and the future.[12] Thus, insofar as the middle can be defined in a chronological sense as what separates the first from the last, the words of the cynical Créon take on an extraordinary importance as they anticipate and define what will turn out to be an inescapable given for the Racinian individual:

> Mais allons. Le remords n'est pas ce qui me touche,
> Et je n'ai plus un coeur que le crime effarouche:
> Tous les premiers forfaits coûtent quelques efforts
> Mais, Attale, on commet les seconds sans remords.
>
> (899–902)

These words, which close the third act of the play, announce an entire Racinian itinerary. For the individual attempting to constitute himself, the "unit" of time is available only during the first of his misdeeds ("les premiers forfaits"). The second crimes are crimes no longer, for they are committed by a character who is in a sense "au repos," at rest, having fully given in to himself. That the "first" crimes are really equivalent to the "last" crimes becomes clear if we look ahead to the final line of *Britannicus*, spoken about Néron by his tutor Burrhus: "Plût aux dieux que ce fût le dernier de ses crimes!" (*Britannicus*, 1758). The "first" crime is indeed the "last" crime — and Burrhus' wish is ironically fulfilled — if we take Créon's words into consideration: Néron's subsequent actions are committed by an amoral being whose ethical sense is entirely extinct, a man incapable of being anything other than himself, a creature who is unable to resist his appalling inheritance and whose actions, insofar as they are not based on choice, cannot be considered to be crimes.

To this extent the phonic resemblance between the words "forfait" and "effort" in Créon's speech is essential: the two words comprise the same phonetic elements (for-fe, ef-for), and can be transformed into each other by two simple reversals, one within the syllable ef-fe and one between the two syllables. What separates all action ("effort") from crime ("forfait"), what ultimately makes of crime the end of effort, is the tragic reversal by which Aristotle defines the unity of time.

But can time in *La Thébaïde* be said to be made up of an Aristotelian tragic reversal? And if the "first" is the "last," where is the middle? The two enemy brothers continue to be on the verge of defining themselves so long as they are opposed as two extremes and have not met in the middle which constitutes their most fundamental instincts for self-definition and self-destruction, and yet once they have met in an effort to define themselves fully, that middle ground becomes a terrain of exclusion. They become not free self-defining individuals, but rather impersonal ciphers in the ongoing history of the house of Laios, their "choice" instantly taking on the face of the inevitable. It is thus only once the brothers stop resisting themselves that they become themselves, but that "becoming" is based upon an exclusion of the very freedom and "individuality" which, paradoxically, existed only through their resistance of themselves. The middle between the two brothers destroys the very unit it is attempting to create, the action of the play being not an initiation ("premier") into the true power of the ethical sense, but rather the final ("dernier") moment which has any relation to ethics whatsoever.

A speech by Polynice in the 1664 edition of the play reveals the illusory relation of virtue and the middle:

> Je ne me connais plus en ce malheur extrême:
> En m'arrachant du trône on m'arrache à moi-même.
> Tant que j'en suis dehors, je ne suis plus à moi;
> Pour être vertueux, il faut que je sois roi.[13]

It might appear that might makes right, that being at the center of power gives one a stabilizing sense of equilibrium and virtue. But this virtual equation of virtue and the center of power is removed in later editions of the play. And Jocaste goes so far as to wonder whether arriving at the center of power doesn't force one to lose one's virtue:

> Dieux! si devenant grand souvent on devient pire,
> Si la vertu se perd quand on gagne l'empire . . .
>
> (1047–48)

Antigone goes even further by adding that being separated from power gives one a moral advantage:

> [Polynice] était vertueux, Olympe, et malheureux.
> Mais, hélas! ce n'est plus ce coeur si magnanime,
> Et c'est un criminel qu'a couronné son crime.
> Son frère plus que lui commence à me toucher:
> Devenant malheureux, il m'est devenu cher.
>
> (1268–72)

Whereas Polynice seems to abdicate all claim to virtue because of what Antigone thinks is his victory over his brother, it is precisely Etéocle's being thrown from power that makes him virtuous in Antigone's eyes. Once the brothers' positions have reversed, virtue also switches places, fleeing rather than residing in the middle. Jocaste's rhyming of "pire" and "empire" reminds us of the double meaning of the word "empire," the noun suggesting a spreading out of power from a center and the verb ("to worsen," from the comparative "pire") dealing rather with a loss of value in the ethical domain: according to Jocaste and Antigone, when one *has* an "empire," one "empire" ("worsens").

This treacherous value of the middle is precisely what is expressed by Etéocle in a statement of non-Aristotelian "reversal": "Il faut, il faut qu'il fuie, et non qu'il se retire" (936). This hoped-for change in the *dynamics* of movement is distinct from the principle of reversal, since it represents no change in *direction* — "fuie" and "se retire" both being acts of distancing — but rather only a change in the source of motion. What Etéocle wants to appropriate for himself is the power of the middle, the power to establish the polarity of his brother's exit: if Polynice "se retire," his moving source is the outside (his destination, the goal of his "retraite"), whereas if he flees, he is pushed out from the middle. Furthermore, the very action of "se retirer," through its related noun forms "retraite" and "trait," forms an ironic commentary on the brothers' meeting:

> Commencez donc, mes fils, cette union si chère,
> Et que chacun de vous reconnaisse son frère:
> Tous deux dans votre frère envisagez vos traits.
> (979–81)

Jocaste's request that the brothers look at each other's "traits" is exactly what leads to their "retraite," each brother moving back in horror, for the "traits" that each one sees are in themselves "re-traits," that is, mere echoes of his own "traits."[14] Catching up with the "traits" on the other side of the middle would mean, like Zeno's arrow ("trait") straining to put its nonunitary moments together to constitute motion, resolving the issue of the interval between the nonunits (moments or brothers). This issue the brothers cannot resolve, as the "traits" of Polynice are overcome by death's own "traits" or arrows (1383) and thus lose any potential power of intentionality or directionality.

The climax of the treacherous middle comes in the brothers' final duel. Yet again a unit seems to be formed which might successfully separate and distinguish them once and for all, since Polynice strikes what appears to be a deathblow against his twin. Once more, however, the unit is no sooner "formed" than it is called into question, and this even before Etéocle has struck back:

> Polynice, tout fier du succès de son crime,
> Regarde avec plaisir expirer sa victime;
> Dans le sang de son frère il semble se baigner:
> "Et tu meurs," lui dit-il, "et moi je vais régner.
> Regarde dans mes mains l'empire et la victoire;
> Va rougir aux enfers de l'excès de ma gloire."
> (1357–62)

The description of Polynice standing over what he thinks is his dead brother features an anaphora which focuses attention on the two lines beginning with "Regarde," a juxtaposition further supported by two other resemblances in the lines: "expirer"/"empire," each immediately following the hemistiche, and "victime"/"victoire," both constituting the lines' feminine rhymes. Moreover, two of the pairs express the alternatives of defeat ("expirer," "victime") and victory ("empire," "victoire") which seem to separate the two brothers at last: Polynice, the former "out," moves in ("empire," from Latin "*im*-perare"), while Etéocle, the former "in," moves out ("*ex*-pirer"). The problem is that the former "in," who has become "out" by "expiring," has also in another sense become "in," since Etéocle is now the "ex-pire," that is, the "former worse" (of the two brothers), or the present better. Polynice, on the other hand, by reaching the center of power, loses the virtuous middle rather than gaining it; being in the middle, which should give one the good, makes one the bad.

The treachery of the middle position continues to the very point of death, even after the middle *seems* to have been excluded, Polynice "chosen" over his brother:

> [Polynice] s'approche du roi couché sur la poussière,
> Et pour le désarmer il avance le bras.
>
> . . . .
>
> Et dans l'instant fatal que ce frère inhumain
> Lui veut ôter le fer qu'il tenait à la main,
> Il lui perce le coeur; et son âme ravie,
> En achevant ce coup abandonne la vie.
> Polynice frappé pousse un cri dans les airs,
> Et son âme en courroux s'enfuit dans les enfers.
>
> (1366–80)

As Polynice tries to take the sword from his brother's hand, Etéocle, far from reversing his brother's action by pulling the sword back toward himself, reinforces Polynice's withdrawal, or rather merely turns it into a "flight" ("il faut qu'il fuie") rather than a backing off. The final spoiling of the excluded middle—the choice of one brother out of two—is thus effected by a change in valence: what was a pull becomes a push, as the dynamics of the middle remain unstable.

But if this is essentially how the brothers end, this is not the end of our discussion. Opposed to the indefinite middle of Jocaste and the two brothers is the character whom we might call the third of the "Frères Ennemis," the third that indeed tries to provide the excluded third which has hitherto been lacking: Jocaste's own brother, Créon, whom Barthes calls the only "individual" in the drama[15] and who alone has—or rather thinks he has—the potential to escape the general morass of nonindividuation.

In Créon's eyes the throne must carry no exclusive power, no element of stability, until he himself is on it; in the meantime, while seeming to favor Etéocle's permanent rule, he manipulates the two brothers as indistinguishable and indifferent opposites:

> D'Etéocle d'abord j'appuyai l'injustice;
> Je lui fis refuser le trône à Polynice.
> Tu sais que je pensais dès lors à m'y placer;
> Et je l'y mis, Attale, afin de l'en chasser.
>
> (851–54)

In revealing the fact that he himself is the one who pushed Etéocle to refuse his brother the throne ("Je lui fis refuser le trône à Polynice"), Créon puts the two brothers in an identical syntactical position, "lui" replacing "à Etéocle" and thus parallel to "à Polynice." Even though in principle one brother is the subject of the action (refusal) and the other its indirect object, the only real subject of the sentence is thus "Je," Créon himself. Like a god serenely manipulating a battle between two armies and granting the upper hand now to one side, now to the other, Créon nonetheless has a final goal in mind—taking the throne himself ("je pensais dès lors à m'y placer").

We may trace Créon's movement toward his goal by looking at three points in the play—roughly speaking, the beginning, the middle, and the end—at which he appears. By connecting these points, like Zeno trying to represent movement, we may sketch out the nature of Créon's trajectory. Here is the first passage, spoken to Créon by Jocaste:

> Mais avouez, Créon, que toute votre peine
> C'est de voir que la paix rend votre attente vaine,
> Qu'elle assure à mes fils le trône où vous tendez,
> Et va rompre le piège où vous les attendez.
>
> . . . .
>
> Et votre ambition, qui tend à leur fortune,
> Vous donne pour tous deux une haine commune.
>
> (223–32)

Créon, like a sort of Zenonian arrow or "trait" is, as Jocaste observes, pure tension: "attente," "tendez," "attendez," "tend," all indicate this latent contained energy of Créon's, as if he were simply waiting for the creation of a unifying process by which his individual moments of plotting might realize their momentum and allow him to spring forward toward his final goal, the throne.

The second passage is the exact midpoint of the play, a place which will interest us in each of the works of Racine that we will be studying. It is at this moment alone, in the speech which Créon recites to Etéocle after receiving the news of his son's suicide, that Créon apparently "stalls," that he seems no longer to be moving toward a goal but rather to come to a halt:

> Ah! dans ses [Ménécée's] ennemis
> Je trouve votre frère, et je trouve mon fils!
> Dois-je verser mon sang, ou répandre le vôtre?
> Et dois-je perdre un fils pour en venger un autre?
> Seigneur, mon sang m'est cher, le vôtre m'est sacré:
> Serai-je sacrilège ou bien dénaturé?
> Souillerai-je ma main d'un sang que je révère?
> Serai-je parricide afin d'être bon père?
>
> (753–60)

Créon points out the absurdity of losing a second son in the name of avenging one he has already lost. By expressing the desire to stop the series of deaths at one, the number which in this play instantly self-destructs, he places himself in the tradition of other resisters of the *lex talionis,* those who, like Athena in the *Eumenides,* understand the nonsense of allowing the fury (or Furies) of an uncontrolled vendetta free play.

The very middle of the play, the line which ends the first half, crystallizes the difficulties of this tragic choice:

> Serai-je sacrilège ou bien dénaturé?
> (758)

Créon's choice between being sacrilegious (avenging his son by killing his nephew or, still worse, his other son) and being denatured (not avenging the death of his own son) closely resembles Orestes' choice between killing his own mother and leaving his father unavenged in Aeschylus' *Choephoroi:* this is the quintessential tragic choice, the choice between two contradictory alternatives neither of which is acceptable but between which no middle is possible. Whichever path is chosen, the wrong persists, because one either leaves the past uncorrected or, by avenging the old wrong, creates a new one: "Serai-je parricide afin d'être bon père?"

Créon's conclusion is to bring the entire system to a halt, to pursue his goals no further, and to seek out "le repos":

> Je me consolerai, si ce fils que je plains
> Assure par sa mort le repos des Thébains.
> Le ciel promet la paix au sang de Ménécée;
> Achevez-la, Seigneur, mon fils l'a commencée;
> Accordez-lui ce prix qu'il en a prétendu,
> Et que son sang en vain ne soit pas répandu.
> (765–70)

Créon tries to make Ménécée's self-negation into "the (very) last blood" shed by the royal family; if Etéocle and Polynice make it up, Créon's own bid for power is over. Thus, even though we are at the drama's midpoint, Créon's apparent resignation makes this sound like an end. Jocaste punctuates Créon's speech by reinforcing this impression of ending:

> Non, puisqu'à nos malheurs vous devenez sensible,
> Au sang de Ménécée il n'est rien d'impossible.
> (771–72)

In the middle of the play Créon becomes "sensible," that is, apparently, "sans cible," without a target, the homonym being suggested by the vocabulary of aiming ("tendre") and arrows ("traits") which we have already discussed. Créon is stopped in the middle, but far short of the bull's eye.

But in fact this tender scenario is nothing but a play-within-a-play; Créon, whose ambition never flags, merely gives this middle the appearance of an end, and we will call this middle parading as an end the theatrical middle. In each of the four plays of Racine we will examine, the theatrical middle will provide the brief (and false) suggestion of a favorable outcome in the precise middle of the drama. In this particular case, it becomes apparent that the middle cannot be an end if we recall the ultimate meaning of the middle for Jocaste, that of "le repos," the moment in which would-be individuals gives up their struggle and becomes what fate and their heritage would make of them. For in this light Créon's seemingly eloquent reconciliation speech of the middle of the play becomes nothing but a prefiguration of his own more fundamental "repos" to come, that which follows his true emergence as a monster: "Serai-je sacrilège ou bien dénaturé?" then becomes a Néron-like rubbing of the hands in anticipation of the limitless field of crime opening up before Créon, not a virtuous rhetorical question but a true question of perverted choice.

And indeed, Créon's monstrous potential shows itself as soon as the middle of the play has passed: "Je ne fais point de pas qui ne tende à l'empire"

(848). This statement again sets Créon's "tendencies" into motion. "Pas" is not a negative here as it was in his "plea" to stop the bloodletting ("Et que son sang en vain ne soit *pas* répandu," 770), but rather a positive indication that the pause or negation of motion (the negative "pas") was itself a pose or a position. Créon's double negation ("*point* de pas qui *ne* tende") signals his attempt at an excluded middle of individuation: by the negation of the spaces, or pauses, between the discrete moments of his plot, the intervals, he will at last reach the position coveted by both—or rather all three—of the enemy brothers, the throne. And it is the law of excluded middle that guarantees his plan: if "no negative" is a positive, then the negation of a negation—the elimination of the intervals between oneself and one's goal, or between the nonunitary "points" of one's trajectory—is a *position,* in this case a position of power. By controlling the theatrical middle, Créon shows that he can both inhabit the middle—play the two brothers off each other, bide his time, even claim to give up the race in the middle—and, when the time comes, exclude it.

But Créon's attempt at constituting himself as an individual is rendered impossible by the play's third time span. Créon, the arrow poised in tension, the embodiment of pure intention, is taken apart—or rather not put together—by a single word thrown out to him, Antigone's last word in the drama, "Attendez" (1420), which becomes like an alpha privative added to Créon's verb of (would-be) motion, "tendre." At the height of Créon's tense anticipation of the realization of his amorous desires, at the moment when his "tending toward" the empire has been realized, Antigone unstrings Créon's bow in a dénouement that unites nothing, but rather, in one final treacherous reversal, unties everything, unravels not so much the threads of the intrigue as the knot by which the nascent heroic individual has tried to seal his superiority, his rise above the middle.

The device of postponement underlying Antigone's cruel imperative, essentially a comic mechanism, signals the profound questioning of genre at the play's end. The brothers' elaborate *pas de deux* is satirized in the brief exchange immediately following Créon's narration of it:

> *Antigone:*
> Adieu. Nous ne faisons tous deux que nous gêner:
> Je veux pleurer, Créon, et vous voulez régner.
> *Créon:*
> Ah, Madame! régnez, et montez sur le trône:
> Ce haut rang n'appartient qu'à l'illustre Antigone.
> *Antigone:*
> Il me tarde déjà que vous ne l'occupiez:
> La couronne est à vous.

Créon:

Je la mets à vos pieds.

Antigone:
Je la refuserais de la main des dieux même.
(1403-9)

The difference here is that the throne is being pointedly rejected rather than ardently sought after, but the same back-and-forth movement of insistence and mimicry is observable here as in the brothers' initial confrontation. It is as if a brief satyr play, a lighthearted drama performed at the end of a tragic trilogy in Athens, were being added on here; the problem of the inheritance of power, which is still the issue, is now turned into a farce.

Is this foray into the domain of satire not an indication of the collapse of the tragedy in the play's final scenes? This transitional point in the play marks the articulation between its extremely tragic subject, what Racine calls "the most tragic subject of antiquity," and the love interest, which Racine considered "foreign to the subject" and which could therefore produce only "mediocre effects" (*Oeuvres complètes* 1:115–16).[16] In fact every tragedy Racine wrote except the first and the last (*La Thébaïde* and *Athalie*) features a love intrigue that is at the very heart of the drama: only at the two extremes is love ex-centric. At the end of *La Thébaïde,* the failed love intrigue is emblematic of the return to the very mediocrity which Créon has tried to escape by excluding the middle. It is as if Créon and Antigone were inhabiting two different genres: Antigone, about to follow in the footsteps of the five characters who have set a good example by choosing death—and the living in this play can do little but look with admiration and envy at the fate of those who have died[17]—thus bids adieu to a Créon who, although he has excluded the middle of political instability in the city, proves to be an eminently mediocre suitor.

Unlike the order "Attendez" which Créon will only too well obey—since the end of the play leaves him in a state of permanent suspension—the other action which Antigone leaves behind as a model for Créon is impossible for him to carry out, that of imitation:

Créon:
Que faut-il faire enfin, Madame?
Antigone:

M'imiter.
(1416)

Following immediately upon the sequence in which Créon and Antigone mime each other's rejection of the crown, Antigone's prescription to imitate her is in fact also one to mime her, to follow her gesture, that of suicide, wordlessly. This order is one Créon cannot follow, for the play cruelly leaves him not only living but also talking; as the character who, along with Jocaste, has by far the most to say,[18] Créon takes up where his sister leaves off, ending the play whereas she starts it, and furthermore ending it precisely where she starts it:

> *Jocaste:*
> Qu'un moment de repos me va coûter de pleurs!
>
> (2)
>
> *Créon:*
> Je ressens à la fois mille tourments divers,
> Et je m'en vais chercher du repos aux enfers.
>
> (1515–16)

Rest ("le repos") is the final failure of Créon's movement toward individuation; the hell in which he will find it ("du repos aux enfers") is the life to which his inability to imitate Antigone condemns him. What Antigone's taunting imperative shows Créon is that to be able to use the excluded middle *in life* is to be able to *represent* life, to give it a closure which it does not possess, or rather which cannot ever adequately possess it. The play not only begins *in medias res,* it also ends there, for the middle is the very problem it can never manage to solve, the place it can never either reach or leave. Créon, the only major character left alive by the play's bloody ending — which even Racine found excessive ("My play's catastrophe is perhaps a bit too bloody" [*Oeuvres complètes* 1:115–16]) — finds nothing but mediocrity left in life. He feels an infinity of indistinguishable, unassimilable, and contradictory sensations ("mille tourments divers") which pull him apart just as surely as the play refuses him any connection that might keep him together.

What is the *rest* of Créon's role, if the play leaves him talking? Créon ends the play not with an excluded middle of heroic individuation, but with a surplus, an excess, a life that has gone on too long and a part that refuses to come to a close: "Vous m'ôtez Antigone, ôtez-moi tout le reste" (1502). If tragedy is a representation, an imitation, a mimicking ("mimesis") of a good and complete ("teleias") action (Aristotle, *Poetics,* VI, 1449b), it has the advantage of having to imitate something which is complete, something which has an end ("telos") to limit and contain its middle. Créon, left in the midst of life, has no such closure.

The ultimate proof of Créon's failure is that he cannot stop talking; the stillness left behind by Antigone's final act of self-exclusion is broken by his inability to leave the play. If Créon is the Racinian individual still to be born, he cannot be still long enough for that birth to take place, for as his apostrophe to the dead princess indicates, he, like a Zenonian arrow, is "still" in motion:

> Vous fermez pour jamais ces beaux yeux que j'adore,
> Et pour ne me point voir, vous les fermez encore!
> (1481–82)

Créon is still so much in the domain of the living that even Antigone's once-and-for-all action of closing her eyes in death seems to him to need periodic reaffirmation ("vous les fermez encore"), for that action has no real stability so long as it is being read and interpreted by living eyes. Créon can watch death's departure here and watch it again and again, but the play, by ultimately emphasizing the mediocrity of the living, blocks his access to the domain of tragic individuation. It is for this reason that although the *Phoenissae* starts out in the domain of a hypothetical ethical middle and, once that middle has proven insufficient, moves into that of the excluded middle which eventually saves the city at the expense of—but also through the constitution of—the individual, *La Thébaïde* obstinately refuses to destroy or to create Créon as an individual. Créon keeps talking because the Racinian individual is still being born.

5

Euripides' *Andromache,* or, *Waiting for Neoptolemos*

Like the *Phoenissae,* Euripides' *Andromache* has above all been criticized for its lack of unity.[1] "Disunified" in focus — Andromache's story? Hermione's story? Neoptolemos' story? — in character — Hermione's change from pursuing fury to whimpering wreck — and especially in time, the *Andromache,* we are led to believe, is the play in which "Euripides neglected . . . more than in any other extant play of his, the internal and external continuity of the fable."[2] Some have thought that the action of the play actually takes several days, since just before the end Orestes and Hermione leave Phthia and, at least according to some critics, go off to Delphi to execute the plot against Neoptolemos which Orestes has already set in motion but has not yet brought to fruition.[3] Since the news of Neoptolemos' death and the arrival of his body in Phthia end the play's action, we may then be tempted to conclude that the whole affair cannot possibly hold within the limits of Aristotle's "mia periodos heliou" ("one circling of the sun").

Even though it has been pointed out that the time scheme of the play is more complex than the above synopsis would lead one to believe,[4] the utter genius of Euripides' plot has not been sufficiently underlined: Neoptolemos, upon whom all of the action of the play depends, whose return is looked to either in hope or in fear by every single major character,[5] is dead not only when Orestes arrives relatively late in the play (957), but already at the very start. We may establish the play's chronology in this way: Orestes arrives in Delphi well before the action of the play begins. There he sets in motion the plot that will culminate in Neoptolemos' massacre, which in fact takes place shortly after Orestes leaves Delphi, still before the opening of the drama. Orestes then travels to Phthia, arriving just when Andromache's crisis has come to a head, and soon after Orestes and Hermione go off to an uncertain future, Neoptolemos' men arrive with his body, having left Delphi shortly after Orestes and thus arriving in Phthia also shortly after him.

The brilliance of this plot cannot be overestimated. Neoptolemos, the "cause" of the play's action in everyone's mind—Andromache herself calls him "ton aition," "the cause" (392)—is dead from the very beginning, and the action of the play develops as a spectacle played out in anticipation of the arrival of an absent and defunct hero. The *Andromache* is an Attic version of *Waiting for Godot*.

Indeed, if the *Phoenissae* is about the constitution of a unit of place, the *Andromache* is about the creation of a unit of time, and the creation of that unit is not undermined by the play's internal discontinuity but rather dependent upon it. The constitution of Neoptolemos as an individual requires a radical break between the overdomesticated world of postwar Phthia and the universe of the final, heroic stand at Delphi. But since Euripides holds Neoptolemos in reserve throughout the play, a carrot held out in front of all the rabbits—characters and audience—anxious for his return, we will follow his example and put off any discussion of this character until the others have gone before him, and as we wait for Neoptolemos we will attempt to analyze this conflict in terms of the two middles we have put into play.

It is Andromache herself who comes closest to representing the virtuous middle, and this particularly in a chronological sense. Andromache resists defining the past as a fully distinct entity separate from the present and thus external to it. She clings tenaciously to her past with a centripetal force which tirelessly attempts to reconcile the two time periods and refuses to recognize them as incompatible.

The pattern of Andromache's attitude toward time is established in the prologue. Her seemingly blasé description of a series of occurrences which some might call cataclysmic—the defeat and sack of Troy, the death of her husband, her child, and her entire family, and her enslavement and concubinage at the hands of the son of her husband's killer—is not merely another example of Euripidean banalization, a term which could also be used of Jocasta's prologue in the *Phoenissae*. Rather, it also reflects the mechanism by which this series of disastrous happenings, as contradictory and as mutually exclusive as its elements might seem (e.g., queen and slave), is held together by Andromache's narration, since hers is a story that is years in the making but seconds in the telling. Indeed, the most surprising aspect of this opening monologue is its insistence upon the continuity of a life which might appear to be a model of disruption. Andromache's first rambling sentence, which strings together a rather astonishing number of subordinate clauses, participles, and connectives ("where," "who," "and," "when") and takes her from her birthplace in Asian Thebes through Troy to her present place of residence, Phthia, is ultimately dependent on the opening noun clause "O form of the Asian land, city of Thebes . . . ,"[6] the following seventy or so words thus being nothing more than an unusually fully elaborated vocative. It is as if the syntactical subordination held together by a force of will the disparate events of Andromache's life.

Andromache's mention of the two countries which mark her point of departure (Thebes) and her point of arrival (Phthia) already suggests a characteristic which might be termed her "continentality." If Andromache is called a "continental" ("epeirotis") by both Hermione (159) and Menelaos (652), it is not only because she is an Asian,[7] but also because she stands upon— and for—*terra firma,* the land mass seen as a center to which the dangers of the ocean, its tides and fluctuations, are safely peripheral. Andromache's first words in the drama, "Form [schema] of the Asian land," already indicate this principle of stability: "schema," related to the verb "echo," "have" or "hold," evokes the idea of continuity—etymologically a "holding together"—which underlies the concept of the "continent," also from Latin *continere.* Andromache's apostrophe to the continent of her birth marks her as the representative of the principle of continuity, the refusal to break away from solid land and give herself up to the uncertainty of the world of flux and change. Although Andromache's is the archetypal story of the displaced person, she allows herself to "move" only as a continent imperceptibly drifts.

The paradox of Andromache's "continentality" is that she survives the tides of change by going with them: it is the adaptability of the virtuous middle which allows her to hold together, to keep her balance in the face of the most extreme hardships. Thus her gruesome tale is marked by patterns of repetition which overcome its breathtaking potential for disruption: being given as a bride to Hector (4) or as a concubine to Neoptolemos (14–15) may be very different experiences, but both are described by the same participle, "dotheisa," "having been given," plus a dative of destination ("to Hector," "to Neoptolemos"). Similarly, the birth of Andromache's two sons is announced by the same verb ("tikto," 9; "entikto," 24); the enormous difference in the status of the two fathers ("posei," "husband," 9; "despote," "master," 25) is swallowed up by their functional similarity. Seeing her husband killed before her very eyes by Achilles (8–9) does not prevent her from looking toward Achilles' son, her present master, for help (49–50), whereas having watched Hector's son be pitched from the towers of Troy, far from making the danger to Neoptolemos' son easier to bear by contrast, appears only to make the present nightmare into a reenactment of the past, a grotesque *déjà vu.* It is precisely because of Andromache's resilience, her ability to stretch between past and present, that she has survived the instability of her trials and tribulations in one piece.

The visual figuration of Andromache's continentality is her clinging to the altar of the goddess Thetis throughout the first part of the drama, since the asylum offered by the goddess is dependent upon not being separated from her palpable image. Andromache's refuge at the goddess' altar emphasizes her status as helpless suppliant and slave, as a woman whose refusal of life dates from the fall of Troy (454–56). Leaving that refuge would be tantamount to Andromache's admission that she is still alive, to plunging once again into the dangerous waters of life, the treacherous currents between the Scyllas and Charybdises of choice. But how to make this unmakable choice? "Menelaos appears to leave the choice up to Andromache; but how can she *choose* between two equally cruel extremities?"[8]

Hermione and Menelaos upset the delicate equilibrium of Andromache's virtuous middle by making her choose between her own life and that of Molossos, her child by Neoptolemos whom Menelaos is threatening with death if Andromache doesn't leave the safety of her asylum. To this extent they might appear to be the enforcers of the law of excluded middle, those who present Andromache with two mutually exclusive alternatives and force her to select only one of them. But although they lack Andromache's sense of equilibrium, Hermione and Menelaos come nowhere near to providing the excluded middle of heroic individuation. Rather, they are themselves inextricably tied to the past; they are nothing more nor less than mediocre, as the play's first occurrence of the word "mesos," "middle," demonstrates:

> For it is not at the point of a spear that [Neoptolemos] got you from Troy,
> but as the daughter of a fine man, with many wedding gifts,
> from a city that is not mediocrely [ou mesos] fortunate.
>
> (871–73)

As these words of Hermione's nurse suggest, only the "unmediocre" prosperity of the city stands between Hermione and her own profoundly rooted mediocrity.

Hermione's inability to distinguish herself in any way is reflected by her failure to create a unit of time, for haunting her is the memory of her mother Helen, a figure whose power she cannot escape:

> For the children of bad mothers
> should flee their ways, those in whom there is sense [nous].
>
> (230–31)

Andromache's reproachful advice to Hermione contains a paradox. Hermione must distance herself from her mother, must separate herself from the past in order to establish herself as a moral unit distinct from her mother. But the precondition for this movement of flight from the past is "nous," the popular meaning of which is "good sense" or "practical intelligence" and which Aristotle links to "phronesis" or "prudence," a quality closely related to virtuous moderation.[9] In order to negate Helen's influence, then, Hermione would need to find within herself the moderation to judge and reject her mother's excesses; but the very act of breaking fundamentally with the past, that is, her mother's inadequate moral model, would go against the virtuous middle. In fact Hermione cannot get free of the past: even though she will never reach her mother's stature, she is doomed to repeat her mother's moral inadequacy.

Menelaos as well is incapable of escaping his wife's sphere of influence. He presents his refusal to punish Helen at the end of the Trojan War as an example of moderate virtue, or "sophrosyne" (686):[10] rather than going to the extreme of venting the sort of rage on Helen which inspired the sack of Troy, he listened to reason and gave Helen a second chance. But Achilles' father Peleus, who comes into the action as Andromache's savior, puts this purported gesture of moderation in another light:

> And having taken [Helon] Troy—I'll go that far with you—
> you didn't put to death the woman [Helen] once she was in your hands,
> but at the sight of her breast, even though you had pulled out your sword,
> you received her kisses, petting the treacherous dog.
>
> (627–30)

The action of taking Troy, "Helon," resembles the name of Helen herself ("Helene"), she of course being one of the main causes of the war.[11] Putting an end to the conflict, far from destroying Helen as its only surviving agent and thus correcting the past, would appear to reconcile Menelaos with his traitorous wife and consequently with the entire prewar period. In Peleus' eyes, Menelaos, by forgiving a woman like Helen, gives in to the entire system of accommodation and compromise which the act of seduction embodies, and by the same token undermines the value of the "reunited" family unit, which is theoretically (and only theoretically) upheld by the war. Going back to Helen means being compromisingly tied to the past.

The confrontation between Peleus and Menelaos over the custody of Andromache and her child which occurs at the middle of the drama is a turning point in several ways. When Peleus takes the floor against Menelaos, the old man becomes the play's first spokesman for the excluded middle, the voice of Achilles once again raging against the injustice of the system of leadership embodied by the mediocre Agamemnon. Achilles, one of the play's most important excluded middles, the father lacking in the relationship of grandfather (Peleus) to grandson (Neoptolemos), once again takes life as Peleus protests against the unearned benefits of the army general:

> But the general [strategos] receives the glory,
> and even though he is only one among countless [myrion] others wielding
>   the spear,
> and does nothing more than a single one of them, he has more renown.
>
> (696–98)

That this is a return to book 1 of the *Iliad* and the argument between Achilles (Peleus' son) and Agamemnon (Menelaos' brother) is clear, and this famous difference of opinion is closely related to the struggle between the ethical middle and the excluded middle. In Menelaos' view, the leader of the army, or *strategos,* represents his men by a *strategy,* that of ensuring their proper organization or interaction. Here is how Menelaos describes the war:

> And Helen got into trouble not voluntarily, but at the gods' prodding,
> and this was of the greatest benefit to Greece [Hellada]:
> for being [ontes] unknowing of weapons and battle
> they moved [ebesan] toward bravery; and context [homilia, "society"]
> is the teacher in all things for mortals.
>
> (680–84)

This paean to "homilia"—related to "homoios," "same" or "similar," and thus suggesting a grouping by assimilation—is nothing but a song of praise to the virtues of the ethical middle, which claims that sense or knowledge exists only in a context. The individual warrior in this view of war is nothing; valor seems to take birth from the interaction of soldiers none of whom on his own is capable of excellence. This impression is reinforced by the ellipsis which Menelaos uses to move from the singular "Greece" ("Hellada") to the unexpressed subject ("the Greeks") of the plural verbs "ontes" and "ebesan." It is as if the collectivity imperceptibly brought forth the "individuals" that constitute it rather than the latter upholding and supporting the collectivity.

In an Achillean perspective, the true leader represents his men not by a strategic organization of the collectivity or by a "contextualization" of his forces, but rather by his separation from his companions, by difference. The Achillean leader, the superlative fighter, the best of the Achaians, is the ideal or the extreme, the ultimate measure of valor which the others can perhaps aim for but which only he himself can ever reach. Achilles, always extreme, a split-second flash of glory, is in some sense not comparable to the "myriad" or countless [myrion] other members of the expedition. He is not assimilable to the collectivity of the Greeks, nor can his uncompromising purity be said to represent them in the way that Odysseus, for example, represents his men. It is not merely that Achilles is better than the others, made of the same stuff but more of it. It is rather that he is what they can never be, an unmitigated impulse to the superlative and the individual which is at the same time an impulse toward exclusion, for the Achillean individual, by nature antisocial, can never participate in the very group which his valor limits and defines. Once the "extreme" leader has forged the unit of the heroic individual, his "integrity"—in a mathematical more than a moral sense, his "wholeness"—does not allow him to be reintegrated into the group. Like the excluded middle, he represents by differentiation rather than accommodation.

Peleus, who introduces the Achillean impulse, is less a figure embodying old age than one who has a relation to an earlier time, the time of heroism and valor before the walls of Troy, and as such he also provides the link to the climactic scene of the play, the account of Neoptolemos' final stand against the Delphians. At the moment of hearing the news that Neoptolemos is dead, Peleus provides the articulation to the world of tragic individuation and the excluded middle by pointing out that he himself—like the times—is out of joint(s):

> I have nothing; I have been destroyed.
> Gone is my voice, gone [to Hades] below are my joints [arthra].
> (1077–78)

When Peleus describes his demise at the devastating news of his grandson's death in terms of a loosening of his joints, the image, which is a conventional one dating at least back to Homer, goes beyond mere convention. What is being prefigured here is the arrival of a final excluded middle in this scene, the joints being necessarily defined as links or midpoints. We are about to witness the final link between the banalized domestic world of the play and the world of tragic heroism in which Neoptolemos' death takes place, between the here-and-now of postwar Phthia and a setting which is even further away in spirit than its geographical distance would indicate.

In fact the entire drama is based upon a kind of time warp, since as we have seen its "final" action, Neoptolemos' murder at the hands of the Delphians, is actually the play's earliest event. The lesson taught to us by this perverse Euripidean use of chronology is that of an extreme discontinuity, the very lesson of the excluded middle itself. The principle of causality which underlies any continuous system is here called into question, as the play's cause—Neoptolemos, the character whose projected or imagined reactions everyone takes as a touchstone for action—is radically separated from its effect:

> The two women [Andromache and Hermione] have been spending the worst or the best of themselves in a situation that made virtue and vice cruelly equal in their irrelevance. Their sufferings were sharp, the decisions they took were concrete expressions of ethos; . . . and yet now an increase in our understanding of actuality [the revelation of the plot against Neoptolemos] has transformed both the wise queen and the erring girl into blind creatures who flutter uselessly in a vacuum of causation.[12]

The cause (Neoptolemos) does not simply disappear, rather, it becomes unreachable, just as the "cause" of Neoptolemos' death (Orestes' spreading of vicious rumors about Neoptolemos' intentions in Delphi), although it leads to the effect (Neoptolemos' death), is not present at that death, not there to be fought against; it sets future action into motion and then goes on its way. But by the same token Neoptolemos' very absence, his arrival as someone no longer existing in the present, not only brings about a shockingly sudden negation of the mediocre world of domestic spats at Phthia, but also provides a unit of tragic individuation. As Paul Friedländer, in what is undoubtedly one of the finest observations ever made about this drama, puts it:

> At last Neoptolemos is brought in as a corpse. Up to now he has been desired or feared as one absent, and also from the beginning of the play called upon again and again, so that as one absent he determines everything that happens onstage. But that is why it becomes so suddenly clear (as strange as it may sound) that in this person resides the unity of the Euripidean drama.[13]

Does Neoptolemos' relation to the world of Phthia not function as a metaphor for the mechanism of human fate in tragedy? Fate is not, as many have mistakenly believed, a complete control of causality such that mortal creatures are—or even think themselves to be—pure "effects," helpless to "cause" their own destinies. Rather, fate is built upon the ultimate inaccessibility of causality, the need for a break between cause and effect. As much as they may believe their lives to be determined by forces other than themselves, humans never fully relegate the belief in causality, and even in their own causality, but the real cause recedes into the inner recesses of an unknowable, unreachable domain. And it is precisely in this sort of unreachable realm that Neoptolemos meets his death.

Neoptolemos' death scene at Delphi is first of all a battle between the one and the many. Repeatedly the nature of the murderous crowd is emphasized: anonymous, heterogeneous, confused, not moved by a single will but rather set into motion by a single whisper, the crowd moves in waves of violence, like a sort of pond into which a single pebble has been dropped; it is pure, agentless reaction. Unlike the climactic confrontation in the *Phoenissae,* this is not a choice of one out of two, but rather a battle of one against many, of the individual against the collective.[14]

On the side of the attackers, then, we find first of all a shocking perversion of the epic convention of naming. Whereas Neoptolemos is named "pais Achilleos" ("son of Achilles") no less than three times in the report of the battle (1119, 1149–50, 1163), and is indeed called by no other name in the entire passage, and even the base and cowardly Orestes is given the (perhaps dubious) honor of his matronymic,[15] the crowd is given no identity more specific than that of its city, "Delphon paidas," "children of Delphi" (1124). Although there in nothing dishonoring in being identified by one's country in Greek epic or tragedy, it is surprising for such a formula to be used in this way in a battle scene, since at key moments the warriors are generally distinguished as individuals. The height of this namelessness comes in the actual instant at which Neoptolemos is dealt the killing blow: the "child of Achilles" (1149–50) is said to fall struck by "some Delphian man" (1151), who is moreover acting "with many others" (1152). This is no head-to-head confrontation of heroes, but rather an attempt at swallowing up the heroic into the indistinct mass of the collectivity.

Similarly, the plethora of weapons used against Neoptolemos indicates the impure nature of this massacre. Starting with a hail of stones (1128) suggestive of an execution more than of a battle, the crowd then proceeds to make use of anything and everything at hand:

> But many missiles at once,
> arrows, mid-strapped spears [mesankyl'], rapid two-pointed javelins
> [amphoboloi],
> and ox-knives fell at his feet.
>
> (1132–34)

The heterogeneous nature of the arms used against Neoptolemos—some of them proper to battle (spears), others meant for other purposes, like the sacrificial knives used to slaughter oxen—is echoed by one of the most important words of the entire sequence, "migades," "mixed up" or "in disarray" (1142), used to describe the flight of the crowd once Neoptolemos has mustered a counterattack. This throng is incapable of any singular action, as Neoptolemos learns when his questioning of it yields no answer: "But no one [oudeis, literally "not-one"] of the countless numbers [myrion] nearby answered anything" (1127–28). This is a "myriad" which is not composed of units.

In the middle of the list of weapons used by the Delphians we find the second word in the drama to contain "mesos," "middle": "mesankyl'," spears having a strap in the middle by which one can throw them. Immediately following is a description of another weapon, an "amphobolos," a double-pointed javelin (literally "both-thrown," i.e., able to be thrown from either end). The combination of these two weapons gives a figurative description of the crowd: motivated by its own mediocrity, propelled by nothing more than the "homilia" or grouping together of its members and thus by a kind of middle of association ("mesankyl' "), at the same time the crowd has no essential valence, positive or negative ("amphoboloi"). It can be thrown or set into motion in either direction of any question, for it is entirely unable to take sides in any authentic way.

Neoptolemos' demise is precipitated by a cry emanating from the "unreachable middle" of the temple:

And an inauspicious clamor in the auspicious silence of the holy buildings
echoed against the rocks; and in a moment of calm, my master
was drawing himself up, shining in his brilliant armor,
when out of the middle of the inner sanctuary [adyton ek meson, "out of the
    unreachable middles"] someone let out
a horrible, hair-raising scream, and stirred up the horde,
turning them around to the attack.

(1144–49)

This use of the word "mesos," its third and last occurrence in the drama, echoes both Hermione's "unmediocre" wealth and the "mid-strapped" weapons of the crowd: but this middle, unlike that of the mediocre nonindividual, precipitates the excluded middle of individuation. And the source of that middle, of the mysterious cry which rallies the anonymous crowd one last time against Neoptolemos, is, it would appear, the gods:[16] Apollo rouses the Delphians to one last decisive strike.

The middle is here synonymous with the inside of the temple, the domain of the gods, and what happens within that domain cannot be known by mortals. Neoptolemos' death represents nothing less than the instant at which past and present are irrevocably and irreversibly separated, the constitution of the unit of time; the gods' snipping of the thread of his life puts an end to an entire generation. Neoptolemos, a pure figure of the past—indeed, we see him only once he is dead—cannot be allowed to survive into this present universe which by his death loses its continuity – and thereby establishes its relation – with the past.

Here is the passage which contains Neoptolemos' final "naming":

> That's how the god who gives oracles to others [Apollo],
> the judge of justice for all humans,
> treated the son of Achilles as he [tried to] give justice.
> And [Apollo] remembered, just like a bad human being,
> an ancient quarrel [palaia neike]. How then might he [or perhaps "how might
>   one"] be wise?
>
> (1161–65)

Neoptolemos is here alluded to not only overtly, as "the child of Achilles," but also covertly, in the phrase "palaia neike," "old quarrels," the two elements of the phrase referring, one by resemblance, one by opposition, to the two elements of Neoptolemos' name, "neos" ("new") and "ptolemos," an archaic form of "polemos" ("war"). If we mix the two components of Neoptolemos' name and Apollo's "old quarrels," we might say that the play's most fundamental opposition is the struggle between "new quarrels," the petty, small-minded bickering of the postheroic world of Phthia, and an "old warrior," one who, even though he is actually fairly young, might just as well be called "Palaioptolemos," since he stands for the heroism of a lost age. In fact it is by his very representation of the old heroic ethic that Neoptolemos harbors in a new age; he forms the separation – and the link – between old and new, his death marking the end of a round in the unending wrestling match between past and present. His separation from the crowd coincides with his extracting (and thus providing) the moment of transition between two eras.

It is not coincidental that this moment of final individuation for Neoptolemos also raises the question of divine injustice, and particularly the injustice of Apollo. Insofar as the forging of the individual depends upon the law of excluded middle, it is an approximation, a representation by difference from and not by resemblance to what it is representing; in short, it is the ultimate act of immoderation. In *The Birth of Tragedy,* Nietzsche emphasizes the relation between Apollo and the process of individuation:

> Apollo . . . appears to us as the apotheosis of the *principium individuationis.* . . . This apotheosis of individuation knows but one law – the individual, i.e., the delimiting of the boundaries of the individual, *measure* in the Hellenic sense. Apollo, as ethical deity, exacts measure of his disciples, and, to be able to maintain it, he requires self-knowledge. And so, side by side with the aesthetic necessity for beauty, there occur the demands "know thyself" and "noth-

ing in excess"; consequently overweening pride and excess are regarded as the truly hostile demons of the non-Apollinian sphere . . . and of the extra-Apollinian world.[17]

Apollo himself is, as Nietzsche points out, the god of individuation, but what Nietzsche might not agree with is the idea that the founding law of individuation is not the measure or the mean, but rather excess, the "overweening pride" of forming a human unit that claims to give godlike protection. It is the middle, the unmarked, the mediocre, the capacity to adapt to any present tense without any special effort of tension or attention, which is the real *inside* of the individual, what is at the heart of his being; but the only possible "measure" of that inside is *outside* of it: one "knows oneself" by knowing one's limits, the boundaries of the individual which mark both his definition and his limitations, and those limits function as an excess pulling him out of this ever-accommodating tendency. Individuation itself is an excess.

In fact Aristotle in the *Nicomachean Ethics* uses Neoptolemos as an example of "akrasia," which is sometimes translated as "unrestraint" but which, given Neoptolemos' link to the "continental" Andromache, I would prefer to render as "incontinence": "At times incontinence [akrasia] will be good [spoudaia], for example Neoptolemos in Sophocles' *Philoctetes;* for it is praiseworthy that he doesn't abide by the things Odysseus had convinced him of, because it is painful for him to tell a lie" (VII, ii, 7, 1146a19–21 [trans. mine]). "Incontinence," presented as an infraction upon the virtuous middle of self-restraint ("enkrateia," VII, i, 1, 1145a15–18), means relegating one's constancy and fidelity to a past model of behavior, one's inner continuity and consistency. It does not mean making up one's mind in any Odyssean way, that is, in the division of one's heart taking the measure of two opposing decisions; rather, it means going to the extreme. And this, Aristotle says, can at times be "good," "spoudaia," the very word used of the "good" action of tragedy in the *Poetics* (VI, 1449b).

Even more than his incontinence in the *Philoctetes,* Neoptolemos' incontinence in the *Andromache* is "good." Opposed to Andromache's "continentality" is Neoptolemos' "insularity": the single time Andromache mentions his name she calls him "to nesiote Neoptolemo," "the insular Neoptemos" (14).[18] Though Andromache and Neoptolemos are faced by the same fundamental conflict, that of finding a point of stability when surrounded by constant, unforeseeable changes, Andromache attempts to remain defined by the middle—her continentality emphasizing what seems to be the victory of solid land over the ocean surrounding it—whereas Neoptolemos remains forever on the edge, poised on the point of land which, though it seems solid, is ever aware of what lies at its borders, aware of itself as a *difference.*

The superiority of Neoptolemos at the end of the play thus resides in the very discontinuity which his presence — and absence — onstage exemplifies, the uncrossable gap between the world of heroic individuation and the mediocre universe of those who are separated from the goal of individuation by much more than the time it takes to get to Delphi. If Apollo's calling for Neoptolemos' death is unjust, it is the "injustice" of the human need to depend upon the stability of a unit, even though that unit inevitably separates itself from the inner nature of those it is representing.

But the radical discontinuity between present and past is not the only relation between time periods established by the end of the drama. In contrast to Apollo's "injustice" at demanding Neoptolemos' sacrifice is Thetis' appearance *ex machina,* the goddess bringing herself down to the level of mortals by more than her physical presence. As a sort of correction of Apollo's excessively harsh punishment of Neoptolemos, Thetis provides an absurdly overindulgent transition into the future, a future which for both Andromache and Peleus represents a return to the past. Andromache will marry Helenos, yet another of Priam's sons, and live happily ever after (1243–52) in a reconciliation with her past life that is disquietingly close to Menelaos' forgiveness of Helen: whether the return to the past is called "Helen" or "Helenos," in terms of tragic heroism it is a compromising return, a recapitulation in a minor mode. As for Peleus, he will go back to his old wife, Thetis herself, and become a god (1253–62), an apotheosis which will allow the old man, or rather the new god, to swim through the ocean while remaining dry (1259). Is this not the dream of having it both ways, of having the fluidity of the waves without losing the "dryness" of firm land?

But only the gods can have it both ways, and from the point of view of the mortal world, the play concludes with what would appear to be two mutually exclusive divine perspectives, Apollo's and Thetis', in a twilight of the gods. But is Thetis' stance of presence any more satisfying than Apollo's demand of absence? If the future returns to the past, the present may connect the two time periods, but where is its capacity for self-determination, for heroic struggle? Thetis' prediction is a sort of divine daydream: the miraculous "rebirth" of a living Troy for Andromache and the apotheosis of Peleus, which are as unsatisfying as "solutions" to the conflicts the play presents as they are tempting as examples of wishful thinking, seriously call into question the value of humans' attempts at solving their own problems. Perhaps Thetis, who is after all Achilles' mother, gives the mortal survivors what they (think they) want, in order to try to show them the dangers of exaggerated continuity, the decidedly unheroic "virtues" of the virtuous middle; but of course those "dangers" could be felt by no one who does not understand the heroic nature of human individuation.

It is thus Neoptolemos, Euripides' Godot *avant la lettre,* dead before the play begins, who is nonetheless its hero, and the unit of time "overstepped" by the transmission of his dead body from Delphi to Phthia might be taken as a commentary on the law of the tragic unit of the individual and its relation to those who are waiting for a simple solution to the problems they hope it will solve. This law or unit cannot but break itself; perhaps the most important thing it provides is the wait itself and the illusory expectation that it will lead to a satisfying solution of the dilemmas which characterize it—illusory precisely because the unit of the tragic individual cannot adequately solve the questions which that wait poses. And yet if the gods gave us what we wanted and thus precluded the need to suffer and to break with the past and with ourselves, they would also take away our only source of individuality. Neoptolemos' negation of himself makes him into an island not of safety but rather of heroic individuation, the first heroic individual in the "Racinian" plays of Euripides. Let us turn, then, to Racine's *Andromaque.*

6

La Guerre de Troi(e)s

Andromaque

> Amour est sans milieu, c'est une chose extrême.
>
> —Ronsard, *Sonnets pour Hélène*

The setting of Racine's play is not Phthia, but rather Epirus (French "Epire"), the land of Pyrrhus rather than the mythological home of his famous father. "Epire," closely related to the word which in Euripides' play describes Andromache's "continentality" ("epeirotis," from "epeiros," "continent," whence Epirus, "continental" [western] Greece), would seem to evoke the solidity of *terra firma*. In Racine's play there is a conspicuous absence of the double geography of Euripides' drama, split between Phthia, the place of waiting and of ultimately futile action, and Delphi, the site of Neoptolemos' climactic death. Indeed, "Delphi," the Latin plural which mediates between the Greek "Delphoi" and the French "Delphes," can itself be reversed to yield the play's first end-rhyme, "fidèle":

> Oui, puisque je retrouve un ami si fidèle,
> Ma fortune va prendre une face nouvelle.
>
> (1–2)

The rhyme of Oreste's opening couplet, "fidèle"/"nouvelle," instantly focuses on the conflict between two possible relations linking past and present or present and future: fidelity, indicative of a movement of continuity, and newness, suggesting a fundamental break.[1] It is as if fidelity, a relation to the past that will be explored and called into question in Racine's play, replaced or rather subsumed the oracular seat at Delphi that endlessly redefines the relation between time periods, as if the play's "single" setting, which conforms to convention (unity of place), already covered up a dual function.

For in spite of the play's much-touted unity,[2] Racine's Epire seems perpetually on the point of exploding into a doubled stage. As Peter France points out, *Andromaque* abounds in scenes played to an absent audience:[3]

> Mais, de grâce, est-ce à moi que ce discours s'adresse?
> (530)

> Daigne-t-elle sur nous tourner au moins la vue?
> (898)

> Vous ne répondez point? Perfide, je le voi:
> Tu comptes les moments que tu perds avec moi!
> (1375–76)

At the same time as the inaccessible loved one is never completely absent from the stage, he or she is also entirely unavailable, and the cast-off lover, although seemingly (and annoyingly) omnipresent, might just as well be invisible for all the attention he or she draws.

Set against this centrifugal potential of the stage is the stifling sense of *huit clos* which Epire, unlike Euripides' Phthia, creates. Phthia, the borders of which are so ill-guarded or perhaps ill-defined that virtually every one of Euripides' main characters breezes either in or out of the place, is quite the opposite of Racine's Epire, which no one, in spite of the boat waiting to carry Oreste and possibly Hermione away, manages to leave. Moreover, the obsessions of Racine's characters wreak havoc on the geographical "unit" of the stage: Hermione is as unpleasantly surprised by Oreste's proximity ("Ah! je ne croyais pas qu'il fût si près d'ici," 476) as she is capable of blocking out his disagreeable presence from her mind by replacing it with the image of the always inaccessible (but always "present") Pyrrhus: "Tout me sera Pyrrhus, fût-ce Oreste lui-même" (1490). Where convention imposes an unwanted unity upon Hermione, a stifling compression which forces her to confront the tiresome Oreste, she builds an emotional partition between herself and the intruder. The irony is that this partition does not establish a unit distinct from the stage itself, a sort of substage that might protect her from an irritating *tête-à-tête*, but rather simply keeps her inside the closed universe of her obsession ("Tout me sera Pyrrhus").

A great deal of the power of Racine's drama comes from its feeling of compression: this is a play composed almost completely of *tête-à-têtes*, no mean feat for a piece whose intrigue is based upon a series of love triangles.[4] It seems impossible for all three members of any of the potential *ménages à trois*[5] to appear simultaneously; it is as if none of the characters were able to compare the two components of unrequited love (loving, being loved) and to come to a definitive decision either to accept second best or to reject once and for all any connection to the unloved lover. The three sides of the triangle cannot be onstage together precisely because the third member can neither be included (captured in the case of the unloving loved one, accepted in that of the unloved lover) nor excluded (recognized as uncapturable or finally and definitively rejected).

Indeed, the dynamics of the play's celebrated "love chain" lends itself to an analysis according to middles and extremes:

$$\text{Oreste} \rightarrow \text{Hermione} \rightarrow \text{Pyrrhus} \rightarrow \text{Andromaque}$$

The arrow in each case indicates a relation of unrequited love, and the entire set-up is simply a condensation of two love triangles, with Hermione and Pyrrhus in the middle and Oreste and Andromaque at the ends. The closure of this site, the "unity" of place, puts its four inhabitants into a sort of closed wave chamber, so that any movement any of them makes toward or away from his or her neighbors, that is, any movement of seeming acceptance or rejection, reverberates down the entire chain which, rather than letting go of either of its end points—putting Andromaque to death or allowing Oreste simply to take back to the Greeks a definitive "no" from Pyrrhus—absorbs the potential energy of escape and keeps the four members of the system in constant motion.

There are in fact two ways of dividing this chain according to middle and extremes. First of all, and in closer conformity to Euripides' play, Andromaque is distinguished from her three co-protagonists by her efforts at resisting the choice they are all attempting to press upon her; her refusal to constitute a unit by an excluded middle of choice assures the "unity" of place by keeping the entire chain waiting breathlessly for her final "yes" or "no." But a second breakdown of the chain takes account of the potential similarity of the two extreme positions: Oreste, who loves but is not loved in return, is the mirror image of Andromaque, who is loved but not loving, whereas Hermione and Pyrrhus are both in a position of knowing both sides of the coin. Thus Oreste and Andromaque could be described as the extremes of the chain, with Hermione and Pyrrhus furnishing its middle; let us begin our analysis with the middle of the chain and work our way outward.

Pyrrhus is the single character who believes that Epire forms a geographical and temporal unit distinct from Troy, and who also, by extension, believes in the myth of the individual as an adequate unit. According to him the outcome of the Trojan War, the excessive, sacrilegious, unjust sack of Troy, put an end to the entire expedition, thus forming a unit of time which is still in force, as he makes clear in his rebuttal of Oreste demanding the life of Astyanax in the name of the Greeks (173–220). The sack of Troy, whatever its injustices, identified a winner and a loser in no uncertain terms.

Perhaps the most convincing evidence that Pyrrhus interprets the sack in this way is that he relates it to the question of injustice:

> Tout était juste alors: la vieillesse et l'enfance
> En vain sur leur faiblesse appuyaient leur défense; . . .
> Mon courroux aux vaincus ne fut que trop sévère.
> Mais que ma cruauté survive à ma colère? . . .
> De mes inimitiés le cours est achevé;
> L'Epire sauvera ce que Troie a sauvé.
>
> (209–20)

Saying that "everything was just" at the time of the sack is a way of saying that nothing was just. Pyrrhus describes the victims as belonging to the two extreme age groups ("vieillesse," "enfance"), those who find it especially difficult to defend themselves, and since the attackers, including Pyrrhus himself, are mainly men in their prime, he is obviously questioning the justice of the enterprise. But as we have seen, the role of the law of excluded middle is to establish a clear-cut, uncompromising position, to make the scales of justice tip one way or the other even if the two sides have an almost equal claim to justice, and this is precisely what happens at Troy. The final defeat of the Trojans alluded to by Pyrrhus puts an end to the gods' endless shifting of the fortunes of war back and forth between the Achaians and the Trojans.

In his reliance on the excluded middle which established the end of the war, Pyrrhus is first portrayed as a potential agent of choice to bring the present crisis to an end: "Haï de tous les Grecs, pressé de tous côtés" (291), Pyrrhus seems able to resist this pressuring encirclement precisely because as a would-be individual trusting in the law of excluded middle, he will put a halt to all vacillation, as his first reassuring response to Andromaque indicates: "Je ne balance point . . . " (287). Pyrrhus is doing nothing less than claiming to have a fixed, unchangeable value. Like a sort of proton in the center of an atom surrounded by whirling electrons, he has a "charge"; not only a protégé (Astyanax), but also an energy potential, an established value.

The charge that Pyrrhus first claims to have, and which the play seems to attribute to him, is a positive one, as the rhyme "Pyrrhus"/"plus" suggests:

> *Hermione:*
> Ah! ne souhaitez pas le destin de Pyrrhus:
> Je vous haïrais trop.
> *Oreste:*
>   Vous m'en aimeriez plus.
>   (539–40)

For Pyrrhus, even a surplus of hatred would at first seem transformable into a plus, an advantage. Hermione originally thinks Pyrrhus' desires to be "plus ardents" than hers (468), and if she vaunts the "virtue" of Oreste, saying of him, "Il sait aimer du moins, et même sans qu'on l'aime" (473), the literal sense of "du moins," which reinforces Oreste's advantages over Pyrrhus (*at least* he has this in his favor), is belied by the suggestion of "lessness" in the term, which opposes Oreste to Pyrrhus as the lesser is opposed to the greater. That Pyrrhus, son of the greatest of the Achaian heroes, has the potential to live up to his inheritance is suggested by Andromaque's high expectations of him: "J'attendais de son [Achille's] fils encor plus de bonté" (939). Even as she walks to what she thinks will be her death, Andromaque persists in believing in this "positive" quality of Pyrrhus:

> Je sais quel est Pyrrhus: violent, mais sincère,
> Céphise, il fera plus qu'il n'a promis de faire.
>   (1085–86)

This "plus" once again seems to represent Pyrrhus' freedom of action: he not only holds to his commitments, but even goes beyond them. His surplus seems to signal a positive charge of individuation, what he gives of himself beyond the measure or the norm.

 And yet, when it begins to become clear that Pyrrhus' "positive" value is contingent upon a positive return, Andromaque's love, when his moral choice turns into nothing more than an investment, a value laid out to garner an interest, Andromaque puts her finger on the real nature of Pyrrhus' supposed plan to save her:

> Voulez-vous qu'un dessein si beau, si généreux,
> Passe pour le transport d'un esprit amoureux?
>   (299–300)

The excess or charge seemingly represented by Pyrrhus' plan is here debunked by Andromaque's characterization of it as a "transport," one of the play's key terms. Nothing more than a temporary imbalance, a swing in one direction, Pyrrhus' "choice" will prove to be a nonchoice precisely because of the endless movement of which it is but a single moment. "Trans-

port" indicates not only an amorous excess or rapture, but also, as its etymology suggests, a carry-over, a constant disequilibrium which provides
or rather imposes an ongoing form of transportation.

This unbalanced nature of "transport" turns Pyrrhus' apparent excluded
middle—his excess as positive value—into a failed virtuous middle:

> Songez-y bien: il faut désormais que mon coeur,
> S'il n'aime avec transport, haïsse avec fureur.
> (367–68)

Pyrrhus' "choice," insofar as it is contingent upon Andromaque's, becomes
a nonchoice, his "transport" being nothing but the movement between love
and hatred which he, along with his partners in indecision, Hermione and
Oreste, will spend the rest of the play undergoing. Andromaque's desire
to impose the correct choice upon Pyrrhus neutrally, that is, for no reason
other than the rightness of the choice, has no place here. The irrevocable
charge of the moral universe becomes a reflection not of so many decisions
made but rather of the incapacity of those faced with the burden of choice
to choose from the enviable but unreachable position of "indifference"—
the zero point between the two opposite charges of love and hatred—which
would signal the end of the play's amorous transportations and thus a return to innocence, or at least to nonguilt:

> *Pyrrhus* (to Andromaque):
> Oui, mes voeux ont trop loin poussé leur violence
> Pour ne plus s'arrêter que dans l'indifférence.
> (365–66)

> *Pyrrhus* (to Hermione):
> Je rends grâces au ciel que votre indifférence
> De mes heureux soupirs m'apprenne l'innocence.
> (1345–46)

Once the emotion of this public transportation system has been set into motion, those who make use of it can no longer escape, for this system, by
prohibiting "indifference," makes them constantly different from themselves,
pulled in two conflicting directions. This is no movement toward virtue,
but rather a futile, endless movement between opposites which prevents
one from either stopping in the middle (indifference) or excluding it (choice).

What attacks the law of excluded middle and the storage units it claims
to guarantee is thus a universe in which the "individual" cannot give freely
of himself, but instead is thoroughly ruled by a system of exchange, trying

to get back at least as much as he has given and ultimately giving only with an eye toward repayment. If payment is one of the play's central metaphors, everyone is always owed or owing and either unwilling or unable to bring the system to a halt:

> Il l'aime. Mais enfin cette veuve inhumaine
> N'a payé jusqu'ici son amour que de haine.
> (109–10)

> Et dans toute la Grèce il n'est point de familles
> Qui ne demandent compte à ce malheureux fils.
> (158–59)

> C'est cet amour payé de trop d'ingratitude
> Qui me rend en ces lieux sa présence si rude.
> (393–94)

This lending system is kept going, the debts prevented from being satisfactorily acquitted by the fact that no character is in full possession of what it is (s)he is meant to give back. For example, Pyrrhus knows that he ought to return Hermione's love, what she calls "un coeur qui m'était dû" (1364), but the original payment tendered has been passed along to another: "Comment lui [to Hermione] rendre un coeur que vous [Andromaque] me retenez?" (344). Ultimately, in fact, the only repayment possible is to see the debt one is owed being demanded by one's debtor with equal despair from the next person higher up on the chain of unreciprocated loves, or unpaid debts, as Hermione recognizes in her anguish:

> Quelle honte pour moi, quel triomphe pour lui [Oreste],
> De voir mon infortune égaler son ennui!
> Est-ce là, dira-t-il, cette fière Hermione?
> Elle me dédaignait; un autre l'abandonne.
> L'ingrate, qui mettait son coeur à si haut prix,
> Apprend donc à son tour à souffrir des mépris?
> (395–400)

The stark reality of this painful dialectic, almost Cornelian in its apparent clarity, its elegant division into hemistiches set off by the switch of the third-person pronoun from subject to object—"Elle me dédaignait; un autre l'abandonne"—uncovers one of the most fundamental mechanisms of this exchange system. The middle position occupied by Pyrrhus and Hermione, that of being loved and loving, not only leads to no excluded middle, as we have seen in the case of Pyrrhus; more important, it leads to no position of possible compromise or equalization. The equality of this middle position, that is, being made to realize that what one is doing to another is being done back to one by someone else, is absolutely unacceptable to those who find themselves in it. The very fact that the middle situation is rigorously, cruelly based upon equality can only be momentarily recognized. In this case, the equalization of Hermione's and Oreste's misfortunes ("mon infortune égaler son ennui") does not put the two cast-off lovers into a truly equal position of commiseration and compassion; rather, their reactions to their newly recognized "equality" instantly recreate an inequality: "Quelle honte pour moi, quel triomphe pour lui."

Like the functioning of the *lex talionis* itself, the middle situation of potential but failed equalization immediately moves into the mode of escalation:

> Je souffre tous les maux que j'ai faits devant Troie.
> Vaincu, chargé de fers, de regrets consumé,
> Brûlé de plus de feux que je n'en allumai,
> Tant de soins, tant de pleurs, tant d'ardeurs inquiètes . . .
> Hélas! fus-je jamais si cruel que vous l'êtes?
>
> (318–22)

Pyrrhus' plaintive reproach to Andromaque, which is based on the conventional metaphor of the enslaved lover, begins with the claim that Pyrrhus himself is undergoing exactly the same sort of suffering that he inflicted on others in Troy. But that initial assessment of equality, that is, of a punishment in some sense equal to the crime, then becomes a claim for inequality, naturally to Pyrrhus' disadvantage: "Burned by *more* fires than I myself set." So that when Pyrrhus sums up his attack with a triumphant rhetorical question—"was I ever as cruel to you as you are being to me?"—it is no surprise if it, too, is based on inequality, or rather on the inequality of equality. Even if Andromaque is merely *as* cruel to Pyrrhus as he was to her compatriots, he would undoubtedly have the distinct impression that cruelty from the receiving end is crueller by far than cruelty from the sending end. The "plus" of Pyrrhus' purported charge of individuality is thus reduced to the feeling of excessive punishment which he offers up as proof of the unfairness of the universe.

By the same token, during the brief time that Pyrrhus and Hermione think their love is on the point of being returned, their (temporary) position of power gives them no generosity—the positive charge which might define the individual—but rather inspires in them a sadistic need to exhibit their good fortune:

Hermione (to Oreste):
Mais que puis-je, Seigneur? On a promis ma foi.
Lui ravirai-je un bien qu'il ne tient pas de moi?
L'amour ne règle pas le sort d'une princesse:
La gloire d'obéir est tout ce qu'on nous laisse.
Cependant je partais, et vous avez pu voir
Combien je relâchais pour vous de mon devoir.

(819–24)

Pyrrhus (to Hermione):
Vous ne m'attendiez pas, Madame, et je vois bien
Que mon abord ici trouble votre entretien.

(1275–76)

Nos coeurs n'étaient point faits dépendants l'un de l'autre;
Je suivais mon devoir, et vous cédiez au vôtre;
Rien ne vous engageait à m'aimer en effet.

(1353–55)

In a theater almost unsurpassed in its capacity for cruelty, these scenes of what might be called emotional exhibitionism are very high even on Racine's cruelty scale. Perhaps their least generous aspect is the ostentatious show of generosity made by both rejecting lovers: both speak in terms of their duty, thus allowing the cast-off admirer an out—the possibility of pretending that nothing has happened between them—which they know will not be taken. Pyrrhus' arrival in particular is a telling commentary on the difference between Euripides' character and Racine's. Whereas everyone impatiently waits for Neoptolemos' arrival in Euripides' play, Pyrrhus' parade of power is gratuitous: "You weren't expecting me, Madame." This shocking example of an "in" relishing his victory over an "out" is punctuated by one of Racine's most sadistically understated lines: the unfinished rhyme ("en effet," answered by Hermione's "Qu'ai-je donc fait?") virtually demands Hermione's explosion of wrathful impotence.

Thus, the equality of the middle position in which Pyrrhus and Hermione find themselves is so repugnant that it results in the creation of a vicious asymmetry by each of these two "middle" characters. The fact of seeing unrequited love from both sides doesn't give them the slightest capacity for compassion or understanding. Let us now turn to the two end positions on the amorous chain.

Andromaque is framed by the character of Oreste, who opens the drama, closes it, and is present onstage at its very midpoint (III, ii, line 824). At the outset Oreste has no individual identity, for he merely "represents" (508, 621) the collectivity, the Greeks who together have decided Astyanax must die. Indeed, the Greeks whom he represents take the place of the Delphians in Euripides' play, for although they remain unseen, the brief description given of them by Oreste makes them thoroughly unimpressive:

> Et je trouvai d'abord ses princes rassemblés,
> Qu'un péril assez grand semblait avoir troublés.
>
> > (59-60)

> J'entends de tous côtés qu'on menace Pyrrhus;
> Toute la Grèce éclate en murmures confus.
>
> > (67-68)

This vision of the Greeks gathered together ("rassemblés") makes of them not only an indistinct mass—"Qui se rassemble se ressemble"?—but also an unheroic one: "troublé," a word often used in the vocabulary of love, suggests a kind of domestication. The "murmures confus" brought out by the mere mention of the name of Pyrrhus once again bring to mind an ill-defined horde such as the one which kills Neoptolemos in Euripides' play, "de tous côtés" emphasizing the multidirectionality of this assembly, which has no clear leader and thus no discernible responsibility or agency.

Another, equally compelling reason for Oreste's lack of identity is his position on the chain of love, the fact that he is loving but not loved. In the universe of *Andromaque,* capturing an identity requires having the power to exclude, to be loved by someone whom one does not love in return, the very power of Oreste's three co-protagonists, for it is by making use of the barrier of unrequited love that these characters ensure their own opacity, their unavailability. Oreste's incapacity for exclusion at the play's outset is evident in his pattern of "yeses" and "nos." Of the four characters, Oreste is the only one to begin with what seems to be an entirely affirmative attitude:[6] he says "Oui" four times (1, 147, 225, 591), including the very first word of the play,[7] before arriving at a "Non" (711), his first word in act III contrasting with the "Oui" which opens act I. But once he has learned to say "Non," the word overwhelms him (737, 760, 816, 1249, 1597, 1642). Even his final ironic "Oui" is as negative as a "Non" ("Oui, je te loue, ô ciel . . . ," 1614).

Thus, excluded himself, Oreste cannot at first exclude, and his discovery of the word "no" marks a crucial juncture in the drama. Oreste's first "No" opening the third or middle act marks the beginning of the play's theatrical middle, the crisis of representation which extends from III, i, through III, iii (the midpoint of the play occurring in III, ii). In contrast to the nonentity of the first two acts we find a character whose position at the edge of an impenetrable network of relations has radicalized him, made him lose his sense of moderation:

> Modérez donc, Seigneur, cette fureur extrême.
> Je ne vous connais plus; vous n'êtes plus vous-même.
>
> (709–10)

It is not so much that Oreste is "no longer himself," as Pylade suggests; it is rather that in his shift between the political domain and the realm of love, Oreste has moved from middle to extreme, from not needing an identity (being a representative of the collectivity) to wanting only an identity.

That identity, Oreste correctly surmises, is his only possible entry into a universe which has thus far used him, even needed him only in order to exclude him:

> Non, non, je le [Pyrrhus] connais, mon désespoir le flatte;
> Sans moi, sans mon amour, il dédaignait l'ingrate [Hermione];
> Ses charmes jusque-là n'avaient pu le toucher:
> Le cruel ne la prend que pour me l'arracher.
>
> (737–40)

Oreste is describing the triangulation of desire: whatever appeal Hermione might have for Pyrrhus depends on the latter's ability to wrest her away from Oreste. Oreste's understanding of the physics of exclusion fundamentally alters his ambitions:

> Non, tes conseils ne sont plus de saison,
> Pylade; je suis las d'écouter la raison.
> C'est traîner trop longtemps ma vie et mon supplice:
> Il faut que je l'enlève, ou bien que je périsse.
> Le dessein en est pris, je le veux achever.
> Oui, je le veux.
>
> (711–16)

Oreste's speech, punctuated by his first "Non" in the drama and his last "Oui" until the very end of the play, reflects his dawning awareness that one must exclude in order to include, that the affirmation of a heroic identity ("Oui, je le veux") depends upon saying "no" to everything that is in one's way, the entire system of mediation here represented by Pylade ("conseils," "raison," "longtemps"). The most important hemistiche Oreste pronounces here, "Le dessein en est pris," looks forward to the beginning of *Phèdre* in a word-for-word anticipation of Hippolyte's opening declaration (*Phèdre*, 1), and what both young men are expressing is their belief in the myth of the individual, the adequacy of intentionality ("dessein"). For the first time Oreste understands that there is no "neutral" individual; so long as he is nothing but a political mediator, he will be nobody. This is Oreste's acceptance of the need for the excluded middle.

This realization opens the play's theatrical middle, and the lesson which that middle will teach Oreste is an eminently theatrical one: the need for the mask, the outside, to cover the middle, the inside.[8] The triply repeated message of the middle of the play is "dissimulez," ordered twice by Pylade to Oreste (719, 800) and once by Cléone to Hermione (855). Dissimulation is the very essence of the theatrical middle, for it is a recognition that the process of individuation itself divides the universe into an outside and an inside, that the unit of the individual is able to create the appearance of a univalent exterior only by keeping ambivalent feelings and thoughts hidden inside, safely inaccessible. Rather than solving the problem of the middle, heroic individuation simple stores it away.

Dissimulation is thus the key to the play's midpoint, which throws together Hermione, playing the role of a Cornelian heroine, and Oreste, who is just beginning to make an attempt at Racinian individuation. Accordingly, Hermione, dizzy with the ecstasy of seeing her love for Pyrrhus momentarily returned, drunk with power, nonetheless almost miraculously has the presence of mind to shake the cobwebs off a bit of Corneille which she had undoubtedly given up all hope of ever being able to use, and proffers it with a flourish that ends the first half of the drama:

> L'amour ne règle pas le sort d'une princesse:
> La gloire d'obéir est tout ce qu'on nous laisse.
> Cependant je partais, et vous avez pu voir
> Combien je relâchais pour vous de mon devoir.
> (821–24)

Hermione's recourse to rules and regulations ("ne règle pas"), to glory, and to duty, the Cornelian holy trinity, gives to the very middle of Racine's drama the same sort of apparently favorable outcome as the middle of *La Thébaïde*. The middle of the play makes a couple of the middle two links in the amorous chain, Hermione and Pyrrhus, sending the two ends, Andromaque and Oreste, off to meet their fates and almost sending the audience scurrying for the exits.

Too soon, however, for the second half of the play, that is, Oreste's response, opens with a brief, muted, but unmistakably Racinian bang: "Ah! que vous saviez bien, cruelle . . . " (825). This prefiguration of countless bitter tirades, including Hermione's own subsequent explosion against Pyrrhus ("Je ne t'ai point aimé, cruel?" 1356), marks Oreste's first foray

into the domain of Racinian individuation. Not only is he unwilling simply
to take what the world gives him, but also he immediately dissimulates that
unwillingness:[9]

> Ah! que vous saviez bien, cruelle . . . Mais, Madame,
> Chacun peut à son choix disposer de son âme.
> La vôtre était à vous. J'espérais; mais enfin
> Vous l'avez pu donner sans me faire un larcin.
>
> (825–28)

Oreste's dignified recovery perfectly matches Hermione's charade. By saying the exact opposite of his recent discovery that any act of possession
is an act of exclusion, he appears to accept the position of also-ran which
everyone in the drama rejects, and thus seems to be bringing to a close
the complex series of love vendettas which constitute the play's hitherto
endless motion.

Oreste is successful in his first try at dissimulation ("Attendais-tu, Cléone,
un courroux si modeste?" 833). But what he doesn't understand is that not
only is dissimulation a necessary precondition for the constitution of the
individual, but also, by the same token, the individual it constitutes is impenetrable. This he discovers too late, when Hermione's orders to Oreste
to kill Pyrrhus have been carried out, and Hermione confronts her despair-
ing suitor:

> Ah! fallait-il en croire une amante insensée?
> Ne devais-tu pas lire au fond de ma pensée?
> Et ne voyais-tu pas, dans mes emportements,
> Que mon coeur démentait ma bouche à tous moments?
>
> (1545–48)

It is when Oreste, no longer transparent or fully open to the world, tries
to reap the benefits of individuation that he is made to see the drawbacks
of its necessary opacity. Racinian heroism depends not on "appearing," the
glory and brilliance of the Cornelian hero, but on wearing the armor of
individuation as a refusal of mediation between an inner and an outer universe. Oreste, like Andromaque, his structural opposite, will survive, while
the middle couple of the love chain perishes—but he will survive in madness. It is a madness symptomatic of the unbearability of dissimulation,
Oreste's ultimate inability to live with the separation between outer identity
and inner feeling.

At the other end of the amorous chain, Andromaque is the exact opposite of Oreste in a number of ways. She is first of all the single character

he never meets onstage, every other combination being present.[10] Thus the two ends of the chain never link up as they might, for whereas Andromaque is at the top of the amorous chain, Oreste, with the support of the Greeks, is at the top politically. The role Oreste is forced to play, that of representing his people, is the very role Andromaque covets: making her way through the present with clear and simple orders from the past is Andromaque's dream as surely as it is Oreste's nightmare.

In fact what Andromaque wishes to be is a leftover, a "reste," someone whose existence in the present is a pure reference to the past. Most would-be Racinian heroes—like Oreste, whose name ("au-reste") is a painful commentary on his miscellaneous position—struggle against the heritage of past determinations; Andromaque asks for nothing more than to be a pure vestige, to act out a role in what Georges Poulet calls "an immense and infinitely complex repetition of an earlier drama."[11] Andromaque even extends this desire to be a "reste" to her son: "Qu'il ait de ses aïeux un souvenir modeste:/ Il est du sang d'Hector, mais il en est le reste" (1121–22).

The fly in the ointment is that Andromaque, although she may be figuratively dead, is literally alive, and so long as she is alive the present may offer her hope and the possibility of change. This becomes clear when Andromaque speaks of the paradoxical nature of Pyrrhus' double role as Astyanax' warden and potential bodyguard against the Greeks: "J'ai cru que sa prison deviendrait son asile" (937). Astyanax' and even Andromaque's "prison" is nothing but Pyrrhus' enforcement of the law of excluded middle, that is, his guarantee that the winners of the war will remain the winners and that the conflict will never be reopened by the next generation. By attempting to provide this security—which, as Andromaque knows, is the only safeguard of her own and Astyanax' survival, such as it is—Pyrrhus also allows Andromaque the hope that she is being protected form the present at the same time as it is being protected from her, that her "prison" will become an "asile." But by furnishing this asylum against the present, Pyrrhus himself takes on the force of a presence; he becomes a part of the very present which he is theoretically keeping from Andromaque, a present she cannot allow herself to accept.

This dreamed-of "asile" is aurally a combination of "Asie" and "île," the two terms which essentially define Andromache and Neoptolemos in Euripides' drama and each of which occurs only once in Racine's play:[12]

> *Pyrrhus:*
> Je songe quelle était autrefois cette ville
> Si superbe en remparts, en héros si fertile,

> Maîtresse de l'Asie; et je regarde enfin
> Quel fut le sort de Troie, et quel est son destin.
> (197–200)

> *Andromaque:*
> Que craint-on d'un enfant qui survit à sa perte?
> Laissez-moi le cacher dans quelque île déserte.
> (877–78)

To say that "this island-refuge is a reminiscence of Euripides"[13] is to say a great deal, for in Racine's play Pyrrhus, the "islander," speaks of Asia, whereas the Asian Andromache, whose first word in Euripides' play was "Asia," longs for a desert island to hide her son. This elegant chiasmus first of all underscores the exchange of roles between Euripides' and Racine's dramas: while Neoptolemos is the hero of Euripides' play, Andromaque is the heroine of Racine's. Moreover the echoes of "Asie" and "île" in "asile" also say something about the very nature of Andromaque's "asile," for that "asile" is based upon the ultimate inseparability ("Asie-île") of the excluded middle—an island of safety—from the "continent" or continuity of life. Andromaque loses the asylum, or rather the island of her excluded middle when she discovers that she is still distressingly attached to the mainland by the narrowest of peninsulas: "Caught between an inexpiable past and an inexorable present, she discovers tragic time, this time-out-of-time which is a promontory swept by all of the winds of temporality."[14] Andromaque leaves the stage when she finds herself about to answer the call—however modest, however vestigial—of life.

For Andromaque is not immune to the transportations which we have seen her co-protagonists undergo. There are a number of ways in which Andromaque before her hasty exit is beginning to be caught in the system from which she escapes by means of her flight. Her closest resemblance is to Pyrrhus, as the final responses of acts II and III indicate:

> *Pyrrhus:*
> Faisons tout ce que j'ai promis.
> (708)

> *Andromaque:*
> Allons sur son tombeau consulter mon époux.
> (1048)

The conflict between first-person plural ("Faisons," "Allons") and first-person singular ("j'ai promis," "mon époux") is of course partly conventional, the "we" form being simultaneously a plural of majesty and a more convenient form for the first-person imperative. But the split is more than conventional:

although Pyrrhus alone has promised to marry Hermione, he seems to need Phoenix to help him carry out his promise ("Phoenix vous le dira, ma parole est donnée," 906), and Céphise starts to play the same role in maintaining Andromaque's own sense of resolve, whence her need to consult Hector in the presence of her servant. Similarly, when Andromaque has resolved to die and says, "Céphise, c'est à toi de me fermer les yeux" (1100), is she speaking only of her death, or may Céphise not already be serving the function of blocking out the temptations of the present for someone who no longer has "des yeux toujours ouverts aux larmes" (449)?

In fact Andromaque seems to be on the brink of participating in the exchange system which the others are caught in, for she, like Pyrrhus, has a surplus:

> J'ai fait plus: je me suis quelquefois consolée
> Qu'ici, plutôt qu'ailleurs, le sort m'eût exilée.
> (933–34)

> Céphise, il fera plus qu'il n'a promis de faire.
> (1086)

If Andromaque, like Pyrrhus, does "more," if she also thinks that he will do "more" than he strictly must, is this surplus a sign of the positive charge of the individual—in this case the generosity of forgiveness (Andromaque) or of guardianship (Pyrrhus)—or an indication of a dangerous excess ("reste") destroying Andromaque's claims of "indifference" toward her captor?

If Andromaque is beginning to resemble those around her, this similarity is not merely an obstacle to her remaining "indifferent" to the play's transportations and thus different from her co-protagonists; it is also fundamentally necessary in order for Andromaque to provide the tragic middle which brings this play to an end, the first tragic middle in Racine's theater. Andromaque's final gesture is her decision to marry Pyrrhus to save her son and then to commit suicide in order to remain faithful to Hector. What makes this gesture into a tragic middle is its utterly and consciously self-contradictory nature. It is a link which is a separation, at the same time a convergence of the encroaching forces which are beginning to touch even Andromaque herself and an explosion of the myth that they can ever be genuinely resolved. It is a stopgap which takes the form of a vacuum seal, a useful harnessing of unbearable pressure in the name of preservation. Andromaque marries Pyrrhus in order to make him a widower, commits him to the bonds of marriage as a prelude to severing the thread of her own destiny, and counters what seems to be her own dawning attachment to her captor with the calculated detachment of her strategy. In sum, her plan is to stabilize the dangerous "reste" of her own life:

> Je vais donc, puisqu'il faut que je me sacrifie,
> Assurer à Pyrrhus le reste de ma vie;
> Je vais, en recevant sa foi sur les autels,
> L'engager à mon fils par des noeuds immortels.
> Mais aussitôt ma main, à moi seule funeste,
> D'une infidèle vie abrégera le reste,
> Et sauvant ma vertu, rendra ce que je doi
> A Pyrrhus, à mon fils, à mon époux, à moi.
>
> (1089–96)

Andromaque's "choice" is not a choice but rather the deceptive representation of a choice. She stages an action, her marriage to Pyrrhus, which in fact "means" the opposite of what it seems to.[15]

The lesson which Andromaque learns is similar to the lesson of Oreste: that the excluded middle of individuation requires not only a choice of one out of two extremes, a hollowing out of the middle, but also the creation of an unfathomable depth, of a unit of storage where the middle will forever remain in hiding. The closest Andromaque comes to providing an excluded middle for the play is in offering herself up as the unit of the individual, the character about whom — or rather inside of whom — we will never know what the nature of her love and her hatred for her husbands past and present really has been.[16] What exactly does Andromaque owe "to Pyrrhus, to my son, to my husband, to myself"? When she claims to be sacrificing "mon sang, ma haine, et mon amour" (1124), whose love and whose hatred has she sacrificed?

All that we can say in answer to these questions is that Andromaque will hitherto be "known" as the unknown heroine, a fact which may explain the heritage she leaves behind her:

> Fais connaître à mon fils les héros de sa race,
> Autant que tu pourras, conduis-le sur leur trace:
> Dis-lui par quels exploits leurs noms ont éclaté,
> Plutôt ce qu'ils ont fait que ce qu'ils ont été;
> Parle-lui tous les jours des vertus de son père;
> Et quelquefois aussi parle-lui de sa mère.
>
> (1113–18)

Is Andromaque's apparent *parti pris* for action ("ce qu'ils ont fait") over character ("ce qu'ils ont été") simply a defense of Aristotle's theory of tragedy,[17] or is it more fundamentally a way of telling us how to interpret (or not to interpret) her final position, that is, narratable in terms of the actions she accomplishes, but entirely unknowable in its essence? At the moment she thinks will bring her death, Andromaque establishes the foundation of a future ritual, the retelling of her story, the chronicle of her "exploits." But if her name, like that of Astyanax' other heroic forebears, has "éclaté," it is rather in the sense of an explosion, an inability to hold in the middle, than in the sense of a brilliant outpouring of glory. The name as an emblem of heroic action and of the boundary surrounding the heroic individual shows us the nature of this foundation by not allowing us to see what is within: we will never know what Andromaque "has been."

7

The Heroic Oath

Iphigeneia in Aulis

More than any other play of Euripides which Racine used, the *Iphigeneia in Aulis* begins *in medias res*. Indeed, the drama's chronological setting is almost instantly given in terms of a middle:[1]

> Sirius, near the Pleiades of the seven directions [heptaporou],
> is rushing along, still in the middle of its path [messeres].
>
> (7–8)[2]

Sirius is in fact a metaphor for Agamemnon's thoroughly indecisive state, since the play begins at a midpoint between two acts of writing: between Agamemnon's first letter to his wife, in which he asks her to bring their daughter Iphigeneia to Aulis, purportedly to marry her off to Achilles but in fact to sacrifice her to the wrathful Artemis, and his second letter, which squarely contradicts the first one by telling Clytemnestra to keep Iphigeneia at home.[3] If in the *Phoenissae* the "choice" between the two brothers doesn't come until the end of the play, and even in the *Andromache* the title character is given a few hundred lines to catch her breath before being forced to choose, *Iphigeneia in Aulis* begins not only at the moment of choice, but in the mean time between two contradictory choices, at a moment of absolute crisis.

Although Agamemnon's indecision, that is, his vacillation over the question of whether or not to sacrifice his daughter in order to raise the winds for Troy, is portrayed as a middle of hesitation, that is, an inability to choose, there is no possibility here for a middle of compromise. Unlike Jocasta who at first hopes for a genuine reconciliation between her two warring sons, unlike Andromache who starts out clinging to a tenuous continuity even in an extreme situation, Agamemnon, in spite of a certain use of the vocabulary of moderation (378–80, 508–9, 685–86), has from the very beginning relegated all possibility of compromise, and this precisely because he has (nominally) accepted the terms of the excluded middle, here represented by the seal ("sphragis," 155; "semantra," 325) with which he closes both his letter and, theoretically at least, the question of whether to say "yes" or "no" to the goddess' demands. The problem is that Agamemnon undermines his use of the seal by "sealing" two opposite and contradictory messages. Thus he locks himself out of a system in which mediation or compromise might be successful without having gained access to a system in which a choice once made would be inviolable. His contradictory letters, like Sirius, are emblematic of his state of mind, his inability either to compromise or to choose. He is a diver who, caught off balance before he has really decided to take the plunge, can no longer find his equilibrium but is not yet in position to jump, divided between his frantic efforts not to fall and the ever more urgent need to find a last-minute strategy for hitting the water safely.

In fact, the demands of the goddess for the sacrifice of Iphigeneia may be interpreted as doing nothing more than revealing to Agamemnon his actual state of mind on the eve of the Trojan enterprise. Artemis is not tearing down a stability that Agamemnon has already erected; rather she is trying to make him understand that he cannot get his wind for Troy until his resolve is strong enough for him to be willing even to sacrifice his daughter to get there. His paradox is that of a mobile immobility: because he cannot stabilize his decision and choose one way or the other (excluded middle), thus ending his movement-as-vacillation, he cannot move forward toward his goal by initiating a movement-as-progression, for what is lacking to him is a unit of motion, his first "action" in the drama being to move backward and to counteract a previous action. Being caught in the middle of his path is for Agamemnon a sort of "aporia," a narrow strait or an impasse, a term which is already suggested by the adjective applied to the Pleiades, "heptaporos," "seven-pathed," and which is then explicitly used to describe Agamemnon's situation: "ton aporon oudenos endeis," "there are no difficult straits that you are lacking" (41). This statement well expresses Agamemnon's paradoxical situation at Aulis, which is based upon a surplus—too many letters, too many decisions, too many emotions—which is at the same time a lack—not enough resolve, no seal strong enough, in short, no unit of decision capable of subordinating all else to the need for setting the Trojan enterprise into motion.

The *aporia* which comes to be virtually synonymous with Aulis harkens back to an earlier *aporia* which led to the initial forming of the pact that is the basis for Agamemnon's expedition against Troy:

> The matter was irremediable [aporos] for [Helen's] father Tyndareus,
> whether to give her away or not to give her away, if he was to touch
> the best fortune. And this idea came to him,
> for the suitors to exchange [sunapsai, "touch"] oaths, and to join [symbalein, "throw together"]
> right hands [dexias] with each other.
>
> (55–59)

This is an allusion to the agreement imposed on Helen's numerous suitors not only to abide by her choice of a husband, but also to come to her husband's aid should anyone fail to respect the marriage. The original *aporia* of selecting a single husband without causing an uprising leads to the solution of the pact, and that "solution" is the direct antecedent of the immobility at Aulis. What Tyndareus tries to do is to unify the crowd of suitors. He has the suitors "touch" ("sunapsai") oaths and "join" ("symbalein") hands—terms whose importance will soon become apparent—in the hope that these gestures might create a feeling of consensus and cooperation which will allow Helen, a figure of universal desire, to be conferred upon one and only one husband.

The choice of a single husband for Helen, which seems to require nothing more than a series of applications of the law of excluded middle—"to give her away or not to give her away," or, more to the point, to give her to suitor x or not—is in fact more complicated than it seems. Even though the "unit" in this case, one husband, is obviously arrived at by a mechanism of exclusion (Helen can marry one and only one suitor), in order for all the suitors to respect that unit they must be involved in an oath of representation by the terms of which each of the suitors "stands for" all of them. If the law of excluded middle were carried to its logical conclusion, Helen's suitors would simply fight each other to the death until only one of them was left. What Tyndareus comes up with to prevent this is a compromise which emphasizes the suitors' underlying similarity, that is, the fact that they are all potential husbands for Helen and that none of them can ever realize that potential without a bloodbath unless all of them agree to respect Tyndareus' and Helen's choice. Tyndareus does nothing less than found a collectivity, the real issue here being the "symbolic" nature of the oath that binds the Greeks together. Only if the oath retains its mediating force, its power of representation, will it provide the solidarity needed for the Trojan expedition.

Tyndareus thus attempts to soften the severity of the law of excluded middle, the law of the individual, by his recourse to mediation and compromise. But the problem of Helen's suitors is an eternal *aporia*. No one can safely have what everyone wants; the desires of the individual and the needs of the collectivity are not always compatible. Tyndareus' "solution" can never eliminate the traces of the conditions under which it was created. The child of the conflict between the founding of a collectivity and the mutually exclusive nature of the desires of the individuals who make up the collectivity, the suitors' pact is a unit, a convergence, a "symbol" covering up a multitude of conflicting and divergent wishes.

And this is precisely the nature of Agamemnon's "seal," for the question of choosing the one from the many is essentially the same whether the "one" is a single suitor or a single course of action. At this early stage of the Trojan expedition, Agamemnon's seal, a metaphor for his heroic resolve (or lack thereof) is not yet airtight, as is clear in his instructions to the messenger who will attempt, and fail, to carry his counterorders to Clytemnestra:

> As you pass by each parting of the ways [poron schiston], look
> everywhere, being on your guard lest some
> chariot carry [komizous'] my child here
> to the Danaan ships. . . .
> Guard this seal which you are carrying [komizeis]
> upon the tablets.
>
> (144–56)

The "poros schistos" or "split way" against which Agamemnon warns his messenger is a metaphor for choice. The messenger is being asked to make sure at every fork in the road that the undesirable choice, allowing Iphigeneia to arrive and thus to be sacrificed, not be allowed passage, as if in the heart of some gigantic computer each split in the path were a bit of information which permitted only the new message—saving Iphigeneia—to be selected. The transmission of the message itself is an integral part of choice: the verb "komizo," "to bring," is used to describe both the undesirable action of bringing Iphigeneia to Aulis (147) and the hoped-for success of the messenger in bringing the seal intact to its destination (156). Thus Agamemnon's *aporia* is closely related to the nature of the "poros"—the path being nothing more than the impasse less its alpha privative—which is a figure for the process of choice. It is precisely because Agamemnon's seal is permeable or "porous," that is, made up of the numerous openings and closings of his own indecision, that it must be reaffirmed at every split in the "poros."

Agamemnon's drama is the drama of representation itself, an exploration of the relationship between the representing unit (integral seal) and what it stands for (contradictory wishes). The problem is that Agamemnon tries to use writing as a guarantor of his will rather than as an expression of a preexisting will. Agamemnon's feelings of hesitation in the face of the enormity of his choice are not in the least condemnable; on the contrary, they are an expression of his humanity, precisely what must be excised before the departure for Troy. According to Bernard Knox, Euripides in this play "fills his stage with human beings who react to changing circumstance with swift and frequent changes of mind which are presented not as deviations from a heroic standard but as normal human behavior."[4] And "normal human behavior" *is* unheroic to the extent that a norm is an average, a middle which erases any difference, one of the components of heroic representation. As Philip Vellacott points out, Artemis in Euripides' play does not raise the winds *against* the Achaian expedition, as in Aeschylus' *Agamemnon*.[5] But if she contents herself with keeping them calm, that "calm" is in fact a representation of two opposing forces, not a truce or a peace but rather a stalemate.

The first character to feel the full impact of the conflict hidden by the Achaian pact is Achilles. When Clytemnestra receives Agamemnon's first letter but not his second one and thus arrives with her daughter, she is greeted by a confused and embarrassed Achilles who is wholly unaware that Agamemnon has used his name to lure Clytemnestra and Iphigeneia to Aulis:

Achilles:
It is shameful for me to exchange [symballein] words with a woman.
Clytemnestra:
Stay here; why are you running away? Touch [synapson] your right hand [dexian]
with mine, as the start of a fortunate marriage-pact.

(830–32)

Clytemnestra's and Achilles' vocabulary ("symballein," "synapson," "dexian") gives as a backdrop to this scene the pact of Helen's suitors ("dexias," "synapsai," "symbalein," all at 58). What is being discovered here is that the pact, or more specifically the seal which Agamemnon has tried to put on his resolutions in his own *aporia* and which is nothing but the descendant of Tyndareus' pact, is not convergent ("symballein," "to throw together"). The two participants in this scene cannot "throw words together" precisely because they are separated by the chasm of deception which lies between Agamemnon's words and his feelings.

This chasm, which is precisely what Agamemnon has been counting on to perpetrate the sacrifice using the name of Achilles as a sort of bait to trap his daughter, separates word and spirit, name and intention:

Clytemnestra:
For your name has destroyed me, by which you should have protected me.

(909)

Achilles:
For my name, even if it didn't raise up the sword,
will murder your child. And the cause
is your husband; but my body is no longer free of guilt.
                                                    (938–40)

The name of Achilles, which Agamemnon can use as a source of protection precisely because of its difference from that in the name of which it is speaking (Agamemnon's lack of resolve), is for Clytemnestra a source of destruction by virtue of the split between name and intention: both the contrast between Agamemnon's purported aim and his real one and the use of Achilles' name against his own wishes. And Achilles, who accepts responsibility for a deed which only his "name" helped to commit, comes to the conclusion that the individual is defined as a necessary defense against the threat posed by the separation of his name and his inner being:

So I would be the worst man among the Argives,
I would be absolutely nothing, . . .
if my name commits murder for your husband.
                                                    (944–47)

Between name and action: this is where Achilles situates the individual. If Achilles accepted the inadequacy of this mediating position of the individual, if he accepted the fact that a meaning and even an action could be attributed to his name against his intentions, he would become "nothing."

This might appear to be an Iliadic Achilles, an Achilles who as the epitome of the heroic individual will not do anything against his will. But in fact Achilles goes on to recognize the potential usefulness of the split between name and action, and he does so in a way which undermines his potential for heroism here:

But King Agamemnon inflicted outrageous violence upon us.
And he should have asked me personally for my name
as a trap for his daughter. . . .
I would have given it to the Greeks, if this was what afflicted
the departure for Ilium; we would not have refused
to increase the common good of those with whom we are fighting.
                                                    (961–67)

This is an utterly astonishing statement. What Achilles is saying is that the false relation between name and action, the deceptive use of his name as a bait, is less important than the recognition of his right to regulate it. If Agamemnon had simply asked permission to use the name of Achilles, the latter would have consented. His objection to the present situation thus hinges not on a question of justice, for he here rejects the idea that word and action must fit together and may never deceive, but rather on the issue of property.

That these words of Achilles have been attacked by critics as "unachillean"[6] underlines their importance here. This Achilles is quite the opposite of the Homeric firebrand who in book 1 of the *Iliad* challenges the Achaian oath of heroic representation by asking what the war has to do with him. If the Euripidean Achilles resembles any Homeric figure, it is rather the shrewd calculator Odysseus, for in spite of Achilles' discovery of Agamemnon's ruse, he is not truly radicalized by it. In fact one of the play's most brilliant inventions is to be found in the moderate portrait it draws of Achilles. Achilles arrives in the middle of the drama[7] and is presented as trying to moderate his men (812–18). He believes it is always right "to rejoice with measure [metrios]," even to the potential excesses brought on by the "swollen sails of good fortune" (921). Unlike his men, who resent having to measure ("ekmetresai," 816) the passage of time, this " 'new' Achilles" is "more prudent than he is bold."[8]

Achilles may seem to recognize the artificial nature of heroic representation insofar as he understands that word and deed can be separated by a whole range of varied motives, but it is not until the end of the drama that he is made to feel what Agamemnon understands from the very start: the pain of heroic individuation, the high price at which it must be bought. This is, of course, the reason for Agamemnon's vacillating attitude toward the sacrifice in the opening scenes; he cannot decide between two things, family and heroism, which he wants with an equal passion. But Achilles must come to this position of hesitation, and this he does only once he has seen Iphigeneia and fallen in love with her.

When Iphigeneia makes her famous speech accepting the need for the sacrifice (1368–1401), Achilles claims to approve of her decision (1407–9), but, paradoxically, seeing her heroic resolve is precisely what makes him vacillate:

> But the desire to marry you comes more strongly to me
> as I look at the sort of woman you are: you are noble.
> Do you see how much I want to be of service to you,
> to take you to my house? And I suffer, as Thetis is my witness,
> because I am not allowed to save you by going to battle
> with the Danaans.
>
> (1410–15)

Although in the course of the play Achilles seems inconsistent in his attitude toward Iphigeneia's sacrifice—he says rather glibly that he would have willingly given his name to lure her to Aulis, but still insists on trying to protect her against the army clamoring for her sacrifice—in fact he does not really hesitate until this moment. Until he understands the value of what will be lost by the sacrifice, until he can say, "I suffer," the story of Iphigeneia and the sacrifice is merely an issue of territoriality: he simply wants control over his "belongings," whether his name or his betrothed. It is only when Achilles finally sees and knows Iphigeneia that he begins to have an inkling of the nature of tragic heroism. It is only then that Achilles contradicts himself in a more fundamental way, as critics have pointed out,[9] alternately characterizing Iphigeneia's decision as "ariston," "the best" (1421)—a word related to "arete," "heroic excellence"—and "aphrosyne," "senselessness" (1430), the opposite of Aristotle's "sophrosyne" or "moderation." The play has come back to its starting point, no further along the path of heroism than in its first scene. Like Agamemnon before him, Achilles cannot help himself from judging heroism from two contradictory perspectives.

For what neither Achilles nor even Agamemnon ever fully own up to is precisely the rite of passage demanded by Artemis and her sacrifice, its basic requirement being the need to go against oneself, to oppose one's feelings, to sacrifice oneself in order to create the heroic individual. The sacrifice of the individual as a reenactment of the gap at the center of the oath of heroic representation comes no more from Achilles than from Agamemnon. It is provided only by Iphigeneia herself.

It is time, then, to examine the import of this sacrifice, and more specifically the ways in which Iphigeneia provides the model of tragic individuation which Agamemnon and Achilles lack. In the section immediately preceding Iphigeneia's first appearance onstage, the play's first stasimon is sung by the young women of the chorus, and it first seems like a paean to moderation:

> Happy are those who with measure [metrias]
> and with [meta] moderate reserve [sophrosynas] partake [meteschon]
> of the bed of the goddess Aphrodite . . .
> May I have moderate [metria]
> pleasure, and respectful desires,
> and may I partake [metechoimi] of Aphrodite's
> domain, but be held far away from excess [pollan, "much"].
>
> (543-57)

The pairing of "meta" and "metrios" in this ode to moderation emphasizes the fact that participation in the joys of love, that is, being "with" ("meta") Aphrodite's powers, must go along with an avoidance of excess. The term that opposes "metrios" is "polys," "much," which is here set against the state of being "metrios" in the same way that it is contrasted to being "isos" or "equal" in the *Phoenissae*.

Nonetheless, the question of the need for greatness or magnitude subtly creeps into the chorus' song. A third term echoing "meta" and "metrios," "mega" ("great"), is introduced:

> But different are the natures of mortals,
> and different are their ways; and what is truly
> noble is always clear;
> and being raised with an education
> brings great things [mega] to virtue [aretan];
> for modesty [to aideisthai] is wisdom . . .
>
> . . . .
> To hunt after virtue [aretan] is something great [mega].
> (558–68)

Even though the chorus never completely loses sight of the value of moderate virtue, as is shown by the term "to aideisthai" ("modesty"), the lesson of Iphigeneia will be the lesson of tragic magnitude ("megethos," the noun based on "megas," "great"), which is as essential to virtue ("arete") in tragedy as moderation is necessary to it in the *Nicomachean Ethics*. The announcement of Iphigeneia's arrival onstage includes a triple repetition of the word "megas": "Great [megalai] are the blessings of the great [megalon]; . . . of what great [megalon] families they [Iphigeneia and Clytemnestra] are born" (590–94).

Thus Iphigeneia's arrival is anticipated by a song which begins in praise of moderation and ends in praise of greatness. Similarly, Iphigeneia's actual arrival in Aulis starts out in moderation but also prefigures the need for the excluded middle of her sacrifice. Here are Clytemnestra's first words to Iphigeneia:

> As for you, my child, leave this horse-drawn carriage,
> setting down your delicate and strengthless extremity [kolon asthenes].
> (613–14)

And Iphigeneia's first response:

O Mother, if I run ahead of you, don't be angry,
I must throw [prosbalo] my heart against my father's heart!

(631–32)

What is first emphasized here is Iphigeneia's humility. She is depicted as fragile, fearful of competition, and sensitive to others. The action of pressing her heart against her father's is described by the verb "prosbalo," related to "symballo," the verb used of Helen's suitors shaking hands to seal their oath. Iphigeneia's gesture is emblematic of her wish not to let her own individual desires intrude upon the situation but rather to adapt herself to others' needs, to act with moderation.

And yet the excluded middle which Iphigeneia will be asked to provide is already suggested by the phrase "kolon asthenes," "strengthless extremity," which is an echo and an anticipation[10] of Agamemnon's arrival home from Troy in Aeschylus' *Agamemnon*. Iphigeneia's modest arrival in Aulis contrasts with her father's excessively prideful homecoming in the course of which Clytemnestra has carpets spread beneath Agamemnon's feet and persuades him to tread upon them (*Agamemnon*, 905–49). Clytemnestra's use of the word *kolon* in the two scenes underlies another, equally important contrast. In the *Agamemnon*, as the Argive queen imagines the Greek army's return trip from Troy, she expresses the hope that the soldiers will act with respect and moderation and thus be allowed safe passage home:

For what they need for a safe return home
is to bend back [kampsai palin] the other member [kolon] for the second half
of the race-course.

(*Agamemnon*, 343–44)

Clytemnestra here uses the metaphor of the racetrack that Aristotle will use in the *Ethics*[11] as she points out that the return trip from Troy is contingent upon moderation. The member must be bent back ("palin") at the midpoint of the race—technically known as the "kampter" and here evoked by the verb "kampsai," "to bend"—and that midpoint negotiated by a movement in the opposite direction if home is to be reached again. By extension we may say that the journey *to* Troy will depend not on flexibility and adaptability, but rather on an extreme desire for glory, a unidirectionality, and this is what Iphigeneia needs to bring to Aulis. Her "strengthless" ("asthenes") member is a metaphor for Agamemnon's own strengthlessness ("ou stheno," "I have no strength," 655), his need for the strength and resolve necessary for the winds to be raised.

Thus the central question of the drama, the question of how human ir-resolution can be represented by heroic resolve, is closely related to the single issue that has most disturbed its critics from Aristotle to the present:

> An example . . . of inconsistent character [is] Iphigeneia in Aulis, for the sup-pliant Iphigeneia is not at all like her later character.[12]

> Either Iphigeneia has changed her attitude fundamentally for reasons which are not divulged and for a dramatic purpose which remains obscure, or her charac-terization is, as Aristotle said, inconsistent.[13]

As Zeno's paradox has taught us, we can never understand the relation be-tween the continuity of life and the discontinuity that constitutes the unit of the individual. The limitations of Euripides' art, its apparent inconsisten-cies, are closely linked to our inability to comprehend heroic individua-tion. This is how Albin Lesky accounts for the play's discontinuity:

> [In *Iphigeneia in Aulis*] the poet lets us see the two endpoints of a develop-ment, first the young girl's fear of death, then her monumental decision and heroic readiness. How the change from one state to the other takes place in his heroine's soul he hasn't shown us, in fact he couldn't show it to us with the means [Mitteln] of his art. . . . Indeed, the poet has not represented the step-wise development from within of his heroine, but rather he has very force-fully let us see the external forces which produce this development.[14]

The means ("Mitteln") of Euripides' art cannot adequately represent the mid-dle of this change across time, since the inner workings of Iphigeneia's soul, which we are not allowed to see, are represented by an outside, the two "endpoints," beginning and end, of her change of heart and the external forces which effect it. What happens in the middle is sealed off to our perception.

Thus, whereas Achilles, as we have seen, tries to take full possession of the mediating function of the individual, Iphigeneia defines the individual by an absence at the center, an abdication of resistance, a thoroughgoing resignation. Achilles, faced with the problematic nature of intention which is proven by the divergence of word (his purported marriage to Iphigeneia) and action (the sacrifice of Iphigeneia), does his all to make the action con-form to the word, that is, to transform the sacrifice into the promised mar-riage. Iphigeneia, on the contrary, ultimately changes nothing but her intention:

Iphigeneia is the only one in the whole tragedy who finds a way out of herself to the universal. . . . The quiet exuberance, the pathetic actions are not natural or primary responses. Even her self-sacrifice is grounded in feeling of power-lessness. . . . The heroic has here assumed the form of the pathetic, because the break between the weakness of man and the triumph of a spirit aspiring to something higher is complete. Even the heroic figure lacks a center, just as the piteous minor characters do. For the vital core is shattered—except that here it is replaced by an ideal.[15]

In order to find "a way out of herself to the universal," to the ideal of tragic heroism, Iphigeneia must leave herself behind, just as she leaves behind the others who are purely "centered on themselves."[16]

What Iphigeneia comes to understand is that in the domain of heroism it is ultimately more important for the word—the oracle, the seal, the sta-bility of the excluded middle which prohibits a movement of reversal once a pronouncement has been made—to remain unchallenged than for it to be "right." The artificiality of the word, the very thing which gives it its power of difference, also means that the word cannot always remain connected to true meaning. Iphigeneia's acceptance of her fate is not a way of saying that Agamemnon no longer loves her, but rather a way of saying that his actions toward her are no longer allowed to represent his feelings for her. This is the very meaning of the sacrifice necessary for heroic representa-tion and the departure for Troy.

Once Iphigeneia has accepted the nature of the oath of representation, once she has seen the gap of falsity and artificiality at its center and decided to offer herself up to fill that gap, she belongs to nobody. Achilles' advice to Clytemnestra to "hold onto" her daughter ("antechou thygatros," 1367), which contains a suggestion of possession ("echo," "to have") by resistance or opposition ("anti-") to a counterforce pulling in the other direction, is bad advice. At the moment of separation from her daughter, Clytemnestra says she will hold onto Iphigeneia's veil ("peplon echomene son," 1460), but in vain. Iphigeneia's acceptance of the sacrifice is the mirror image of Tyndareus' oath, for whereas the latter moderates the harshness of Helen's choice of a husband, Iphigeneia's willingness to die recognizes that the al-ways recurrent needs of the law of excluded middle have made themselves heard in the terms of Artemis' demands.

Iphigeneia's heroism leaves a "silence in the middle":

And everyone was stupified when they heard
the courage and the virtue [areten] of the maiden.

And standing in the middle [en meso] Talthybios, whose task it was,
ordered a respectful silence for the army;

. . . .

And the son of Peleus took the basket and the holy water at the same time
and moistened the area around the goddess' altar in the shape of a circle.

(1561–69)

If Iphigeneia cannot be "had" by any one individual, it is because she is "in the middle" ("en meso") of the entire Greek army. She "belongs" to no one, least of all to herself, because it is only her sacrifice which establishes the boundaries of individuation. The circle which Achilles describes around the altar of the goddess is also a circle around Iphigeneia. Although it is a metaphor for unity and for the sealing of the Achaian pact, it also shows the difficulty of reaching the stature of Iphigeneia's heroic gesture. Only by remaining at a fixed distance from the circle does the middle define its outlines.

The heroic individual is thus constituted by an act of willing exclusion in the middle, Iphigeneia's explosion of the myth of the adequacy of the mediating "I" to make word and action join in a seamless fit. If the actual moment of the sacrifice requires silence in the middle, this is because tragic individuation is a function of the inadequacy of the oath of heroic representation. Clytemnestra's characterization of the story of Iphigeneia's miraculous last-minute rescue as a "myth" ("mythous," 1617) correctly labels the status of survival in the creation of the heroic individual. The relation of the zero point of the sacrifice (excluded middle) to the world of survival (virtuous middle) is a myth, the very source and mechanism of this tragic theater, that is, something which must be believed in but not fully understood, for if one gets too close to it, one can no longer be taken in by this heroic representation. Iphigeneia's miraculous, last-minute substitution and departure are described by the word "thean," "spectacle" (1588), the very essence of "theater," an act of seeing from afar. If the writing of two contradictory letters is what ushers Iphigeneia into the theater of individuation, it is with the equally unclear status of myth that she is whisked away by the goddess, for it is upon the dual status of Iphigeneia, both alive and dead, protected and killed by the mask of heroism—"having died and seeing the light of day" (1612)—that this tragedy depends and ends. And, in a mythopoetic reversal, it is with two Iphigeneias that Racine is going to begin and with "one" that he is going to end. Let us turn, then, to these two Iphigeneias, and to Racine's *Iphigénie*.

8

Middle, Model, Muddle
An I.O.U. from Racine to Euripides

In the preface to *Iphigénie,* Racine admits that in spite of a number of elements which separate his own tragedy from Euripides', his debt to the author of the *Iphigeneia in Aulis* is considerable: "So those are the main areas in which I have slightly distanced myself from Euripides' economy and his use of the legend. But as far as the passions in the play go, I have contrived to follow him more precisely. I confess that I owe him a good number of the places in my tragedy that have met with the greatest approval."[1] Racine is here acknowledging a debt; his preface to *Iphigénie* takes the form of an I.O.U. But what exactly does Racine "owe" to Euripides?[2]

When he enters into the specifics of his play, Racine seems to explain what he does *not* owe to Euripides:

I have mentioned all these various opinions [the different versions of the Iphigeneia myth], and especially the passage from Pausanias, because he is the author to whom I owe the fortunate character of Eriphile, without whom I would never have dared to undertake this tragedy. What kind of impression would it have made if I had sullied the stage with the horrible murder of a person as virtuous and as lovely as I had to depict Iphigénie? And on the other hand what kind of impression would it have made if I had resolved my tragedy with the help of a goddess appearing *ex machina* and a metamorphosis which might have been somewhat plausible in Euripides' time, but which would be too ridiculous and unbelievable in ours?

I can therefore say that I was very fortunate to find among the Ancients that other Iphigénie, whom I have let myself depict however I please, and who, when she falls into the very same misfortune which her own jealousy has tried to impose upon her rival, in some sense deserves to be punished, although she is still not completely unworthy of compassion. (*Oeuvres complètes* 1:670)

The first Iphigénie, the daughter of Agamemnon and Clytemnestra, is not only virtuous, but even too virtuous. Racine "must represent" her in such a way that her death, which is imposed by the myth unless the ridiculous *deus ex machina* of Euripides' ending is adopted, is too shocking to be the basis of a tragedy. As anyone who is familiar with Racine's play knows, the day is saved (and the tragedy can thus be written) thanks to "that other Iphigénie," the mysterious daughter of Theseus and Helen whose identity is revealed only at the play's end and who is her virtuous cousin's opposite in terms of their (apparent) personalities, and more specifically her lack of virtue, for this is one case in which the absence of virtue is a virtue. Being able to represent this other Iphigénie in any way he pleases is what allows Racine to write his tragedy.

The most important debt of Racine to Euripides might then appear to be Iphigénie herself. If Racine describes her as "a person as virtuous and as lovely as I had to depict Iphigénie," it is largely because Euripides has made his character into a model of virtue. But is it not precisely because of this unassailable ethical model that Racine feels the need for "that other Iphigénie"? Eriphile may seem to be precisely what Racine doesn't owe to Euripides. And yet is Racine's need for her not generated by the Euripidean heroine? Eriphile is a foil, a character defined by negation. She is everything Iphigénie is not, or more precisely, everything Iphigénie is not willing to recognize herself to be. To this extent, whatever Iphigénie as an upholder of heroic virtue claims to be determines what Eriphile is not, and Racine "owes" Eriphile to the virtue of Iphigeneia. It is as if the ambiguity of Euripides' transformation of his protagonist into a model of heroism—an ambiguity which, as we have seen, dominates the end of his drama—brought forth Racine's doubled Iphigénie.

Iphigénie and Eriphile are the two components of a single personality attempting to form itself. Iphigénie herself wonders aloud whether she and Eriphile can ever be separated:

> Vous ne pouviez sans moi demeurer à Mycène;
> Me verra-t-on sans vous partir avec la reine?
> (665–66)

> Je vois ce que jamais je n'ai voulu penser:
> Achille . . . Vous brûlez que je ne sois partie.
> (672–73)

These admonitions of Iphigénie to Eriphile have the impact of an internal dialogue. Iphigénie, who has been described as one of Racine's most Cornelian characters, the epitome of virtue and duty, is here speaking to the part of herself, Eriphile, in which nonvirtuous desire is lodged, so that the question of whether she will be able to leave Aulis without Eriphile becomes the question of whether she can extricate from within herself the desire which is in conflict with her virtue.

Thus Iphigénie and Eriphile are two parts of the same character from the very beginning, from their first shared appearance onstage, their meeting with Agamemnon:

> Vous n'avez devant vous qu'une jeune princesse
> A qui j'avais pour moi vanté votre tendresse.
> Cent fois lui promettant mes soins, votre bonté,
> J'ai fait gloire à ses yeux de ma félicité.
> Que va-t-elle penser de votre indifférence?
> Ai-je flatté ses voeux d'une fausse espérance?
> (561–66)

"Vous n'avez devant vous qu'une jeune princesse": this means not only "Eriphile is no one to feel inhibited in front of," but also "There is only *one* princess here, not two." Iphigénie's assurances to Eriphile of Agamemnon's devotion are the language of duty speaking to desire. Eriphile, who revels in her status as unloved, rejected daughter, is also Iphigénie's hidden desiring function, which by the very nature of desire can never have enough, so that this "Iphigénie" cannot be sufficiently reassured of her father's devotion. Iphigénie assuring Eriphile of Agamemnon's paternal affection is the dutiful Iphigénie trying to make desire accept the very limitations which are inimical to desire.

Although Iphigénie and Eriphile have the same object of desire, Achille, and although the masochistic nature of Eriphile's desire has been commented upon, the precise nature of Iphigénie's love for Achille has not been sufficiently emphasized. At the outset, there is no conflict between virtue and desire for Iphigénie: she describes Achille as "Cet amant . . . / Qu'un père de si loin m'ordonne de chercher" (598–600), an order which is supported by Clytemnestre's initial approval (640). But whereas Iphigénie at no time openly revolts against her father's plans for her own sacrifice, that exemplary bit of obedience draws our attention away from her refusal to reject Achille:

> Vous voyez de quel oeil, et comme indifférente,
> J'ai reçu de ma mort la nouvelle sanglante.
> Je n'en ai point pâli. Que n'avez-vous pu voir
> A quel excès tantôt allait mon désespoir,

> Quand, presque en arrivant, un récit peu fidèle
> M'a de votre inconstance annoncé la nouvelle!
> Qui sait même, qui sait si le ciel irrité
> A pu souffrir l'excès de ma félicité?
>
> (1033–40)

The seemingly moderate Iphigénie, a model of self-control who seems to live the purity of her exclusively positive vision ("J'ai cru n'avoir au ciel que des grâces à rendre," 550) as a sort of norm or average and not as an extreme, recognizes her "excess" only here: "l'excès de ma félicité." She even reverts to a sort of nascent Eriphilism as she wonders whether the heavens can put up with the very sight of her happiness.

In this light the confrontation between Iphigénie and Eriphile (II, v) takes on the impact of a meeting of Iphigénie with herself, of her conscience with her desire. It is absolutely essential to remember that when this scene takes place, Iphigénie has just been instructed by Clytemnestre to forget Achille (645–56) but has not made the slightest response to her mother's orders. In fact her indirect reply will take the form of a cry of astonishment, anguish, and resistance directed more to herself than to Eriphile, or rather toward the part of herself that is Eriphile:

> Oui, vous l'aimez, perfide!
>
> (678)

This is a discovery not only that Eriphile has been in love with Achille from the very beginning, but also that Iphigénie herself, now turned "perfidious" because her love is no longer in line with her filial duty, is still in love with Achille in spite of the dictates of her conscience.

Thus the most important sacrifice in Racine's drama is not the sacrifice of Iphigénie's life, but that of her love for Achille, and it is a sacrifice which she rejects:

> Achille trop ardent l'a peut-être offensé,
> Mais le roi, qui le hait, veut que je le haïsse;
> Il ordonne à mon coeur cet affreux sacrifice.
>
> .   .   .   .
>
> Dieux plus doux, vous n'avez demandé que ma vie!
> Mourons, obéissons.
>
> (1504–11)

The "sacrifice" that Iphigénie refuses to make is that of her desire for Achille, and when she says "obéissons," her gesture of obedience (offering up her life) is designed to take our attention away from a more serious act of revolt against Agamemnon's authority than a refusal of the sacrifice of her life would be. Continuing to love Achille against the demands of virtue means creating an internal division, a split embodied by Eriphile, the "wanting" Iphigénie. Iphigénie nowhere openly admits either to herself or to anyone else that her love for Achille is in any danger of undermining her status as the most virtuous of daughters. It is Eriphile alone who bears the brunt of her reproaches, Eriphile who is labeled as perfidious. Iphigénie's heroic illusion is that Eriphile, the nonvirtuous lover, is not a part of her, is not "another Iphigénie."[3]

It is Eriphile who embodies the radical break at the heart of heroic representation, the element of negativity and unremitting opposition which Iphigénie spends so much of her time and energy refusing to recognize. Eriphile is defined as what the others are not:

> Ne les contraignons point, Doris, retirons-nous.
> Laissons-les dans les bras d'un père et d'un époux,
> Et tandis qu'à l'envi leur amour se déploie,
> Mettons en liberté ma tristesse et leur joie.
>
> (395–98)

In her first words onstage, Eriphile imagines simultaneously liberating her own sadness and the joy of those around her. The perennial outsider, she is "excluded . . . from the action, . . . held in check at the margins, wandering like a shadow around the luminous, magical circle of power she cannot get into."[4] She is what Roland Barthes calls "the only free being in Racine's theater,"[5] her single and overpowering freedom residing in her power to say no. Eriphile embodies the capacity—which Iphigénie either lacks or refuses to recognize—to be unsatisfied, not to possess; an antiheroic capacity that might be said to define desire itself, for desire never has what is wants, never transforms its lack into a capacity for storage, and to that extent it is utterly incompatible with the goals of the law of excluded middle.

Even though she is "excluded" and "at the margins," Eriphile is nonetheless in the middle:

> Savez-vous quel serpent inhumain
> Iphigénie avait retiré dans son sein?
> (1671–72)

Eriphile is not only the unmediable opposite of Iphigénie, she is also the essence of Iphigénie, for Iphigénie needs Eriphile—that is, needs to negate her—in order to constitute herself. Iphigénie draws her strength from this hidden element at her center in the same way that the first part of her name, "iphi-," "strongly or courageously," is found, albeit less conspicuously, at the center of "Er-iphi-le," a name which Racine seems to have adapted from "Eriphyle" (the wife of the seer Amphiaraos who is completely unrelated to this story)[6] and which aptly describes its bearer ("love of strife"). It is her own oxymoronic nature (the "good" Iphigénie based on repressing the "bad" one) that Iphigénie attempts to deny. What she wants is strength ("iphi") without internal strife ("eris").

Thus if Eriphile is hidden in the middle, it is not as a moderating influence, but as a kind of tragic vortex violently drawing everything into itself. When Agamemnon tries to send his daughter back home and thus provide what would be an excluded middle to his endless vacillations,[7] Eriphile, by making Iphigénie's flight known and preventing this reversal from taking place, becomes a figure of Agamemnon's desire as well as Iphigénie's. In spite of his decision to send his daughter away and give up his aspirations to power, it is the "Eriphile" within him, his desire to have it all, the secret pocket of regret for lost glory that love for his daughter cannot make disappear, which makes his decision public and compromises it, thus imposing the sacrifice.

It is precisely at the moment Eriphile reveals Iphigénie's attempted flight from the camp that she reaches the status of monster (1675–76) which epitomizes her paradoxical nature. The monstrous is what goes against the laws of combination. It is the product of a fundamentally incompatible pairing, for its existence suggests that in the conflict between the two poles (parents) which produced it, there is no possibility either of compromise (virtuous middle) or of resolution by choice (excluded middle). The monstrousness of Eriphile is a commentary on the immeasurability of desire and the impossibility of regulating and regularizing it. She is the daughter of Helen and Theseus, the former being a figure of infinite desirability and the latter, as his name suggests (related to "tithemi," "to establish," "to constitute," used of laws among other things), known primarily as a lawmaker, one who, as will become apparent in *Phèdre,* prides himself on the destruction rather than the production of monsters in spite of—or perhaps because of—his own ambiguous relation to desire. The paradox of the monstrous Eriphile resides in the fact that in spite of her extremity, she is never on the outside; she is like the monster in the middle of the labyrinth. By a topology possible only in tragedy, she is the extreme that is in the middle. In order to be "correctly" sacrificed (which she is not), she would have to be flushed out.

Thus, we find ourselves forced to modify our initial description of Eriphile as "what the others are not." Many critics have emphasized the fundamental separation between Eriphile's world and that of the others in the play.[8]

As Barthes puts it, Eriphile is the "rupture" which can never be overcome, and Agamemnon, who is representative of the departing Greeks, is unlike Eriphile precisely because he himself "is not monstrous but *mediocre, an average* [moyenne, "mean"] *soul.*"9 Eriphile may indeed be anything but mediocre, but she is in the hearts of all of those trying to depart for Troy. She may stand for an ineradicable difference, but it is an internal difference, not one which distinguishes her from the others but one which separates the others from themselves.

Eriphile can be summed up as the necessary but not sufficient, the imposition of conditions which guarantees no satisfactory result. This is already apparent in the terms of the oracle:

> "Vous armez contre Troie une puissance vaine,
> Si, dans un sacrifice auguste et solennel,
>   Une Fille du sang d'Hélène,
> De Diane en ces lieux n'ensanglante l'autel.
> Pour obtenir les vents que le ciel vous dénie,
>   Sacrifiez Iphigénie."
>
>   (57–62)

The oracle is divided into two parts which seem to give the same message but which take very different forms. The second sentence is based on a fairly direct relation of cause and effect which will, moreover, be borne out by the end of the tragedy, the miraculous raising of the winds at the moment of Eriphile/Iphigénie's death. But the first sentence, the more useful part of the oracle insofar as it refuses to identify the correct victim—and nothing prevents people from discovering the truth as efficiently as making them think they already know it—is neither a command nor a recommendation, nor even a prediction of what will happen. It is rather a prediction of what will not happen, since it takes the form, "If not x, not y": if Helen's blood does not flow onto Artemis' altar, the expedition will not be able to leave. Although this statement may seem to refer to the same miraculous ending, its form makes it into a completely different utterance, for it is merely a *sine qua non.* It says that the sacrifice of Iphigénie will provide something *without* which the expedition cannot leave for Troy. The form, "if not x, not y," looks ahead to the oracle delivered to Eriphile, "Un oracle . . . / Me dit que sans périr je ne me puis connaître" (428–30), which doesn't guarantee that she ever will know herself even if she does perish.

Thus Eriphile is born—and, more important, dies—under the sign of the necessary but insufficient. Even her death does nothing to guarantee that the Greeks are not arming a power which, at some level, will always continue to be "vain." Indeed, the entire oracle harkens back to Racine's description in the preface to *Iphigénie* of "the fortunate character of Eriphile, without whom I would never have dared to undertake [entreprendre] this tragedy." Racine tells us that he would never have dared to write this tragedy without Eriphile, yet another statement which takes the form, "if not x, not y." If her discovery (or rather invention) is what leads to the "enterprise" of the tragedy as well as the enterprise against Troy, is it an enterprise that reaches its goal? Can Racine, in spite of his outstanding debt to Euripides' virtuous Iphigeneia, be a successful "entrepreneur"?

Euripides' Iphigeneia, as we have seen, may be taken as a model of virtue that tallies up and pays the dues of heroic representation. But as we approach the end of Racine's play, we may well wonder what Racine's debt to this model of virtue ultimately is. When Eriphile seizes the sacrificial knife and, instead of having her throat cut as the ritual demands, plunges it into her middle, has Racine opted for the benefits of a salutary excluded middle by the terms of which virtue is simply rewarded and evil punished? Or, by undermining the proper execution of the sacrifice, is he saying that the debt of heroic representation cannot be so easily acquitted? As we are about to look at Racine's ending, let us first follow Eriphile's lead by focusing not on its end but on its middle, the site which she never allows us either to reach or to leave.

As usual with Racine, what we find in the middle of this drama is the middle parading as the end:

> *Eriphile:*
> Souffrez que loin du camp, et loin de votre vue,
> Toujours infortunée et toujours inconnue,
> J'aille cacher un sort si digne de pitié,
> Et dont mes pleurs encor vous taisent la moitié.
> *Achille:*
> C'est trop, belle princesse. Il ne faut que nous suivre.
> Venez, qu'aux yeux des Grecs Achille vous délivre,
> Et que le doux moment de ma félicité
> Soit le moment heureux de votre liberté.
>
> (889–96)

At the precise midpoint of *Iphigénie,* we find the happy illusion that Eriphile can be "liberated," that desire can be freed from its relation of opposition to will and duty and exiled ("far from the camp") from the midst of the assembled Achaians who are on the verge of affirming their pact of heroic representation. The real illusion here is that if desire were extricated from the center of the heroic individual, the will which opposes desire could persist, that heroic will, which seems to take the form of an affirmation, is anything other than a negation of desire. Achille's words question the definition of Eriphile as the extreme opposite of whatever is presented to her. His intention of simultaneously freeing her happiness and his own would correct the all-important words of Eriphile's entrance onstage: "Mettons en liberté ma tristesse et leur joie" (398). Doing this would be tantamount to doing away with the principle of strife and conflict that Eriphile embodies. And so it is that the closest the play comes to affirming heroic representation in a "simple" way—in spite of the claims of some that the drama actually ends happily or "well"[10]—is its midpoint.

It is no accident, then, that Eriphile's final word before this midpoint is "half" ("moitié"). Her tears, which look ahead to Iphigénie's final action in the play ("pleure son ennemie," 1786), are a form of silence, or more precisely of half-silence. They are simultaneously a sign that something is trying to be expressed—Eriphile's desire for Achille, which she never admits either to him or to Iphigénie—and that it will not be given full expression. This entirely liminary status of Eriphile's tears goes along with her own position as what can be neither completely silenced nor completely expressed. Half outside and half inside, Eriphile and her half-silent tears thus teach a lesson at the play's midpoint: that heroic representation allows external expression of only half of oneself, and silences the rest. The lesson of the play's middle can be divided into two half-lessons. It teaches the limited nature of heroic representation to those who know how to read Eriphile's half-speech and half-silence. But it also provides the opposite lesson to those who, like Achille, are incapable of such a reading: the useful illusion of freedom. Heroic representation can wear the mask of liberty at the play's midpoint because as a sort of filtering mechanism which allows only half of the truth to be expressed (yes, the sacrificial altars are ready, but who is the victim?), the midpoint serves the essential function of preventing those who are under its spell from looking further within. The valence of the middle's lesson is thus both negative and positive. It is negative to the extent that it shows the essential element of falsity in heroic representation, and positive in the sense that nonawareness can be a benefit, a form of protection.

And it is only at the middle of the play that this fundamentally imprisoning position seems able to be made compatible with liberty, for the very next lines, the opening of the second half of the tragedy, reveal the true nature of the problem and spoil the middle's attempt at solving it:

> Madame, tout est prêt pour la cérémonie.
> Le roi près de l'autel attend Iphigénie;
> Je viens la demander. Ou plutôt contre lui,
> Seigneur, je viens pour elle implorer votre appui.
> (897–900)

This ceremonial readiness, echoing the announcement of Andromaque's confidante ("Mais tout s'apprête au temple, et vous avez promis . . ." *Andromaque*, 1063) just before the Trojan queen's suicide vow, is the quiet before the storm. The announcement of "contrariness" ("ou plutôt contre lui," coming in the middle of a line) or opposition in the relation between Iphigénie and her father initiates the second half of the drama and, at its innermost moment, makes the middle profoundly discontinuous, the empty façade of a happy ending. It is at this moment, the moment that proves the inadequacy of her father's devotion and thus puts an end to her illusions of any simple, nonexclusionary heroic representation, that Iphigénie is forced to know herself—that is, the Eriphile within her—and to die as herself. If the oracle which appears to name Agamemnon's daughter is ultimately interpreted as referring to Eriphile, the oracle meant for Eriphile could also apply to Iphigénie:

> J'ignore qui je suis, et pour comble d'horreur
> Un oracle effrayant m'attache à mon erreur,
> Et quand je veux chercher le sang qui m'a fait naître,
> Me dit que sans périr je ne me puis connaître.
>
> (427–30)

"Le sang qui m'a fait naître" is Agamemnon, and Iphigénie's horror at his betrayal, which she silences as effectively as Eriphile silences her love for Achille, is what allows her to know herself and to "perish" at the same time.

Thus if the second half of the tragedy is what forces—more than it allows—Iphigénie to know herself, in the course of that knowing the Iphigénie who set off to look for self-knowledge "perishes." Iphigénie's desire to be completely and seamlessly identified with her father leads to a realization of what she—and he—must do without if the Trojan expedition is to begin. What Iphigénie must learn is that the heroic individual's interior being cannot be fully externalized, that the process of tragic individuation demands that the individual deny what is on the inside in order to affirm what is on the outside.

But if Iphigénie is the only character who perhaps understands the nature of what must be sacrificed in the process of heroic individuation, once the curtain falls upon her—at the middle of the play, which is in some sense her end—we can never again answer by a simple "yes" or "no" the question of what Iphigénie has understood in this process. To this extent Lucien Goldmann thoroughly misunderstands Iphigénie's character when he condemns the disunity of the play on the grounds that the scene in which Iphigénie confronts Eriphile ("Oui, vous l'aimez, perfide!")—the all-important scene which largely establishes the relation between Iphigénie and her "other"—has no followup, that Iphigénie "will never again recall her jealousy, even though it is quite justified."[11] It is not so much that Iphigénie "doesn't remember" her attack on Eriphile, but rather that she internalizes her attitude toward Eriphile. Her process of individuation requires a reabsorption of the entire issue of the conflict of duty and desire—embodied by her relation to Eriphile—which is as much a form of remembrance or storage as a form of "forgetfulness."

In the face of this opacity of individuation, all we can say is that Iphigénie provides the model of the formation of the tragic hero to which the others are left to look at the end of the play. Their illusions certainly haven't been shattered: perhaps they even take Iphigénie's final gesture of weeping as a simple sign of relief rather than as half-silent tears like those of Eriphile, simultaneously demanding and resisting interpretation. And whatever Iphigénie has or has not understood or remembered, it is upon them that the model of heroic representation is imposed as a simplified course of action rather than being exposed as a complex process of exclusion and inclusion.

This, then, is the difference between the middle that the play leaves Iphigénie in and the middle that it leaves the others in. For Achille, Agamemnon, Ulysse, and even Clytemnestre, the outcome of the play is a middle in the sense that it is the end of the beginning of the expedition, the moment of a successful departure, a reaffirmation of heroic representation and heroic virtue. For Iphigénie, who knows the nature of the Achaian union from the inside, for whom virtue is based upon denying a series of debits, losses, and exclusions more than upon any simple attribution of credit to the virtuous man or woman, who has understood that the end of the war can bring no joy less ambivalent than the beginning and who from the start learns to mourn her enemy,[12] it is the beginning of the end of the war.

But is *Iphigénie,* the next-to-last play Racine wrote before abandoning tragedy, the end of the beginning or the beginning of the end of the tragic middle period of his own life? Is this a play about the constitution of the heroic individual or one about his or her destruction? Perhaps the question is itself the answer: even more than *Andromaque, Iphigénie* shows us the process of individuation only to leave us, at the end of the tragedy, on the outside, wondering what the status of the individual thus constituted can be. The account of Iphigénie mourning—as perhaps we are, in spite of ourselves—her "departed" other leaves us finally with the question of which Iphigénie the play's title refers to, and thus of whether it is the story of what is lost in the process of individuation or that of the exterior obtained by that loss.

Indeed, is the feeling of loss which so subtly ends Racine's play a refusal of tragedy itself, or an affirmation of it? The difficulty of answering this question is suggested by Racine's comments about Euripides in his preface to *Iphigénie:*

> In seeing the impression created in the theater by everything I have imitated from Homer or Euripides, I have been pleased to recognize that common sense [le bon sens] and reason are the same in every century. The tastes of Paris have proven to conform to those of Athens. My public has felt moved by the same things which in earlier times brought tears to people's eyes in the wisest Greek *polis* and which made people say that among poets Euripides was extremely tragic [extrêmement tragique], *tragikotatos,* that he had a marvelous gift for stirring up compassion and terror, the true effects of tragedy. (*Oeuvres complètes* 1:671)

Racine pays tribute to Euripides' extremity: "extrêmement tragique" is in fact a loose translation of the superlative "tragikotatos," "the most tragic." He even suggests that extremity is what links him to Euripides across the centuries. In a tragic perspective, "le bon sens"—what better way to describe the virtuous middle in three short words?—includes recognizing its own limitations. Paris "conforms" to Athens in its recognition of the extreme emotions which recur in every era and which tragedy is meant to moderate.

But this does not mean that Racine has fully accepted the lessons of tragedy. If his Iphigénie would undoubtedly be willing to recognize her debt to Euripides' virtuous model but not her debt to the Eriphile within her, perhaps Racine would feel a certain affinity for his heroine's refusal. His play is designed to draw its power from extreme emotions—and to the general tragic emotions he mentions in the preface, compassion and terror, we might add hatred, jealousy, and betrayal in the case of *Iphigénie*—but also from his heroine's ability to attribute those emotions to her other. Euripides' lesson, the lesson of the always-recurrent extremity at the center of the human heart, never loses its double value for Racine: it is both an attraction and a repulsion. It is, among other things, what will ultimately lead him to try to leave tragedy behind him. In this way Racine is like his own heroine. The debt that Racine owes to Euripides is not only learning the lesson of extremity, but also being able to attribute that lesson to another.

9

"A horse! a horse!
my kingdom for a horse!"
Euripides' *Hippolytos*

What better play than Euripides' *Hippolytos* to approach the end of our tragic middle? If it is one of the features of the tragic middle to have no real end in the sense of a final conclusion or solution, the *Hippolytos* allows us to go back to where we started, to the Aristotelian tragic middle, and even earlier than the beginning, to the Socratic and Platonic sources of Aristotle's thought which are nearly contemporary with Euripides. Even in terms of Racine's relation to Euripides, the *Hippolytos* represents a movement backward toward a source. The last play of Euripides which Racine used, it is also (arguably) the earliest Euripides play he used, dating probably from 428,[1] and it seems to have participated in a contemporary philosophical debate that will allow us to come closer to defining the tragic middle.

Bruno Snell has seen in the *Hippolytos* a meeting-ground of tragedy and philosophy, and more specifically the site of a struggle between Euripides and Socrates over the question of virtue. He comments on Phaedra's tirade against the inadequacy of moderate virtue ("to sophronein," *Hippolytos*, 399) in this way:

> To whom is Phaedra here replying? To ask the question amounts to as much as answering it. We are acquainted with this point of view from Plato's early dialogues, but in Xenophon Socrates too speaks like this: "When asked whether he believed that those men were wise and weak [sophous te kai akrateis] who knew what had to be done but nevertheless did the opposite, he answered: Rather are they unwise and weak, for I believe that all those who choose from possibilities do what appears most to their advantage."[2]

According to Socrates, one cannot be wise and weak ("akrates," immoderate, being the opposite of "enkrates" or "self-restrained") at the same time.

Socratic virtue sees no inconsistency between true wisdom and the virtuous middle.

For Socrates, knowledge and virtue are, if not synonymous, profoundly compatible. And it is this view which, as E. R. Dodds points out,[3] Aristotle no less than Euripides rejects:

> The unrestrained man [akrates] does things that he knows to be evil, under the influence of passion [dia pathos], whereas the self-restrained man [enkrates], knowing that his desires are evil, refuses to follow them on principle. . . . How can a man fail in self-restraint when believing correctly that what he does is wrong? Some people say that he cannot do so when he *knows* the act to be wrong; since, as Socrates held, it would be strange if, when a man possessed Knowledge, some other thing should overpower it, and "drag it about like a slave" [*Protagoras*, 352 B]. In fact Socrates used to combat the view altogether, implying that there is no such thing as Unrestraint [akrasias], since no one, he held, acts contrary to what is best, believing what he does to be bad, but only through ignorance. Now this theory is manifestly at variance with plain facts.[4]

According to both Euripides and Aristotle, "pathos," a central element of tragedy, can undermine one's knowledge of good and evil by preventing one from choosing the good. But Socrates seems to have thought (and taught) that the keystone of moral action is education, that to know the good *is* to choose it.

In Aristotle's system theoretical knowledge, as we have seen, may be in tension with the virtuous middle. And in Euripides tragic individuation is based upon the need for an excluded middle. But Socratic virtue would appear, or so Snell argues, to depend upon negating the radical lessons of Euripides no less than Aristotle's system will partly be a reaction against Socratic (or Platonic) idealism:

> If we suppose that Socrates taught "virtue is knowledge" and "if men do not act correctly, it is because they do not think correctly" as early as 428 B.C., and that Euripides is attacking him for it in *Hippolytos,* then there is a further question to be looked into: is it possible that Socrates by contradicting the sentence spoken by Medea "my *thymos* [rage] is stronger than my sound considerations" first arrived at the cardinal tenet of his teaching? . . . The fundamental and radical element of the idea . . . certainly did not originate without a thesis to which there was an antithesis. . . . Finally, this discussion between Euripides and Socrates, who was ten years his junior, illuminates dazzlingly the turn which Attic thinking takes with Socrates: Euripides brings the passions into play as they are in human life. . . . Socrates, however, demands knowledge in order to remove the evil. . . . Socrates' interjection strikes the very marrow of tragedy.[5]

The "radical element" of Socrates' teaching, the idea that knowledge and ethical action can be unified in a single concept of knowledge of (or as) the good, depends upon denying an equally radical "teaching" of Euripidean tragedy: the idea that education itself is not enough. For Euripides the tragic individual is, to borrow E. R. Dodds' term,[6] essentially irrational (in a mathematical as well as a psychological sense). He or she is built not on a ratio, but on an unnamable relation between incompatible parts:

> Phaedra feels that the moral blame is upon her. And different, too, is her attitude to the old values of shame, honor, and *sophrosyne*. Phaedra—and Medea before her . . . —seem to say: it is all very well for man to keep up his reputation, and of course it is nice to be wise and to constrain oneself—but that has become rather a platitude, it does not cover my situation; one must take into more serious account something else, that alone gives value to an individual.[7]

That "something else" may in fact not be anything fully describable. But one thing it is not is the virtuous moderation of "sophrosyne." The union of knowledge and ethical action upon which Socratic virtue is based is not what constitutes the tragic individual. If tragedy teaches us anything, it is that the unit of the individual is based on disunity, that it is forged from an endless struggle to hold together disjunctive forces.

With this in mind, let us now turn more specifically to Euripides' *Hippolytos*. Froma Zeitlin observes that "the true objective of the [*Hippolytus*] . . . might be called the education of Hippolytus."[8] But the lesson the play actually offers Hippolytos is not especially clear. What is it that Hippolytos is supposed to learn?

The problems involved in reading the *Hippolytos* as a *Bildungstragödie* are indicated by one of tragic theater's most remarkable passages, Hippolytos' description of the "unmixed" meadow:

> I bring you this woven crown from the unmixed
> meadow, my lady [Artemis], having fashioned it [myself],
> [the meadow] where no shepherd thinks it right to graze his flock,
> and no iron has ever come, but instead the bee
> crosses the unmixed meadow in the springtime,
> and modesty [Aidos] cultivates it with rivers of dew,
> and it is for those who have learned nothing [didakton meden], but
> in whose nature it is
> to have moderate virtue [to sophronein] in all things equally,
> to reap the harvest; and bad people have no rights here.
>
> (73–81)[9]

Hippolytos' meadow is a paradise of moderation. "Aidos," "modesty," which in Hippolytos' description waters the meadow, is discussed by Aristotle in the *Nicomachean Ethics* (IV, ix, 1128b10–36; we will turn to this passage presently). What is extraordinary about this vision of moderate virtue is that in it Hippolytos rejects all notion of the learning process by which Aristotle will come to define the doctrine of moderation: "didakton meden," "nothing is learned." Hippolytos claims he is already moderate; what does he have to learn? A profound contradiction underlies Hippolytos' vision.[10] The moderation of his meadow is based not upon being aware of the extremes and keeping them in balance, but rather upon ignoring them. The unmixed meadow has an inside but recognizes no outside. It is at the same time pure—unalloyed, uneducated,[11] unaware of the precarious equilibrium which we find in Aristotle's virtuous middle—and moderate. In other words, it is the dream of a middle which is all-inclusive ("in all things equally"), a topological contradiction.

And yet Hippolytos ends this speech with a line which suggests that his pose does have an element of exclusion:

And may I bend around [kampsaim'] the finish line [telos] just as I started my life.

(87)

Hippolytos is here applying the purity of the unmixed meadow to himself, and saying that as he enters into the second part of his life, he hopes to remain as innocent as he has been in the first part. The instability of this wish is indicated by the conflict between the vocabulary of the middle and that of the end. "Kampto," "to bend," is generally applied in racing terminology to turning around the midpoint of the race, that is, bending around the stadium's far end ("kampter") and heading back toward the finish line, which is the same as the starting point. But Hippolytos uses the verb in speaking of the act of finishing the race. What Hippolytos really wants is for the middle of his life to be the end of his development; he wishes to live his entire life in the middle of innocence. That "kampto" can be used of the action of guiding horses around the bend of the racetrack[12] may help to bring out the underlying meaning of Hippolytos' words here. "Hippos," "horse," is the first element of Hippolytos' name, and this suggests that his reason for wishing the second half of his life to be like the first, and its middle to play the role of its end, is that what he most fears is knowing himself, that is, having to finish the race in the second half of his life with a knowledge of himself forced upon him at its midpoint. The very need to express this wish marks Hippolytos' dawning realization that his life is turning its back on something, that the infinite middle of the meadow is about to be invaded, and that his desire for purity is in fact an exclusion.[13]

What is about to invade his territory is, of course, Aphrodite:

> *Servant:*
> How then can you refuse to speak to a revered divinity?
> *Hippolytos:*
> Which one? Be careful not to make a slip of the tongue.
> *Servant:*
> This one standing at your door, Cypris.
> *Hippolytos:*
> I greet her from afar, because I am pure.
> (99–102)

Hippolytos' attitude toward Aphrodite—and by extension sexuality—is not based on ignorance, but on denial. For the purity of the meadow to be maintained, it would have to exclude Aphrodite entirely, since it is, as we must remember, based upon "not learning." To have Aphrodite standing at one's door suggests that one sees her every time one arrives or leaves home, and not to invite her in under those circumstances is tantamount not to remaining innocent of her, but to rejecting her.

Hippolytos thus refuses geography only to rely on geography. He first extracts any potential element of spatiality from his description of the meadow, and then, when faced with an aspect of life he doesn't wish to allow access to that meadow, he depends upon distancing himself from it to protect himself. The longer Hippolytos lives, the more things will have crossed his path, and the more serious a threat their contact will pose to his dream of the homogeneous middle.

This spatial element of the individual which Hippolytos both uses and denies is once again apparent in his expression of despair over his unjust condemnation:

> Alas! if only I could stand opposite myself
> and look at myself, how I would have wept at my sufferings!
> (1078–79)

What Hippolytos wishes for here is exactly what he needs: to exile himself from himself, to realize that personality is based on distance and opposition, on the opacity and spatiality of the individual and his need to recognize the inside and the outside that constitute him. The irony here is that the wish, in its "if . . . , then . . . " form, is untrue, its contradiction the same as the one which defines the unmixed meadow. What Hippolytos means is that if he could stand in his father's place and judge himself, he would pronounce himself innocent. But if Hippolytos really stood in Theseus' place, that is, if as an adult he had sufficient self-distance to look at himself as others look at him, he would not weep but would rather, in all likelihood, do precisely what Theseus is doing, that is, condemn him(self) on the basis of appearances. Were he to be outside of himself he would no longer have the privileged, inside information of his own innocence. That "innocence," which is itself based on never leaving the safety of an infinite, undefined interior, would be lost. Hippolytos does not see to what extent his own defense is solipsistic. He wants to look at himself from an "opposite" perspective in order to have the capacity of the other for judgment, but at the same time he wants to remain himself to a great enough degree to find himself unquestioningly innocent.

Hippolytos defends himself purely on the basis of essences, by saying that he cannot have committed the actions he is accused of because they do not represent what is in his heart:

> I swear that I never touched your matrimonial bonds,
> nor even wanted to — the idea never even occurred to me.
>
> (1026–27)

The single most shocking lesson Hippolytos cannot fathom is that the world of adults accepts the split between inner feelings and outer manifestations of feelings. Perhaps Theseus would even be indifferent to the thought that Hippolytos coveted his stepmother, so long as he could be certain that he would never touch her. Because Hippolytos refuses to recognize the layers, the internal separations of the individual, because he finds the thought of desiring his stepmother almost tantamount to violating her, his defense rests upon proving more than he ever could or need prove — utter blamelessness of mind and soul — and neglects to prove what he might be able to demonstrate — his physical innocence — if only he could see himself from the outside; if only he understood the movement of opposition in the formation of the individual.

The character who understands this movement of opposition, indeed, who sacrifices herself rather than giving in to it, is Phaedra. That Phaedra embodies the very same dilemma as Hippolytos at a further stage of awareness and development[14] is apparent in her metaphor of the mirror, which echoes Hippolytos' desire to look at himself from an opposite perspective:

> It is said that the only thing which matches life to the end is this:
> a just and good conscience, for anyone to whom it is present.
> But what reveals [exephen'] the wicked among men, when it comes,
> setting a mirror before them as before a young maiden,
> is time; may I never be seen in that group!
>
> (426–30)

In order not to be revealed by the mirror of time, Phaedra will leave behind a mirror image of herself, a reversed or opposite image which "represents" her desire for Hippolytos by means of an attack on him (the accusatory letter).[15] Phaedra does exactly what Hippolytos wishes he could do but cannot do. She looks at herself from the opposite perspective, that is, as others interpret her and as she hopes they will remember her. But in so doing, she, unlike Hippolytos, recognizes her divided nature. It is the very process of reversal linking Phaedra to her image which she hopes will save her glorious name. Thus Phaedra's desire never to be revealed ("exephen'," from "ekphaino," related to Phaedra, "the brilliant one") by time entails not only keeping what is inside of her hidden, but also representing that inside in reverse, creating an outside which, the opposite of what is within, blinds those who would find out her secret passion and limits their understanding of her to her "brilliance," her name.

It is thus Phaedra's experience of profound disunity which is the source of her heroic individuation. Her situation is not consonant with Socratic virtue, as David Claus remarks:

> Only if we define the "self" as a single, finite, and continuous psychological entity capable of containing the interaction of reason and emotion, thereby giving us responsibility for the control of our emotions, can we begin to place moral success in something as intangible as the condition of the psychological life, something internal and personal as opposed to external and social, and thus allow Phaedra to examine herself in Socratic terms. To the extent that Phaedra's view of herself remains traditional, reason and passion must appear to her mind as forces that either are, or are capable of becoming, discontinuous.[16]

It is precisely because Phaedra feels the discontinuity of her character, the impossibility of making reason and passion mesh, that she also feels the need to stabilize the struggle within her. "The fact that Phaedra probably does not assume a proportional relationship between reason and passion"[17] does not make her simply throw up her hands in helpless despair, blaming the world for her misfortune. Rather, this lack of proportionality, the absence of a definable ratio between these two forces, is what leads her to form the unit of the individual.

The process of that formation is described in the three stages Phaedra has gone through in attempting to save her virtue from the demon of illicit passion:

> When love had pierced [etrosen] me, I examined how
> I might best bear it. So I started out
> from that point by keeping my disease silent and hiding it.

> For there is no trusting the tongue, which even though it knows
> how to give warnings to those who are outside
> brings the greatest share of woe onto itself.
> Second I resolved to bear my folly best
> with moderate virtue [sophronein], conquering it in that way.
> And third, since by these means I wasn't reaching my end
> of bettering Cypris, I made up my mind to die,
> the best — no one will contradict me — of resolutions.
>
> (392–402)

If Hippolytos is in the stage of preawareness of the element of exclusion in the process of individuation, Phaedra starts out at the next stage. When love has invaded her boundaries ("etrosen," "penetrated," "wounded") as nothing has yet invaded Hippolytos', she tries to reestablish the strength of those boundaries by keeping the trespasser locked up inside. This internalization leads naturally to her second stage, the illusion that her dilemma can be solved by virtuous moderation ("sophronein"). The difference from Hippolytos' recourse to that ethic is that Phaedra has gone through the intermediate step of realizing the utterly problematic nature of the middle because of the immoderate emotion which the goddess has put there, all-consuming passion. It is the last of the three stages which Phaedra will hold to [18]: the decision to sacrifice herself to the needs of her virtue. Since her first two strategies have not exhausted the goddess' powers, Phaedra decides to give up her life altogether, emptying the middle which cannot be "cured" by virtue.

The most compelling evidence that Phaedra's decision to die is an excluded middle comes in her all-important discussion of "aidos," "shame" or "modesty," which Hippolytos places in his unmixed meadow and which Aristotle discusses in the *Nicomachean Ethics:*

> And it is absurd that, because a man is of such a nature that he is ashamed if he does a shameful act, he should therefore think himself virtuous, since actions to cause shame must be voluntary, but a virtuous man will never voluntarily do a base action. Modesty can only be virtuous conditionally — in the sense that a good man would be ashamed *if* he were to do so and so; but the virtues are not conditional. And though shamelessness and not shrinking from shameful actions is base, this does not prove that to be ashamed when one does shameful acts is virtuous — any more than Self-restraint is a virtue, and not rather a mixture of virtue and vice. (IV, ix, 6–8, 1128b27–36; Rackham, p. 251)

In the practical world of Aristotle's ethics, the virtuous middle depends upon action, "praxis," and "aidos" seems to resist any simple relation to action. Its potential virtue lies in the anticipatory blush it can cause in the person imagining a shameful action, thus stopping him from committing the action, whereas the retrospective blush of shame one feels once a shameful action has been committed has nothing virtuous about it, since the immoderate action has in that case already been done. The real problem is that "aidos" is operative only in the conception of action or its recollection; at the moment of action itself it has no function.

And this is precisely what Phaedra's critique of "aidos" points out:

> And there are many pleasures in life,
> and long chats and leisure, an evil enjoyment,
> and *aidos*. And there are two forms of *aidos*, one being not bad,
> the other being an onerous burden for any household; but if only the right time
>   [kairos] were clear,
> there wouldn't be two of them having the same letters.
>
> (383–87)[19]

Phaedra too refuses the qualification of "good" to "aidos"—the furthest she will go is to call the better form of it "not bad"—and although she does not explain the nature of its two forms, she suggests that time alone ("kairos," "the right time"), the present tense of action itself, separates them. The first meaning of "kairos" is "right measure," "moderation,"[20] whence the more common and specific meaning, "right time." Phaedra's words are a complaint about the difficulty of realizing the potential moderation of "aidos," of identifying the precise moment in the middle between the conception of wrong action and its recollection, or between the two forms of "aidos."[21] Phaedra's comments are nothing but a theoretical version of the frequent narrative technique of the criminal recounting his crime: "And the next thing I knew was that I had done it," the actual moment of committing the crime being a sort of dimensionless point.

If the "kairos" is thoroughly unclear, then the middle which distinguishes virtue from crime is insufficient. Phaedra decides that only the assurance of the excluded middle can protect her vacillating virtue because time, the domain of the virtuous middle, has become an unmediable torture for her since Aphrodite's assault, every passing moment a mocking temptation:

> Already on other occasions, in the long time [en makro chrono] of the night,
> I have thought about how mortal life is corrupted.
>
> (375–76)

"Chronos," time as a series of always-renewed moments, is as infinite and unremitting as "kairos," the single moment which is the right one to choose, is elusive. To pinpoint the precise moment when one "decides" to commit a crime is as unfeasible as seizing the passage of time itself. It is impossible either to keep the two forms of "aidos" strictly apart or to make its two meanings converge upon one integrated concept that would leave no leeway for the carrying out of shameful action.

Phaedra's act of simultaneously writing an accusatory letter and deciding to die is a way of saying that the chronological middle ("kairos" or right moment) in which action should take place serves no moral purpose, that it is no help in preventing one from falling into error. Like an excluded middle which artificially stabilizes any hesitation or ambiguity within, Phaedra's letter seals her final resolution to resist her passion and to die; to this extent it is more successful than Agamemnon's two contradictory letters. It is of course true that Phaedra's action is based on a lie, but it is at the same time a lie that represents an underlying truth, the truth of her unshakable refusal to pass the middle ground separating the two forms of "aidos."[22] It is no more a lie than it is a lie to shout "Fire!" rather than "Help!" in order to attract immediate attention if someone's life is in danger. And it has no less disastrous consequences.

Phaedra's attempt at an excluded middle purports to teach Hippolytos a lesson by showing him the immoderate nature of his refusal to recognize the power of love. Her final words are "[Hippolytos] will learn to be moderate [sophronein mathesetai]" (731).[23] But rather than at the end of the drama, Phaedra's last speech comes at its precise midpoint.[24] The excluded middle ends the first three plays of Euripides which Racine used; only the *Hippolytos* places it in the middle. The *Hippolytos* gathers to its center the two peripheral acts of the *Iphigeneia in Aulis,* the acts of writing and self-sacrifice which begin and end that play, so that the message which Phaedra seals with her death leaves her survivors the time to learn the nature of the artifice involved in this act of heroic "virtue." Let us look more closely at the lessons which are taught by the second half of the play.

It is in the middle of the play that Theseus arrives back home, and it takes him little time to take up the difficult ethical questions which Phaedra has left behind. In spite of his much-commented-on obtuseness, he pronounces one of the most important speeches in all of tragic theater:

> Alas, mortals should have some clear proof in
> friendship and a way of discerning souls,
> both the person who is true and the one who is not a friend,
> and all humans should have double voices,
> the just one [dikaian] and another, however it might be [hopos etynchanen],

so that the one thinking unjust things [tadik'] would be refuted
by the just one [dikaias], and we would not be deceived.
(925–31)

In the second part of this statement, Theseus makes a clear distinction between "unjust" [tadik'] thoughts and the "just" [dikaias] voice which he wishes
would refute them. Why then does he begin his wish for "double voices"
with a thoroughly unclear distinction between the two voices, one being
just and the other being "however it might be"?[25]

It is absolutely essential that Theseus does not instantly divide the world
into just and unjust, as if everything fit easily into this binary distinction.
He does not deny the existence of an amoral world of circumstance and
accident, of "tyche" (related to the verb "etynchanen"). The universe of everything that is cannot be seamlessly divided between the just and the not-just,
for these categories are mere approximations, quantifications based on the
law of excluded middle (a thing must be x or not-x).

But Theseus goes on to say even more about the relation between justice
and the law of excluded middle. He says that the categories of just and unjust, as artificial as they are, are still necessary if any system of justice is
to function:

Alas, how far will the mortal heart go?
What end [terma] of [its] audacity and boldness [thrasous]
                                                    will there be?
For if it is swollen from one generation to the next,
and the later one is more excessively [eis hyperbolen] evil-doing
than the earlier one, the gods will have to add to this earth
another one, which will contain
those who are unjust and evil by nature.
(936–42)

The only way to teach virtuous action is to use the example of nonvirtue.
Theseus does not imagine ridding the world of excesses like audacity and
boldness (Aristotle gives "thrasos," "boldness," as an example of excess[26]),
but rather relegating the nonvirtuous to a separate world, for he needs that
second world in order to teach virtue to the first one. In his view the teaching of virtue depends on a recognition of and a resistance to nonvirtue. The
"hyperboles" or excesses of vice cannot be eradicated, but they can be used
to define a geographical unit, the very "termata" or limits of civilization
beyond which Theseus tries to drive his son:

Hippolytos:
Alas, what will you do? Won't you wait for time
to reveal the truth about us, or will you drive us from the land?
Theseus:
Beyond Pontos [the Black Sea] and the limits [termonon] of Atlas,
if ever I could, that's how much I hate you!

(1051–54)

Hippolytos' position challenges Theseus' role as the mythological lawgiver of Athens. His "crime" is his refusal to recognize the excluded middle, his punishment expulsion. The civilizing tool of the legendary father of Athenian civilization is exile.

What, then, is the political and moral lesson taught by Hippolytos' exile and death? Pulled along by the horses whom he has nourished (1240) and whose name he bears ("Hippo-lytos," "breaker [or] looser of horses"), Hippolytos in going toward his exile is transported by his problematic relation to himself. The means of his death is that very relation. He cannot go forward into the middle of his life, into his prime,[27] without being separated from himself in a way he refuses to understand.

What sets off the panic leading to Hippolytos' fatal injury is a monstrous bull flushed out by a gigantic wave:

And then [the wave] swelled and, spewing foam all around [perix aphron]
in great quantity with a sea rumble,
moved toward the shore, where the four-horse cart was.
And with a commotion and a triple breaker
the wave put forth [exetheken] a bull, wild and monstrous.

(1210–14)

The wave which sends the bull onto the shore, the very image of powerful, irrational excess, strongly recalls Aphrodite, Hippolytos' persecutor, by the use of the term "aphros," "foam," which is the first element of her name, the legendary medium of the birth of the goddess being the foam of the sea.[28] That this violent wave is the precise opposite of Hippolytos' entire pose of virtuous moderation is suggested by the phrase "perix aphron," "the foam all around," "aphron" being close to the adjective "aphron," "unreasonable," "insane" (with omega rather than omicron, and a different accent), which can be used by contrast to "sophron," "moderate," "reasonable," the word used of Hippolytos by Phaedra (731) and Theseus (949), ironically; by himself, repeatedly; and by Artemis, with some bitterness (1402).

This imposition of excess upon Hippolytos comes only indirectly from Phaedra, its immediate source being Theseus' condemnation of his son. The action of the wave expelling the monstrous bull, "exetheken," "put [or] set out," recalls the name Theseus, the legendary king who "sets forth" ("tithemi") the laws of Athens. The purging of Theseus' kingdom ultimately depends on the behavior of Hippolytos' horses. The future of Theseus' reign, like that of Richard III's kingdom, would appear to ride on a horse:

And straightaway a terrible fear falls upon the young horses;
and the master, quite used to the horses' ways [hippikoisin ethesin],
seized the reins [henias] in his hands,
and pulls [helkei]—like a ship-pilot on the oar—
on the straps, straining his body backward [es toupisthen].
But the horses, biting the forged bridle-bit with their jaws,
became riled [bia pherousin].

(1218–24)

Hippolytos' horses, the cause of his death, seem to be the enforcers of Theseus' royal will. The description of Hippolytos as he loses control over them is remarkably close to the passage in Plato's *Phaedrus* which describes the two conflicting parts of the soul,[29] figured as two horses, one good and one bad, when their "driver," a man in love, lays eyes on his beloved:

Now when the charioteer beholds the love-inspiring vision, and his whole soul is warmed by the sight, and is full of the tickling and prickings of yearning, the horse that is obedient to the charioteer, constrained then as always by modesty [aidoi], controls himself and does not leap upon the beloved; but the other no longer heeds the pricks or the whips of the charioteer, but springs wildly forward [bia pheretai]. . . . And as the charioteer looks upon him [the beloved], . . . he is afraid and falls backward in reverence, and in falling he is forced to pull the reins so violently backward [eis toupiso helkysai tas henias houto sphodra] as to bring both horses upon their haunches. (*Phaedrus*, 253E–254C)[30]

The phrase *"eis toupiso helkysai tas henias"* ("to pull the reins so violently backward") echoes no less than three terms in the *Hippolytos* passage. Does Hippolytos not appear to be a kind of Platonic lover? We find ourselves back at the beginning, with the question of Platonic (or Socratic) virtue. Hippolytos, who may think that being accustomed to "horse ethics" ("hippikoisin ethesin," 1219) is enough to keep his steeds always in control, would undoubtedly believe he had only "good" horses and not the "mixed" pairs which, as Socrates explains to Phaedrus, every human charioteer must content himself with (*Phaedrus* 246A). The monster of excess which makes Hippolytos' horses buck finds its analogue in the *Phaedrus* in the form of passion, precisely what Hippolytos refuses to recognize.

But in a sense Platonic virtue requires one to forget (or to ignore) the myth of the two horses, which is the closest Plato ever came to admitting that knowledge and virtue do not always go hand in hand:

> Eros has a special importance in Plato's thought as being the one mode of ex-perience which brings together the two natures of man, the divine self and the tethered beast. For Eros is frankly rooted in what man shares with the animals, the physiological impulse of sex (a fact which is unfortunately obscured by the persistent modern misuse of the term "Platonic love"); yet Eros also supplies the dynamic impulse which drives the soul forward in its quest of a satisfaction transcending earthly experience. It thus spans the whole compass of human per-sonality, and makes the one empirical bridge between man as he is and man as he might be. Plato in fact comes very close here to the Freudian concept of *libido* and sublimation. But he never, as it seems to me, fully integrated this line of thought with the rest of his philosophy; had he done so, the notion of the intellect as a self-sufficient entity independent of the body might have been imperilled, and Plato was not going to risk that.[31]

In the *Phaedrus,* one of the so-called middle dialogues, Plato comes to a problem which he will refuse to integrate into his thought: the need for a "bridge" between "man as he is" and "man as he might be." His theory of forms refuses to distinguish between the two: "The theory of Forms in its general intention and result identifies the ideal with the real; it is the doctrine that the ground of values and the ground of natural fact are the same."[32] According to the theory of forms, what is is not strictly separable from what should be. The form, defined as a kind of perfection or ultimate good, profoundly informs all manifestations of it.

Euripides is reported (by Aristotle) to have participated in a different way in the age-old conflict between what should be and what is: "Sophocles said that he portrayed people as they ought to be and Euripides portrayed them as they are" (*Poetics,* XXV, 146b).[33] In his tragedies Euripides challenges the adequacy of ethics, but far from leaving ethics aside, unexplored, he repeatedly questions the real nature of ethics. And this, ultimately, is the "lesson" of the *Hippolytos:*

> Through the mouths of all the chief characters of this play its author emphati-cally denies that enlightenment can make men good. . . . I believe that it was part of Euripides' purpose to suggest, in opposition to the Socratic intellectual-ism, that while a false ethical theory may provide a convenient mask for a dan-gerous impulse, the true springs of conduct lie deeper. . . . The last link in

the chain of disaster is not Hippolytus' self-control, but his lack of it. *Sophronein mathesetai,* cries Phaedra (v.731). . . . As Phaedra does violence to *aidos* in the name of *aidos,* so does Hippolytus to *sophrosyne* in the name of *sophrosyne:* each is the victim of his own and the other's submerged desires masquerading as morality. . . . Here, to my mind, lies the unity, structural and intellectual, of the *Hippolytus.*[34]

The "unity" of the *Hippolytos* is the disunity of what should be and what is. What lies hidden inside of Hippolytos can never be recognized so long as he holds to *sophrosyne* as a universal principle.

When Hippolytos refuses to accept the excluded third, the third which he is really excluding is the third dimension: the spatial nature of heroic representation, the necessary depth of the individual. Hippolytos asks to have his face hidden in death ("krypson de mou prosopon," 1458), echoing Phaedra's wish to be hidden ("krypson kephalen," 243) because of her shame at loving Hippolytos, but the similarity of the gestures is belied by a difference of intentions. Phaedra asks to have her head ("kephalen") hidden, the head being three-dimensional, a figure for the hidden depths of her intrigues. By contrast Hippolytos wants to cover his face, "prosopon," a synonym for "prosopeion," "mask."[35] The final irony of the play is that by eliminating all possibility of depth, Hippolytos finds himself not protected by an eternal inside, the unmixed meadow which precludes all need for learning, but rather revealed as a creature lacking a dimension, as Zeitlin puts it, "all surface and no depth."[36]

Must we then conclude that the only way to self-knowledge would be to leave the middle of the unmixed meadow and to confront the extremes at its borders?

> For Hippolytos the division is decisive: the chosen few get moderate virtue [sophronein]; the others get evil. Phaedra knows it isn't as simple as that. She knows that only time reveals one to oneself in one's wickedness. But are wicked people the only ones who know themselves? The text seems to say so. The honest individual lives with values like modesty, virtue; that is enough for him. He lives in the moment, in the identity of his being, in sameness. He doesn't know illness and change, the slow transformation of one's being, the modification of one's features.[37]

The virtuous middle may present itself as the place of the good. But it is not the place of knowledge, even less so of self-knowledge. Although its endless mediations are worked out across time, it remembers nothing. Tragic recognition is the experience of an extreme, of an imposed and unwanted alternative—be it only the choice of an interpretation one has hitherto managed to reject—which can no longer be refused. And if Hippolytos is spared anything at the end of the play, it is the burden of this recognition, the pain of this learning, for if he could learn this lesson, he would not have to die, or even go into exile. He could be allowed back into Theseus' kingdom.

10
Excluding the Excluded Middle
Phèdre

As we have seen, the *Hippolytos* is the single play of Euripides used by Racine which most emphasizes the artificial nature of the excluded middle. By placing Phaedra's suicide letter in the middle of the drama rather than at the end, Euripides gives us the time not only to witness the revelation of the letter's falseness, but also to begin to understand that Theseus' own ethical system is based on a similar artifice, the "exiling" of excesses rather than their abolition, which can never be accomplished. Theseus' lesson in exiling Hippolytos is that there is no such thing as "natural," unlearned virtue, that true virtue requires one to recognize the possibility of vice and not to choose that possibility. This is the very lesson which, carried to its extreme, has led Phaedra to write her letter in order to present a virtuous exterior to the world.

To the extent that Phaedra's gesture is a heroic "solution" the inadequacy of which the drama unmasks, it is the epitome of Racinian tragic individuation: it offers the model of an exterior that hides rather than reveals an interior. The itinerary of Racine's first three Euripidean dramas leads us to one final Euripides play which itself seems to become the quintessential Racinian tragedy, a drama about the disjunction between outside and inside and about trying not to recognize what is at the center of one's being.

Racine eliminates Phaedra's suicide letter from his play, but I would like to suggest that the letter embodies the very principle upon which his play is based: repression. Repression is a representation by opposition, the (unsuccessful) attempt at choosing between two contradictory possibilities. The principle underlying Phaedra's suicide letter becomes generalized in Racine's play and creates a kind of milieu of communication for all of the characters, a milieu based on the meeting of two impulses each of which vainly tries to exclude the other: the revelation and the dissimulation of their desires.

Francesco Orlando, in his remarkable Freudian analysis of *Phèdre,* quotes several passages from Freud particularly applicable to *Phèdre* which show to what extent the relation between the conscious and the unconscious is based on the individual's inability to enforce the law of excluded middle:

> I quote now from another of the earliest . . . of the *Introductory Lectures:* "It is important to begin in good time to reckon with the fact that mental life is the arena and battle-ground for mutually opposing purposes or, to put it non-dynamically, that it consists of contradictions and pairs of contraries." . . . "Proof of the existence of a particular purpose is no argument against the existence of an opposite one; there is room for both. It is only a question of the attitude of these contraries to each other, and of what effects are produced by the one and by the other." . . . The strictest, closest confliction discussed by Freud [is] that which qualifies all manifestations of the unconscious as *compromise-formations.* One after the other Freud thus qualifies jokes, as we have seen, and dreams, parapraxes, which are "the outcome of a compromise; they constitute a half-success and a half-failure for each of the two intentions"—and symptoms, which are "the product of a compromise and arise from the mutual interference between two opposing currents; they represent not only the repressed but also the repressing force which had a share in their origin." . . . Usually, within the silence of this compromise, the voices of the opposing parties are reconciled only in that they both cry out as being unreconciled.[1]

Mental life is the interaction of mutually exclusive purposes ("a particular purpose" and its "opposite one") neither of which can manage to exclude the other. And if the language of dreams, jokes, and symptoms provides a sort of "compromise" between contradictory purposes each of which wins a "half-success" and a "half-failure" in its endless struggle with its opponent, that compromise is not a true virtuous middle, a "reconciliation," but simply a way of communicating that the milieu of communication itself is the site of an irresolvable problem.

Even though *Phèdre* does not incorporate Phaedra's suicide letter and the artificial nature of her virtuous pose in Euripides' play into its own events, Racine's entire play is about the tragic nature of inner communication. The *Hippolytos* reveals the artificiality of Phaedra's representation of herself in her writing, the excluded middle that manages to stop all communication between the two warring parts of her soul only because it is accompanied by her death. But *Phèdre* explores the stubbornly persistent milieu of communication between the conflicting and contradictory parts of the Racinian individual.

The first character to make an unsuccessful attempt at an excluded middle is Hippolyte. Hippolyte's first words in the drama already give an example of what Freud calls "mutually opposing purposes" or, to use the vocabulary of *Phèdre,* "desseins":

> Le dessein en est pris: je pars, cher Théramène,
> Et quitte le séjour de l'aimable Trézène.
>
> (1–2)

This initial plan of Hippolyte's is a flight from his own desires, "l'aimable Trézène" being a covert allusion to the true cause of his departure, Aricie,[2] whom Hippolyte does everything he can to put out of his mind. Hippolyte is denying what is inside of him by a process of representation. The Hippolytos of Euripides, who, unlike Hippolyte, seems to be a creature with no desires, admits that he has seen representations ("graphe," *Hippolytos* 1005) of love, what Racine would undoubtedly have called "dessins" or "desseins," since the two words were confused in the seventeenth century.[3] This confusion underlines to what extent the initial intention ("dessein") of Racine's Hippolyte depends on the distance and the artifice guaranteed by the selective representation of his inside by his outside.

Hippolyte's misunderstanding of the complexity of the relation between inside and outside is reflected by the play's opposition of the terms "sein" and "dessein." Although the two words have no etymological link, the rhyme "sein"/"dessein" occurs twice in the play (511–12, 747–48). The relation between the terms is particularly important in Hippolyte's genealogy. The breast ("sein"), or rather the lack of a breast, is what characterizes the race of his mother, the Amazon Antiope. This is reflected in the iconography of the Amazons—often depicted as having only one breast—as well as the common etymology of their name (alpha privative plus "mazos," "breast").[4] The lack of a breast, which is often interpreted as a sign of the Amazons' rejection of female sexuality, also suggests a nonmaternity, a nonseparation of cause (mother) and effect (child), of underlying motives and intentions, or, in Hippolyte's case, of "sein" and "dessein." Similarly Hippolyte's "dessein," to leave Trézène before admitting that he has fallen in love, reflects his desire to choose only one-half of his father. He attempts to censor the narration of Thésée's various adventures and to exclude "Cette indigne moitié d'une si belle histoire" (94), that is, his father's amorous escapades, leaving only his heroic exploits.[5]

Thus Hippolyte starts out in a position that is diametrically opposed to that of Euripides' Hippolytos. By trying to live in the dimensionless inside of the unmixed meadow, Hippolytos denies the need for the excluded middle, and his punishment for this is exile and exclusion. The *Hippolytos* is a play about exile, or being forced to leave the middle. *Phèdre,* by contrast, is a play about escape: from the beginning Hippolyte asks only to leave behind "l'aimable Trézène," that is, the very possibility of love ("aimable") which is his frightening internal dilemma. What he wishes to appropriate from the start is the power of the excluded middle. By choosing as his heritage the nonsexual halves of his father and his mother, he believes that he can preclude any potential conflict within himself and thus obtain the desired unity of his own personality.

Hippolyte spends the entire play attempting to leave Trézène,[6] as several critics have noted.[7] The problem is that although his intention of leaving is his "dessein," it is not necessarily his "destin." The two words are juxtaposed from the very beginning of the play:

> Le dessein en est pris: je pars, cher Théramène,
> Et quitte le séjour de l'aimable Trézène.
> Dans le doute mortel dont je suis agité,
> Je commence à rougir de mon oisiveté.
> Depuis plus de six mois éloigné de mon père,
> J'ignore le destin d'une tête si chère.
>
> (1–6)

Even less clear to Hippolyte than the relation of his "sein" to his "dessein" is the relation between his "dessein" and its (and his) ultimate "destin." Hippolyte may intend to leave, but he is at a loss to imagine where he might go, since Théramène has already searched for Thésée everywhere that might be searched: "Et dans quels lieux, Seigneur, l'allez-vous donc chercher?" (8). Hippolyte's movement is purely centrifugal, going away from his center, and toward nothing:

> J'ignore jusqu'aux lieux qui le peuvent cacher.
>
> (7)

> Et je fuirai ces lieux que je n'ose plus voir.
>
> (28)

The conjunction of two lines which Hippolyte himself does not put together shows that he is running away from something and not toward anything, that he has a "dessein," but not yet a "destin," a destination, or at least that his "dessein" and his "destin" are discontinuous.

What Hippolyte doesn't understand is that a "dessein" is a message and that it must be received as well as sent, that intention is separated from realization, its destination and its destiny. Hippolyte's "dessein"—and let us not forget that there is an etymological link between "dessein" and "signe"[8]—conforms to the communication model "destinateur"/"message"/

"destinataire" of which Roman Jakobson speaks,[9] and Hippolyte at the start knows only the "destinateur" of his message, himself. He doesn't know where his message is destined to end up. If the communicative process is, as Umberto Eco defines it, "the passage of a signal . . . from a source . . . to a destination,"[10] communication is itself a movement between "dessein" and "destin."

In fact the way in which Hippolyte's message is encoded, something which should take place at the level of "dessein" or intention, provides the model for virtually all important communication in the first half of the play. Hippolyte's message is not simply that he loves Aricie; an integral part of the message is that he is resisting the message, that he wishes to flee it. This is the model of the "aveu à contre-coeur" of which the first two acts offer no fewer than four examples: Hippolyte to Théramène and to Aricie, and Phèdre to Oenone and to Hippolyte.[11] The unwilled confession is a product of mutually exclusive purposes, the desire to keep one's guilty secret inside (Phèdre) or to flee it (Hippolyte), and the equally strong impulse toward confession, to which only Phèdre ultimately admits: "Je t'ai tout avoué, je ne m'en repens pas" (312).

A still more important deformation of the model of normative communication comes in the status of the "destinataire" in the case of unwilled confession. Hippolyte, a purely centrifugal force, would like to be able to take refuge from himself in a neutral medium which would be a kind of benign halfway house between confessing and thus getting his hidden desires off (or rather out of) his chest ("sein") and allowing them to reach their goal ("destin"). The ideal of the unwilled confession would be to speak without being heard, to send the unwanted message off to be absorbed by an obliviating universe in which it would fall on proverbial deaf ears. This ideal may help to explain why Hippolyte's initial "confession" of his love for Aricie ("Aurais-je pour vainqueur dû choisir Aricie?" 102) in response to Théramène's question ("Aimeriez-vous, Seigneur?" 65) seems not to have been heard, since Théramène essentially repeats his question ("La charmante Aricie a-t-elle su vous plaire?" 137). Phèdre, by the same token, allows herself to let out her secret to Oenone, for there is a difference between speaking and being heard by the wrong (or right) ears, and Phèdre hopes to protect herself by means of this distinction. Indeed Oenone, when she hears Phèdre's secret, for the first and only time has nothing to answer: "Déjà même au tombeau, je songeais à vous suivre" (338).

The ultimate perfidiousness of this seemingly euphemizing medium of communication—the middle that allows the sender to rid him- or herself of a dangerous message without running the risk of having it arrive at its destination—is to disappear, to transform itself unannounced from an obstacle into a transparency. Like the comic stunt of the door which opens just as the hero is about to break it down and which, by no longer stopping his momentum, makes him fall, this newly conducive middle unexpectedly makes way for the message. At the moment of finally letting her message arrive at its destination, Hippolyte's horrified ears, Phèdre says: "Ah! cruel, tu m'as trop entendue!" (670). She does not say that she has spoken too much, but that she has been heard too well. Even when she does at last say, "je n'ai que trop parlé" (740), she instantly goes on to identify the true source of the excess as being the receiving and not the sending of her message: "J'ai dit ce que jamais on ne devait entendre" (742).

And yet it is the prerogative of the tragic medium of communication to change valences indefinitely, and this is demonstrated by its role first in preventing and ultimately in allowing Phèdre to receive the message of Hippolyte's passion for Aricie. Hippolyte confesses his love to no fewer than three characters, Théramène, Aricie herself, and Thésée, but the one "destinataire" who is missing from his list, the one who gets his message indirectly, through Thésée, is Phèdre. It is at the moment of hearing the fatal phrase revealing Hippolyte's love for Aricie, "Qu'il l'aime" (1188), from Thésée rather than from the original "destinateur" of the message that Phèdre decides once and for all to let Hippolyte meet his destiny ("destin"). The middle between "dessein" and "destin" is not simply a way for Hippolyte to carry out his intentions, to connect his plans with their realization. It is rather the barrier and conduit, or more precisely the valve which demonstrates the complex nature of tragic communication. The path the message leaves on may not be able to determine or even foresee the one which takes it to its final destination.

Hippolyte thus begins the play trying to appropriate the security of an excluded middle that would allow him to escape from a part of himself. Like her namesake in Euripides' play, Phèdre embodies the same dilemma as her stepson but at a further stage of development. The tragic time leading up to the play's events dates from Phèdre's arrival in Trézène:

> Cet heureux temps n'est plus. Tout a changé de face
> Depuis que sur ces bords les dieux ont envoyé
> La fille de Minos et de Pasiphaé.
>
> (34–36)

But in fact Phèdre begins to base her existence on an excluded middle long before her arrival in Trézène. Hippolyte's (and the play's) first description of Phèdre as "The daughter of Minos and Pasiphaé" immediately establishes Phèdre's two contradictory extremes, the forces of conscience and of animal passion. As Lucien Goldmann puts it:

[Phèdre] asks life for a kind of totality that is all the more utopian and illusory in that it is a totality made up of a union of values which in the empirical reality of daily existence are contradictory. What she wants, what she thinks she can get, is the union of glory and passion, of absolute purity and forbidden love, of truth and life.

But in the empirical world that she takes to be pure and real, all she meets is average men who are terrified by her monstrous demands.[12]

Goldmann is correct in saying that Phèdre is caught between two contradictory values, but he is mistaken in his belief that she attempts a "union" of the two poles which generate her character. What Phèdre initially attempts to do is to eliminate one of the two poles, that of her monstrous sexuality, to exclude it completely at the expense of the other pole, her duty and her conscience.

Phèdre at the outset is an effective conscience not only for herself—and the fact that Athens selects her over Hippolyte and Aricie shows to what extent her life has been a model of duty—but also for Thésée, as Hippolyte's words indicate:

> Cher Théramène, arrête, et respecte Thésée.
> De ses jeunes erreurs désormais revenu,
> Par un indigne obstacle il n'est point retenu;
> Et fixant de ses voeux l'inconstance fatale,
> Phèdre depuis longtemps ne craint plus de rivale.
>   (22–26)

Thésée is no longer kept away from home by an unworthy obstacle, yet another amorous adventure. Rather he is kept at a distance from himself by the "worthy" obstacle of Phèdre, the barrier between the two halves of his being, since she has forced him to choose between the heroic and the amorous. Phèdre represents the end of doubt and vacillation over the fundamental value of Thésée's character and her own.

Thus, in terms of the image of the labyrinth which is at the center of the drama no less than the monster is at the center of the labyrinth, once the monster of illicit and unbridled sexuality—the excluded pole of Phèdre's and Thésée's personality—has been killed, the path out of the labyrinth becomes the path of an artificially constituted virtue. At every fork in the tortuous road one must simply choose one from two: right from left or, more precisely, right from wrong. The univalence of the path out of the labyrinth is suggested by contrast to Oenone's description of the infinite paths to death: "Mille chemins ouverts y conduisent toujours" (231). The thousand paths leading to death are a metaphor for the infinite possible roads which an essentially amoral being like Oenone can take through life. Their open-endedness is entirely antithetical to the closure provided by the law of excluded middle, the closure necessary to find the one and only path out of the labyrinth. Exiting from the labyrinth reiterates the process of killing the monster of sexuality which forms the unacceptable pole of the heroic individual.

Why then does Phèdre's arrival in Trézène transform its (and her own) moral landscape? To answer this, we must look at the way Phèdre enforces her excluded middle when she first sees and falls in love with Hippolyte:

> Je le vis, je rougis, je pâlis à sa vue;
> Un trouble s'éleva dans mon âme éperdue;
> Mes yeux ne voyaient plus, je ne pouvais parler,
> Je sentis tout mon corps et transir et brûler.
> Je reconnus Vénus et ses feux redoutables,
> D'un sang qu'elle poursuit, tourments inévitables.
>
> (273–78)

Phèdre's blood first flows away from her center as she blushes ("rougis") and then back toward it as she turns pale ("pâlis"), and this reenacts her own movements in reaction to her unwanted passion. Her first strategy is to continue to apply to it the same exclusionary mechanism which has defined her own virtue and Thésée's in the pre-Trézène period: to exile it, which in this case means exiling Hippolyte (295–96). Her blush recalls the Euripidean Phaedra's invective against "aidos" (shame): in this case anticipatory "aidos" may keep Phèdre "innocent" but it will not extricate the source of her temptations. But the palor which follows her initial blush, the return of the blood toward the heart, already suggests that no centrifugal force will be strong enough in the long run to keep this invading passion from reaching her center.

Nonetheless, in spite of its ultimate futility, Phèdre's tactic of exiling Hippolyte at first seems to be a victory of sorts for the excluded middle:

> Je pressai son exil, et mes cris éternels
> L'arrachèrent du sein et des bras paternels.
> Je respirais, Oenone; et depuis son absence,
> Mes jours moins agités coulaient dans l'innocence;
> Soumise à mon époux, et cachant mes ennuis,
> De son fatal hymen je cultivais les fruits.
>
> (295–300)

It is not that Phèdre is "soumise" or "obedient" to Thésée, but rather that both Thésée and Phèdre are obedient to the principle of self-exile that is the key to their "virtue." Phèdre precipitates the development of Hippolyte's "desseins," his intentionality, by tearing him from the paternal breast ("du sein et des bras paternels").

Phèdre's arrival in Trézène, her return to Hippolyte, teaches her that her excluded middle will not work, that her innocent exterior can hide her interior but cannot protect itself from the dangers of the middle:

> Grâces au ciel, mes mains ne sont point criminelles.
> Plût aux dieux que mon coeur fût innocent comme elles!
> (221–22)

What finally reveals Venus' "feux redoutables" is the return of "doubt" — etymologically, "doubleness" — to a moral being who had attempted to exclude it. Only when she sees Hippolyte for a second time — "J'ai revu l'ennemi que j'avais éloigné" (303) — does Phèdre realize the failure of her excluded middle. The third step which completes her initial blush (attempt at fleeing the middle) and palor (inevitable return to the middle) is the act of bleeding: "Ma blessure trop vive aussitôt a saigné" (304). Only death can finally enforce the law of excluded middle.

If we compare the three stages of Phèdre's struggle against her passion to the three stages of Phaedra's resistance in the *Hippolytos* (391–402), we find that in Racine's play the possibility of moderation is ruled out from the very beginning. Euripides' Phaedra, as we have seen, first hopes to silence her passion (393–97) and then to moderate it (398–99). Only as a last resort does she decide on the excluded middle of her death and suicide letter. But Racine's Phèdre skips the first two stages. She immediately exiles Hippolyte, as a way of protecting against the vacillations of her virtuous pose. What this tells us, in effect, is that Phèdre is not only at a further stage of awareness than Hippolyte, but also that she has an understanding that surpasses Euripides' heroine. When Racine's Phèdre falls in love with Hippolyte, she has already been basing her life on an excluded middle. She already knows that no less extreme solution can protect her (and Thésée's) virtue. It is as if in the radicalized universe of Racine's greatest play his heroine incorporated the knowledge of her namesake's struggles.

Thus if the excluded middle in the *Hippolytos* comes at the earliest point of any Euripides drama Racine used, Phèdre's knowledge of the excluded middle long precedes the opening of Racine's play. But although Phèdre's recourse to the excluded middle comes earlier than Phaedra's, Racine's heroine also lives to see its failure. Her intention of following her Attic predecessor's suicidal lead fails:

> Voulez-vous sans pitié laisser finir vos jours?
> Quelle fureur les borne au milieu de leur course?
>
> (188–89)

Phèdre's arrival in Trézène teaches her that her excluded middle can be enforced only by her death "in the middle of the course" of her life. Although Phèdre's reaction to her failed excluded middle is her decision to die, before she dies she will speak, for she too is subject to the reawakening communication between the different parts of her being. Before she can secure her excluded middle by her death, the middle reasserts itself as a medium of communication.

What Phèdre's return, the failure of the excluded middle, sets off is a series of communications, the middle reaffirming itself as the articulation between the different and opposed parts of the personality which the excluded middle tried to keep strictly segregated. The chain of awakened and reawakened passions, going from Phèdre to Thésée to Hippolyte to Aricie, is a latter-day version of the game of dominoes in *Andromaque*. The character at the top (Phèdre, Andromaque) is a sort of model to whom all the others react. It is as if Phèdre's arrival marked a particularly potent full moon which set everyone to baying, a moment of collective abandon.

Thus Phèdre's arrival in Trézène produces an incurable moral disorder not only in Phèdre herself, but also in everyone around her. Phèdre's return to Hippolyte and her realization of the failure of her excluded middle sets off a chain reaction that drives all of the drama's major characters out of their previous moral stances, beginning with Thésée:

> Qui sait même, qui sait si le roi votre père
> Veut que de son absence on sache le mystère?
> Et si, lorsque avec vous nous tremblons pour ses jours,
> Tranquille et cachant de nouvelles amours,
> Ce héros n'attend point qu'une amante abusée . . .
>
> (17–21)

> Oui, Prince, je languis, je brûle pour Thésée.
> Je l'aime, non point tel que l'ont vu les enfers,
> Volage adorateur de mille objets divers,
> Qui va du dieu des morts déshonorer la couche.
>
> (634–37)

> Je n'avais qu'un ami; son imprudente flamme
> Du tyran de l'Epire allait ravir la femme;
> Je servais à regret ses desseins amoureux.
>
> (957–59)

What Théramène suspects, Phèdre supports and Thésée, in spite of his feeble self-justification, confirms. Thésée, "De ses jeunes erreurs désormais revenu" (23), has now "returned" from "returning" from his amorous ways, or, to put it more simply, has gone back to his pre-Phèdre state. The failure of Phèdre's own excluded middle brings along with it the breakdown of her role as Thésée's conscience; no longer can she keep his philandering side at a distance. Phèdre herself senses this when she depicts Thésée in the underworld as having gone back to precisely the same state in which she found him, "Volage adorateur de mille objets divers," the latter phrase recalling (and rhyming with) Aricie's disdainful dismissal of the court Thésée originally paid Phèdre as "un hommage à mille autres offert" (447).

Phèdre's arrival in Trézène thus leads to Thésée's departure from it in search of his lost sexual freedom, and this departure in turn sets off Hippolyte's sudden awakening to desire. The chronology of his passion for Aricie meshes almost perfectly with that of Thésée's departure ("Depuis près de six mois, honteux, désespéré," 539; "Depuis plus de six mois éloigné de mon père," 5). Even Aricie is subject to this small-scale communal hysteria:

> Tu sais que de tout temps à l'amour opposée,
> Je rendais souvent grâce à l'injuste Thésée,
> Dont l'heureuse rigueur secondait mes mépris.
> Mes yeux alors, mes yeux n'avaient pas vu son fils.
> (433–36)

When did Aricie first see Hippolyte? Undoubtedly, to carry the conjunction of events to its logical conclusion, when Phèdre arrived in Trézène and admitted herself defeated, thus causing Thésée to leave Trézène, thus causing Hippolyte to "see" Aricie for the first time, thus causing Aricie to see him. It all goes back to Phèdre's fateful second look at Hippolyte.

When Phèdre fails to put an end to her life "in the middle of its course," she is condemned to live through the middle of the play. And it is this moment which marks the final undermining of her decision to die, her return to life and to hope:[13]

> De l'austère pudeur les bornes sont passées.
> J'ai déclaré ma honte aux yeux de mon vainqueur,
> Et l'espoir malgré moi s'est glissé dans mon coeur.
> (766–68)

This passage closely echoes the treacherous ambiguity of "aidos" in Euripides' *Hippolytos*. The two forms of "aidos" may indeed be separated by a "borne," a dividing line between "pudeur" and "honte," but Phèdre has stepped over that dividing line. Even though she has not satisfied her desires, "pudeur" has already yielded to "honte." Thus Phèdre's arrival at the middle of the play—which Euripides' character only barely touches—means that for her the show is over.

Here, then, is the middle of *Phèdre:*

> *Phèdre:*
> O toi, qui vois la honte où je suis descendue,
> Implacable Vénus, suis-je assez confondue?
> Tu ne saurais plus loin pousser ta cruauté,
> Ton triomphe est parfait, tous tes traits ont porté.
> Cruelle, si tu veux une gloire nouvelle,
> Attaque un ennemi qui te soit plus rebelle.
> Hippolyte te fuit, et bravant ton courroux
> Jamais à tes autels n'a fléchi les genoux.
> Ton nom semble offenser ses superbes oreilles.
> Déesse, venge-toi; nos causes sont pareilles.
> Qu'il aime . . . Mais déjà tu reviens sur tes pas,
> Oenone? On me déteste, on ne t'écoute pas?
> *Oenone:*
> Il faut d'un vain amour étouffer la pensée,
> Madame. Rappelez votre vertu passée:
> Le roi, qu'on a cru mort, va paraître à vos yeux;
> Thésée est arrivé, Thésée est en ces lieux.
>
> (813–28)

The wish in the middle of *Phèdre,* expressed by the subjunctive "Qu'il aime," marks the single moment when Phèdre conceives of the possibility that what has hitherto been her refusal of passion might be mediated, that it might take a form other than death. In the middle of the *Hippolytos,* Phaedra excludes her middle once and for all; she dies by the exercise of her own will. In the middle of *Phèdre,* Phèdre loses her excluded middle—and by the same token any possibility of will—for she touches her middle and stops struggling with it.

The "dess(e)in" of the entire play is to bring Phèdre to this movement of revelation of the middle that she has spent so much energy trying to keep inside. The irony is that the revelation of Phèdre's innermost desires leads not to an act of individuation, but rather to Phèdre's complete assimilation to Venus and the consequent loss of her heroic identity: "Goddess, take your revenge; our causes are the same." The lesson of Phèdre's self-revelation is that in Racine heroic individuation, the constitution of a coherent unit of character, is only a potential, a process by which one moves toward unity of personality—along a path which forces one to use the law of excluded middle—and flees all irreducible ambivalences, or monsters, in one's center. But if one ever understands how artificial this centrifugal movement is, if it ever comes to seem inauthentic, that is when the heroic illusion which forms the basis for any conception of unity of personality is destroyed. That is when one loses the only trump card proper to the human condition, and more particularly to the tragic effort to transcend it, the possibility of struggle itself; when one becomes, like Phèdre, or like Néron in *Britannicus,* a monster, a creature which no longer fights against itself, which has accepted its contradictory and irresolvable nature. In becoming a simple agent of the goddess, Phèdre loses the heroic potential of being like the gods by fighting against them, of defining herself by fleeing herself. If heroism is itself, like the idea of the unity of the individual, artificial, fully understanding its artifice means no longer being able to use it.

Phèdre's disappearance in the middle of the play is reflected by a key omission in her wish for Hippolyte's love: "Qu'il aime" has no direct object. Because Phèdre forgets herself in her wish, it becomes a simple reiteration of the goddess's wish. Hippolyte will indeed love, but he will not love her. The formal and ironic realization of Phèdre's wish will take the most economical and cruellest form possible, Hippolyte's message "transmitted" by Thésée which simply supplies the missing word: "Qu'il *l*'aime" (1188).

At the very moment of releasing what is essentially an oracular utterance, Phèdre is interrupted, in the middle of a line, and the entire play reverses. Oenone retraces her steps, the king comes back from his "death." Only Phèdre cannot turn back. The word which marks the middle of the play, or rather the rhyme which opens its second half, is "lieux"—"Thésée est en ces lieux"—and Phèdre understands perfectly well that the reestablishment of this "mi-lieu" signals her own end: "Il vit; je ne veux pas en savoir davantage" (834). The middle of *Phèdre,* like the middle of the *Hippolytos,* marks the death of Phèdre, but here her death is not the expression and the guarantee of a failing heroism but rather the death of a heroic morality at the expense of life.

This reassertion of the power of the middle is ultimately what reestablishes Phèdre's mortality, what undermines her heroic decision to die in order to keep her middle excluded, and thus what distinguishes her from the gods. *Phèdre,* unlike the *Hippolytos,* puts only mortals onstage. The gods are not present and are not asked to speak, and speech often takes the supremely mortal and unheroic form of gossip:

> On dit même qu'au trône une brigue insolente
> Veut placer Aricie et le sang de Pallante.
>
> (329–30)

On sème de sa mort d'incroyables discours.
On dit que, ravisseur d'une amante nouvelle,
Les flots ont englouti cet époux infidèle.
On dit même, et ce bruit est partout répandu,
Qu'avec Pirithoüs aux enfers descendu,
Il a vu le Cocyte et les rivages sombres,
Et s'est montré vivant aux infernales ombres,
Mais qu'il n'a pu sortir de ce triste séjour,
Et repasser les bords qu'on passe sans retour.
(380–88)

Cependant un bruit sourd veut que le roi respire.
On prétend que Thésée a paru dans l'Epire.
(729–30)

The stage is linked with the outside by a series of "on dit," or "rumors," and if this fact is manifestly true of the external events of the drama—the passage of power in Athens, Thésée's "death," his miraculous return—it also characterizes the nature of the drama's milieu of communication: no word can be spoken in isolation, stopped or stabilized at its source. Once spoken, the word follows a path of its own.

Thus "partout répandu" is one of the play's key phrases, suggesting not only the word's capacity to spread out and separate itself from its source, but also the acceleration of the transmission of messages. Although Phèdre may be the last to find out about Thésée's "death" ("Et ce malheur n'est plus ignoré que de vous," 320), she seems instantly informed of the rumors surrounding its circumstances, since the "bruit partout répandu" of his return to infidelity is incorporated into her delirious description of Thésée to Hippolyte ("Je l'aime, non point tel que l'ont vu les enfers, / Volage adorateur de mille objets divers," 635–36). Indeed, the rumor of Thésée caught in the underworld and unable to cross the Acheron in the other direction becomes a metaphor for the nature of language in the play:" "Malheureuse, quel nom est sorti de ta bouche?" (206), Phèdre's initial reaction to Oenone's mention of Hippolyte's name, echoes the Homeric image of scandalous or shocking words crossing the barrier of the teeth and unable to be taken back. The mouth itself, the link between inside and outside, then becomes the "bords qu'on passe sans retour."

The unidirectionality of speech, always being spread out ("répandu") and disseminated ("sème") from a center which loses control of it by releasing it into the world, is what distinguishes humans from the gods. This is a drama in which almost no attempt at repeating a scene, a frequent tech-

nique in Racine, succeeds.[14] Phèdre's wish to replay her confrontation with
Hippolyte by Oenone's proxy leads instantaneously to the announcement
of Thésée's return (III, iii), thus aborting the plan. Thésée's wish to inter-
rogate Oenone a second time (1458) coincides with the news of her death
(1466), and his willingness to listen to Hippolyte's pleas of innocence a second time ("Qu'il vienne me parler, je suis prêt de l'entendre," 1482) has
precisely the same effect (1492). The climax of this series of failed returns
to the source of the word comes when Thésée unsuccessfully asks Neptune
to return his curse to him, undelivered (1483–84), and the ironic reversal
of the series takes place in the play's final scene, in which Phèdre, in spite
of Thésée's request not to reexamine her original accusation ("Je consens
que mes yeux soient toujours abusés," 1599), insists on rectifying his mis-
reading of it (1617).

The play's most important "on dit," in Théramène's climactic description
of Hippolyte being dragged to his death by his horses, contains a fleeting
hint of a silent and victorious divinity:

> En efforts impuissants leur maître se consume;
> Ils rougissent le mors d'une sanglante écume.
> On dit qu'on a vu même, en ce désordre affreux,
> Un dieu qui d'aiguillons pressait leur flanc poudreux.
>
> (1537–40)

This "affreux dit" may well be an echo of Aphrodite, whose presence is
already suggested by the image of the "écume" (the goddess born of the
foam).[15] It is particularly appropriate that the play only hints at Aphrodite's
name and her presence here, for the goddess' victory consists in large part
of her absence and her silence: unlike her Euripidean counterpart, and also
unlike the characters in Racine's play, she is not forced to speak. The "affreux dit" thus characterizes the undeniable difference between mortals and
gods which the play makes felt at every moment by the nature of human
speech itself. When Phèdre's excluded middle has failed, she is left in the
midst of her mortal condition, the condition of *homo loquens,* caught by
the need to relegate her words to a treacherous medium which keeps apart
what it shouldn't keep apart (source of word/ultimate path of word) and
puts together what it shouldn't put together (confession or curse/delivery
or execution thereof).

The emblem of Phèdre's return to communication as a signal of the end
of her excluded middle is the "fil," the thread which her sister Ariane gave
to Thésée to help him find his way out of the labyrinth and which Phèdre
in the transitional speech leading to her full confession to Hippolyte rejects:

> Pour en développer l'embarras incertain,
> Ma soeur du fil fatal eût armé votre main.
> Mais non, dans ce dessein je l'aurais devancée.
> L'amour m'en eût d'abord inspiré la pensée.
> C'est moi, Prince, c'est moi, dont l'utile secours
> Vous eût du Labyrinthe enseigné les détours.
> Que de soins m'eût coûtés cette tête charmante!
> Un fil n'eût point assez rassuré votre amante:
> Compagne du péril qu'il vous fallait chercher,
> Moi-même devant vous j'aurais voulu marcher,
> Et Phèdre au labyrinthe avec vous descendue
> Se serait avec vous retrouvée ou perdue.
>
> (651–62)

This "fil" takes us instantly back to Hippolyte's confusion between "dessein" and "destin," since the "fil" belongs to both domains. First of all the thread indicates Ariane's intention ("dessein") to help Thésée. Phèdre's replacement of her sister is expressed in these very terms ("dans ce dessein je l'aurais devancée") and "dessein" takes on its full ambiguity as both Ariane's intention ("dessein") and Phèdre's picture or image ("dessin") of the scene.

The underlying supposition of the "fil du dessein" is that one can touch the center of the labyrinth and get back out again, that one can confront the problem of the middle, kill the monster, and turn around. According to the myth of heroic intentionality, one is not immobilized by the knowledge of one's middle. One can go back to the world of action while carrying with one an awareness of the middle, a link with it. The problem is that Phèdre, once she has understood the inadequacy of the law of excluded middle, the impossibility of systematizing the middle's chaotic force, no longer believes in this link. She knows that in order to exclude the middle one must die. It is thus the "fil du dessein"—intentionality as an element of the heroic illusion—which Phèdre in her resketching of the incident eliminates: "Un fil n'eût point assez rassuré votre amante."

Once Phèdre recognizes the danger and the inadequacy of the thread of heroic intentionality, the only way she can use the thread to her moral advantage is to sever it, to turn the "fil du dessein" into a "fil du destin" cut short by the "Parque homicide" (469) whom Hippolyte mentions in speaking of his "dead" father. It is not a mere coincidence that the "fil fatal" is thus associated with Hippolyte and his father; an extremely revelatory printing error in a recent edition of *Phèdre* may be taken as a further commentary on the ambiguous status of "fil":

> Un fils [*sic*] n'eût point assez rassuré votre amante. (658)[16]

The inadequacy of *filiation* as a normative link between the generations is the real issue in *Phèdre,* an issue which has been largely missed in spite of (or perhaps because of) the disproportionate attention paid to the incestuous element of Phèdre's passion.

The "fil" of filiation, the thread tying one generation to the next, is in fact not singular, but plural, its plurality ("fils" as "threads") hidden but not erased by the "singular" definition of the relation of father and son ("fils"). The problem is that the "fil" as a metaphor for the passage of time (relation between father and son) is either bidirectional ("fil du dessein"), allowing one to get to the middle ("sein," center of the labyrinth) and then turn around and escape it, or unidirectional ("fil du destin"), like scandalous language emanating from a source to which it refuses to return and intent to arrive at its fateful goal. The irreversibility of time is precisely what distinguishes humans from gods. It is the very essence of the mortal condition, as well as of Racinian tragedy:

[In Racinian tragedy] it seems that we observe the process by which things finally become "fated" even as we look on, and force us to recognize that they indeed had to happen as they did. . . . Racinian fatality is Phèdre's "Qu'ai-je dit!"; it is irreversibility.[17]

What, then, makes the Word so terrible? First of all, the fact that it is an act, that the word is powerful. But above all, the fact that it is irreversible: no word can ever be taken back.[18]

The ambivalence of the "fil" is thus that whether it is reversible or irreversible, it still defines a mortal and an immoral (rather than an immortal or moral) condition. One can never take back what has been said, but one can always go back on one's intentions.

Phèdre, caught by the conflict of intention and destiny, that is, by her attempt at making the thread of her intention coincide with the thread of destiny by cutting it at the right time, misses her moment, her "kairos."[19] Failure to snip the "fil du destin" means that it becomes the "fil fatal" (related to Latin *fari,* "say," i.e., "the thread of saying") unsevered, the passage of time which is the most serious threat to Phèdre's heroic resolve. While Phèdre talks about her death and about the untouchability of her own center, she is still living, spinning out her discussion. And her own "affreux dit," the frightful revelation of herself, marks her distance to the goddess who may or may not be visibly pushing a goad into her side as into the side of Hippolyte's monster, but who is nonetheless victorious over her because of Phèdre's relation to her own center.

Once Phèdre is ethically defunct, what will constitute Thésée's moral sense when he returns from hell? And if the road to hell is paved with good intentions, what is the road back from hell paved with? This is the road which Thésée alone manages to travel, and it is clear that his return from hell — along with his entire adventure there — is a return to the side of Thésée which Phèdre can no longer exclude. As the founder of Athenian civilization, will Thésée leave behind Phèdre's attempt at an excluded middle, and leave us to conclude that it is simply false to try to exclude the middle, that Phèdre is wrong, and that she is punished for her attempt?

This lesson would already be disturbing enough, for who doesn't need the excluded middle in order to create himself? But *Phèdre* is more disturbing still. "Hamartia" or "tragic error" has generally been interpreted as what compromises the hero's or the heroine's identity. But *Phèdre* shows us that individuality, an essential element in the tragic hero's identity, is in itself the "hamartia," that it is the artificial nature of tragic individuation which is the hero's success and failure, or rather "half-success" and "half-failure." And as if to prove that the "moral" of the play is the contradictory nature of tragic morality, the falsity but also the need for the excluded middle, the end of *Phèdre,* what follows the middle of the play which excludes the excluded middle, recreates another excluded middle and thus reaffirms its necessity.

That excluded middle is the message — or rather the nonmessage, the empty place of the message[20] — sent by Hippolyte to Thésée:

> "Dis-lui qu'avec douceur il traite sa captive,
> Qu'il lui rende . . ." A ce mot, ce héros expiré
> N'a laissé dans mes bras qu'un corps défiguré.
> (1566–68)

> Que malgré les complots d'une injuste famille
> Son amante aujourd'hui me tienne lieu de fille!
> (1653–54)

In Hippolyte's final words as they are reported by Théramène, the middle is missing, since his last wish, "Qu'il lui rende," indicates the "destinateur" ("il," Thésée) and the "destinataire" ("lui," Aricie), but not the message. The middle in this communication system is lacking,[21] as a profound questioning of the heritage left by the drama. What is Thésée supposed to "return" to Aricie? What will mediate between the tragic time of the play and the future? Hippolyte's death leaves him "disfigured"; the empty place of his message thus has nothing but a new "face"—a mask, a unity or an appearance of unity—to put on. But is it advisable, or even possible, to "change faces" at the end of this catastrophe as Phèdre and the others did at the beginning, to take off the tragic mask as Racine claims to do when he leaves tragedy behind after *Phèdre,* as if the problem of the tragic middle had been resolved?

Thésée's "solution," the middle that he furnishes to fill the nonmessage and the nonheritage which refuse to link him directly to his dying son, is adoption. *Phèdre* tells us in the end that one cannot choose, but one can adopt. What is the difference between these two concepts?

Let us first of all emphasize the paradoxical nature of Thésée's adoption of Aricie. Racine follows the tradition whereby Pandion—a descendant of the autochthonous founder of Athens, Erechtheus, and in this play Aricie's grandfather—adopted Aegeus (497), whereas Pallas, Aricie's father, was Pandion's natural son. This is a play which ends by having the adopted son (or rather grandson), Thésée, readopt the family that has already adopted him, Aricie "taking the place" ("me tienne lieu") of his daughter. This "place" that she takes—the place of adoption, of substitution for the middle left empty by Hippolyte's dying words—indicates the metaphorical value of adoption as an emblem of the complex relation which links civilization to its origins, to the monsters from which it tries to liberate itself. When Pandion, a descendant of the Earth and thus the representative of the monster, adopts Thésée's father, his action has the value of a provisional acceptance, a sanction of the civilization which will be imposed by Thésée's family and embodied by Phèdre and her excluded middle. By killing the Minotaur, Thésée seems to go even further in this direction, for he rids Athens of the monster which has been haunting it, and he goes directly from that exclusion to the exclusion of half of his personality by Phèdre. The city's moral future, and his own, seem assured.

But killing monsters can be tiring; and then, there may be monsters which one doesn't wish to kill. In order to come back from hell, Thésée in fact feeds monsters rather than slaying them (969–70). Thésée's "adoption" of Aricie means that the artificial morality which he as a civilizer represents has recognized the race of the monster which it defines itself as denying. This is a way of reestablishing a middle of communication between the generations, and also a way of providing a link between father and new-found daughter, but that middle is a tragic middle. The excluded middle that Phèdre provides for Thésée is what gives him his heroic virtue, his identity as a great civilizer. But it is the artificiality of civilization itself which must periodically be recognized by the questioning of the law of excluded middle, just as it is recognized by tragedy itself. The tragic middle reestablishes a continuity which has been broken, but the break is an internal part of its message. If the final words of Racine's tragic theater assure us that "the orphan has a father" (*Athalie* 1816), it does not say that the son or daughter has one. In tragedy it is the interruption of the normative relation, its negation, which is needed in order to define it. The tragic middle is a tragic recognition. It recognizes the need to accept the interior distance which defines the individual, the discontinuity, or in positive terms the contiguity at the very heart of individuation; and, from the opposite perspective, the need for adoption, the need to accept for oneself, as if one were not separated from it by a terrifying void, what one defines as other, the irreducible other by opposition to which one defines oneself, the enemy or the monster.

Thus the sense of continuity at the end of *Phèdre,* the rejoining of the generations, the definition of a unit of time, is based upon a sort of double negation. What links Thésée and Aricie is a double distance, a double adoption, a double questioning of the relation of outside to inside, and the lesson which this double questioning leaves us with is that the middle is not simply the inside itself, the monster which must be killed, the internal boundary between the conscious personality and what it must deny in order to constitute itself, but more fundamentally the relation between the inside and the outside, the endless checking and testing of the authenticity and the viability of the individual which constitutes tragedy itself. Adopting the monstrous, accepting the limitations of the excluded middle, is not a return to a moral or a virtuous middle, but the final step into the tragic. As the philosopher Clément Rosset, whose aim is to found a philosophy of tragedy, puts it: "The concept of moral instinct cannot be more accurately defined than the feeling of what is *unknown to the tragic. "*"Denying that contradictions are unsolvable" means "denying tragedy itself, and wanting to resolve contradictions . . . from moral, anti-tragic motives."[22] Thésée thinks the road from hell is the road out of tragedy, for his future, the foundation of Athenian civilization, has a moral content. But if he fully understood that moral content, he could never get out of the world of tragedy.

Part 3
After the Middle

Leaving the middle means leaving humanity.

—Pascal, *Pensées*

11
To Speak or Not to Speak

Once he said, *I shall stop speaking,* he should not have continued to speak.
— "Sentiments de l'Académie sur la tragi-comédie du Cid"

If Thésée thinks in the end he has left tragedy behind, does Racine believe that he himself can do so as well? This question brings us back to our starting point, the division of Racine's life into three parts, with the theatrical period corresponding to the middle. As striking as the remarkably even division of Racine's life into three is his expressed desire and ambition to exclude that middle, to make the three parts into only two parts, beginning and end without any middle to link them, his refusal of all synthesis. In the final stage of his life, Racine completely disclaims his theatrical career, marrying a woman who in over twenty years of married life barely learns the titles of his tragedies, forbidding his children from reading his profane plays, and generally doing what François Mauriac in his biography of Racine calls backtracking ("revenir sur ses pas"[1]), seemingly trying to erase the middle period of his life and leave only the two extremes.

This is Racine's attempt at applying to himself the law of excluded middle. The "contradictory statements" of Racine's life are not so much the two "ends" or extremities of his biography as they are the two fundamentally opposed tendencies which seem to have inhabited the man, neatly summed up by the much-quoted Third *Cantique:*

> Mon Dieu, quelle guerre cruelle!
> Je trouve deux hommes en moi:
> L'un veut que plein d'amour pour toi
> Mon coeur te soit toujours fidèle.
> L'autre à tes volontés rebelle
> Me révolte contre ta loi.[2]

If Racine managed to exclude the middle of his life, the theatrical period, he would manage to limit himself not only to the two ends of his life, but also to a single image of himself. If the middle is excluded, the third period is equivalent to the first, and there is only one, "faithful" Racine.

But how does tragedy lead Racine to spend the final third of his life denying what he spent the middle third of his life affirming? Has he, as the sanctimonious pose that follows his midlife crisis suggests—and to reverse the terms of Thésée's own escape from hell (and thus from tragedy)—escaped from hell *by leaving tragedy behind?* Has Racine been "purged" of his extreme, immoderate emotions? Will a successful catharsis allow him to leave the theater and go home, cured of his passions?

If catharsis as a principle of tragedy interested Racine considerably more than it did most of his contemporaries,[3] it is not only a poetic practice, and a medical practice which obsessed the seventeenth century,[4] but also a very ancient social practice, that of the scapegoat or ritual victim, as René Girard observes:

> The word *katharsis* refers primarily to the mysterious benefits that accrue to the community upon the death of a human *katharma* or *pharmakos*. The process is generally seen as a religious purification and takes the form of cleansing or draining away impurities. Shortly before his execution the *pharmakos* is paraded ceremonially through the streets of the village. It is believed that he will absorb all the noxious influences that may be abroad and that his death will transpose them outside the community. This is a mythical representation of what does in fact *almost* take place. The communal violence is indeed drawn to the person of the surrogate victim, but the final resolution cannot be described as the expulsion of some substance. The interpretation thus approaches the truth but fails to attain it because it fails to perceive three essential facts: the mimetic nature of reciprocal violence, the arbitrary choice of the victim, and the unanimous polarization of hostility that produces the reconciliation.[5]

It is the acute polarization of the community, the crowd united against the sacrificial victim, which leads to reconciliation. By defining the "katharma," or victim to be purged, as an opponent to the collectivity, as being what they are not, the community is able to reaffirm itself. It is thanks to this excluded middle, a polarization into contradictory opposites one of which must be selected at the expense of the other, that the group, its solidarity newly redefined, can return to the moderation of everyday life, the world of compromise and reconciliation.

Girard goes on to point out that Aristotelian tragic catharsis is remarkably similar to ritual, communal purification:

On closer inspection, Aristotle's text [the *Poetics*] is something of a manual of sacrificial practices, for the qualities that make a "good" tragic hero are precisely those required of the sacrificial victim. If the latter is to polarize and purge the emotions of the community, he must at once resemble the members of the community and differ from them; he must be at once insider and outsider, both "double" and incarnation of the "sacred difference." He must be neither wholly good nor wholly bad. . . . Having accompanied the hero part of the way, the audience suddenly perceives him as wholly "other" and abandons him to his fate, his superhuman ignominy and glory. The spectator may shudder with "pity and fear," but he must also feel a deep sense of gratitude for his own orderly and relatively secure existence.[6]

Aristotle's tragic hero is, as we have seen, "in between,"[7] that is, in the middle between good and bad, and the hero's violent downfall can be interpreted as bringing a salutary end to this unbearable status. The exclusion of the hero leads to the establishment of tragic magnitude. It gives the hero a newly established value, a majesty in suffering which makes him purely other. His exclusion leads the audience back to "prudence," to what Aristotle would call "sophrosyne," no less than it seems to lead Racine to a renewal of his moral convictions.

But as Michel Butor observes, the only way Racine can "exclude" his tragic middle is by creating a persona *for himself,* a mask with a seemingly unambivalent value—fidelity to the king and to the glorification of his reign, fidelity to the writing of History, fidelity to God, to family, and to country:

It would be absurd to cast doubt on Racine's attempts to put his life in order. He wants to seem like a good Christian. Yes, it is almost a question of life or death for him: it is the only way he can deflect all those widespread condemnations of the theater, to which he remains very much attached. It is true that the surest way would be to *be* a good Christian, to be a true believer. But how can he fully contain all of those demons which his poetry has loosed? From that time on he creates a character for himself, a mask in which he locks himself up. And that is exactly the impression he made on a number of his contemporaries.[8]

The safest way for Racine would be to return to the ethical middle, that is, not to feel the painful disjunction between his inner and his outer being and thus the inauthenticity of the unit of the individual keeping the inside in and the outside out. But "after" tragedy—and in fact tragedy "comes after" (pursues) Racine in his old age much more than his old age "comes after" (follows) tragedy—that middle is unavailable to him. The best he can do is to put on a mask and to lock himself up inside of it in the hopes of keeping in "that demon which lives inside of him."[9] In constituting himself fully as an individual, Racine gives up exploring the complex relation between the inner being and the outer being that makes up the ongoing *process* of individuation which alone, as Racine's theater tells us, leaves the potential individual any room for struggle and development.

Racine's renunciation of tragedy brings into play another philosopher whose relation to Racine has not received a sufficient amount of attention: Plato. In his preface to *Phèdre*, Racine mentions Socrates in speaking about the relation between tragedy and virtue:

> What I can assure you of is that I have never written a tragedy in which virtue is brought further to the fore than it is in this one. . . . That is the proper goal which any man who writes for the theater must give himself. And that is what the first tragic poets generally had in mind. Their theater was a school in which virtue was as well taught as in the philosophers' schools. Thus Aristotle took the trouble to set forth the rules of the dramatic poem; and Socrates, the wisest of philosophers, was not above taking things from Euripides' tragedies. We can only wish that our own works were as solid and full of useful instruction as these poets' works. Perhaps that would be a way of reconciling tragedy with many people known for their piety and their doctrine who have recently condemned tragedy and who would be more favorably inclined toward it if authors thought as much about instructing their public as about amusing them, and if they therefore followed tragedy's true intention. (*Oeuvres complètes* 1:747)

Racine claims that Plato (or at least Socrates) was in profound agreement with Euripides over the moral content of tragedy. The *Hippolytos* has already shown us to what extent this hypothesized harmony between Plato and Euripides—like the preface to *Phèdre* itself, which Francesco Orlando calls "one-sided" when compared to the "much more complex reality of the text"[10]—is oversimplified and artificial. Indeed, the *Phaedrus,* which Racine knew[11]—and let us not forget that in French Phèdre refers indifferently to Phaedra or to Phaedrus—might possibly have given him this impression of consonance between Euripides and Plato, the tortured lover straining at his horses closely recalling Hippolytos' death. Moreover Racine implicitly puts Aristotle and Plato together in their relation to tragedy, Aristotle establishing its rules and Plato (through Socrates) using Euripides' tragedies as illustrations of ethical problems.

But as Girard states, Plato's relation to tragedy was altogether different from Aristotle's:

> The fundamental duality of tragedy led to the opposing formulations of Aristotle and Plato. Given his time and place, Aristotle was correct to define tragedy in terms of its cathartic qualities. But then, Aristotle is always "correct." That

is why he is so great, and so one-sided in his greatness. Aristotle is above and beyond the crisis of tragedy. He incorporates into his theory all the meanings and reasons that pertain to the misunderstanding of this crisis. In choosing Aristotle as their mentor the formalistic literary critics could not have done better, for Aristotle views tragedy solely from the perspective of order. In his view the art of tragedy affirms, consolidates, and preserves everything that deserves to be affirmed, consolidated and preserved.

Plato, by contrast, is closer in time and spirit to the crisis. . . . Paradoxically, it was Plato's own acute insight into the nature of tragic inspiration that provoked his hostility to drama. He saw tragedy as opening a window onto the dark and dangerous origins of social values, as somehow posing a challenge to the very concept of civic order. . . . The poet, like many a modern intellectual, reveals an ambiguous attitude toward those beings whom the stricken city has driven from its precincts in an effort to regain its lost unity. . . . The city, says Plato, must protect itself from subversion; therefore it must rid itself of subversive elements. Sophocles must join Oedipus on the road to exile.[12]

Girard is alluding to the tenth book of Plato's *Republic,* a text which Racine knew even better than the *Phaedrus*[13] and which develops Plato's reasons for wanting to exclude tragedy from his ideal republic:

But we have not yet brought our chief accusation against it [tragedy]. Its power to corrupt, with rare exceptions, even the better sort is surely the chief cause for alarm. . . . I think you know that the very best of us, when we hear Homer or some other of the makers of tragedy imitating one of the heroes who is in grief, . . . abandon ourselves and accompany the representation with sympathy and eagerness, and we praise as an excellent poet the one who most strongly affects us in this way. . . . But when in our own lives some affliction comes to us, you are also aware that we plume ourselves upon the opposite, on our ability to remain calm and endure. . . . Reflect that the part of the soul that in the former case, in our own misfortunes, was forcibly restrained, and that has hungered for tears and a good cry [pepeinekos tou dakrysai] and satisfaction, because it is its nature [physei] to desire these things, is the element in us that the poets satisfy and delight, and that the best element in our nature, since it has never been properly educated by reason or even by habit, then relaxes its guard over the plaintive part, . . . and it is no shame to it to praise and pity another who, claiming to be a good man, abandons himself to excess in his grief [akairos penthei]. (*Republic,* X, vii, 605C–606B)[14]

Tragedy reinforces our tendency to cry and complain, "to pepeinekos tou dakrysai." It waters the passions, instead of what it should do, which is to dry them up. The only things that poetry ought to be allowed are hymns and praises of God. Age-old quarrel between philosophy and poetry. (Racine, *Oeuvres complètes* 2:908)

Tragedy affects the weaker part of the soul, the part which loses control and abandons itself to "excess"—"akairos penthei," or "grieves intemperately" (i.e., in a way that goes against "kairos," the right amount or the right time)—and this would appear to Plato to be the principal source of its danger. Plato here recognizes that tragedy brings pleasure, and even a natural kind of pleasure, since the part of us that it satisfies has as its "nature" ("physei") the need for "a good cry." But Plato does not consider a good cry to be good, since it is a way of giving in to the conflict of the various parts of our being rather than forcing reason to keep them in balance.

What tragedy challenges is *measure*(s):

> The same magnitude [megethos], I presume, viewed from near and from far does not appear equal. . . . And have not measuring [to metrein] and numbering and weighing proved to be most gracious aids to prevent the domination in our soul of the apparently greater or less or more or heavier, and to give the control to that which has reckoned and numbered [metresan] or even weighed? . . . But this surely would be the function of the part of the soul that reasons and calculates. . . . And often when this has measured [metresanti] and declares that certain things are larger or that some are smaller than the others or equal, there is at the same time an appearance of the contrary. . . . And did we not say that it is impossible for the same thing at one time to hold contradictory opinions about the same thing? . . . The part of the soul, then, that opines in contradiction of measurement [metra] could not be the same with that which conforms to it. . . . That which puts its trust in measurement and reckoning must be the best part of the soul. . . . This, then, was what I wished to have agreed upon when I said that poetry, and in general the mimetic art, produces a product that is far removed from truth in the accomplishment of its task, and associates with the part in us that is remote from intelligence, and is its companion and friend for no sound and true purpose. (*Republic*, X, v, 602C–603B; Shorey, pp. 449–51)

Measure, "to metrion," is closely related to "to meson," the virtuous middle.[15] There is nothing tragic about "magnitude" (and let us not forget that "megethos" is also the term used by Aristotle of tragic magnitude) if one can find a way to go beyond the apparent changes of magnitude inherent to the imperfect nature of perception—and this can also be a metaphor for the instability of (moral) perspective in tragedy—by relying on measure as a kind of universal. Measure alone can subordinate any changes of perspective to an eternal truth, the abstract measure of a thing being akin to its ideal form. Measure alone can resolve contradictions of perspective when two views appear opposite. And indeed, this passage, recalling an earlier passage of the *Republic* (IV, xii, 436B), provides us with the first written record of the law of noncontradiction ("it is impossible for the same thing at one time to hold contradictory opinions about the same thing"), the very law which Aristotle will pair in the *Metaphysics* with the law of excluded middle.

May we then conclude that a belief in measure, a synonym of the virtuous middle, is consistent with the laws of noncontradiction and excluded middle? On the contrary, this is the moment that separates Plato and Aristotle, for the law of excluded middle is largely a reaction to the Platonic theory of ideal forms. Plato may have attempted to eliminate contradiction, but he never excluded the middle:

> The origin of the doctrine of the Excluded Third is apparent in *Aristotle's* opposition to the *Platonic* assertion of a Third or mean between Being and Not-Being.
>
> *Plato* set on one side Ideas, as that which *is,* on the opposite side, matter, as that which *is not* (but nevertheless made it the substratum of sensible things), and between the two as the Third, sensible things. . . . Their true place must be considered to be the mean between Being and Not-Being. . . .
>
> *Aristotle,* on the other hand, allowed no mean between the members of the contradiction, between Being and Not-Being.[16]

Aristotle feels the need to exclude the middle because the middle is for him, as for Racine, an unsolvable problem. His reaction to that problem is to establish two separate domains, two units of philosophical inquiry, ethics and metaphysics, which, as we have seen, do not necessarily converge even if they have close affinities. But Plato asserts that there is no problem, that is, no irreparable incompatibility between the ideal and the real, between what should be and what is. And this is why he rejects tragedy; for tragedy is an expression of this incompatibility.

Indeed, the only third which Plato does exclude is the poet:

> The painter, we say, will paint both reins and a bit. . . . But the maker will be the cobbler and the smith. . . . Does the painter, then, know the proper quality of reins and bit? Or does not even the maker, the cobbler and the smith, know that, but only the man who understands the use of these things, the horseman? . . . And shall we not say that the same holds true of everything? . . . That there are some three arts concerned with everything, the user's art, the maker's, and the imitator's. . . . In heaven's name, then, this business of imitation is concerned with the third remove [triton] from truth, is it not? (*Republic,* X, iv-v, 601C–602C; Shorey, pp. 445–47)

> Plato comes back again to Homer and to dramatic poetry, which he continues to exclude from his republic. . . . The poet is only the third worker. The first is God; the second is the man who acts upon God's idea; the third is the poet who represents what is made. (Racine, *Oeuvres complètes* 2:907)

Rather than excluding the third, and separating ethics from metaphysics, Plato excludes from his republic the tragic poet who is at the third remove from the truth, the poet whose work expresses the very separation which Plato and his idealism refuse to recognize. And Racine follows Plato's advice by attempting to exclude the poet inside of himself at the moment of integrating himself, if not into the Republic, at least into political life, the service of his king.

But in excluding the tragic poet in himself, can Racine exclude the excluded middle? The excluded middle has a double (and incompatible) status for Racine. It is first of all one of the central laws of his tragic theater; but it is also the law by which he tries to exclude that theater. Can Racine use his tragic system to get out of the system? *Phèdre* is followed by a long period of silence, and if that silence is part of the message of *Phèdre,* it does not indicate simply that Racine has left tragedy behind, but rather that we must know how to interpret the meaning of silence.

It is, once again, the *Republic* and Racine's notes to it that can help us in this task. Here is Socrates' description of philosophers:

> And those who have been of this little company and have tasted the sweetness and blessedness of this possession and who have also come to understand the madness of the multitude sufficiently and have seen that there is nothing, if I may say so, sound or right in any present politics, and that there is no ally with whose aid the champion of justice could escape destruction, but that he would be as a man who has fallen among wild beasts, unwilling to share their misdeeds and unable to hold out singly against the savagery of all . . . —for all these reasons I say the philosopher remains quiet, minds his own affair, and, as it were, standing under shelter of a wall in a storm and blast of dust and sleet and seeing others filled full of lawlessness, is content if in any way he may keep himself free from iniquity and unholy deeds [katharos adikias te kai anosion ergon] through this life and take his departure with fair hope, serene and well content when the end comes. (*Republic,* VI, x, 496C–E; Shorey, pp. 53–55)

And Racine's notes to this passage:

> The philosopher or the just man [le juste] is a man who lives among wild beasts. . . . The just man is a man who has fallen in the middle [au milieu] of ferocious beasts; he must keep silent, if he does not wish to be torn apart. He withdraws under a little roof, and from there he sees the others covered with rain and mud, fortunate to finish his life without getting dirty [sans être sali]. (*Oeuvres complètes* 2:910)

Is Racine this "juste [au] milieu"? Racine identifies the Platonic philosopher as a just man, that is, an ethical man. Is the tragic silence of the end of Racine's life just silence? Once Racine no longer allows himself tragic catharsis, it is not surprising that catharsis comes to mean nothing more "purifying" than the absence of dirt; Racine translates "katharos adikias te kai anosion ergon," "clean of injustice and unholy deeds," simply as "sans être sali." But if, as Racine's final annotation to the *Nicomachean Ethics* suggests, "Virtue consists more of doing the good rather than of not doing the bad" (*Oeuvres complètes* 2:934),[17] what has become of virtue as a positive ethic?

No one who has seen a tragedy and let it reach its goal, his innermost fears, can ever again believe in the simplicity of any moral system. And yet, to the extent that life continues when one leaves behind (or tries to leave behind) the experience of tragedy — be it that of an evening at the theater or that of an entire literary career — that "continuity" is based on the power to forget, or not to understand too well. Thésée's adoption of Aricie requires that he not fully fathom the implications of his own gesture. As tragedy demonstrates, morality demands a blocking mechanism, an inability or a refusal to see everything that is. Seeing too much, as the tragedy of Oedipus shows us, leads to blindness. But it may also lead, as the tragedy of Racine should tell us, to silence. And it is not a silence that comes from having nothing to say, but rather a silence that expresses contradictory statements which, were they to be uttered, would tear one apart ("he must keep silent, if he does not wish to be torn apart").

We began with Aristotle, who was born some twenty years after Euripides' *Phoenissae* was produced posthumously. Let us end with Pascal, who died at the very moment (1662) when Racine was preparing to launch his theatrical career. Nowhere is the tripartite division of Racine's own life so well described as by Pascal's depiction of the three stages of human life:

> The world judges things well, for it is in the natural ignorance which is the true place of man. The sciences have two extremities which meet: the first is the pure natural ignorance in which all men find themselves at birth; the other extremity is the one reached by great souls who after making their way through everything that men can know find that they know nothing and recognize that they are in the same state of ignorance from which they started, but it is a knowing ignorance which understands itself. Those in between who have left natural ignorance behind but have not managed to reach the other kind dabble in a smug sort of science [science suffisante], and play at wise men [font les entendus]. They disturb the world and judge everything badly.[18]

The middle period between the "natural ignorance" of the young and the "knowing ignorance" of the old is indeed a theatrical middle: those "in between" these two forms of ignorance act out the role of understanding, "font les entendus" being essentially a theatrical metaphor.

But where shall we place this theatrical middle in the life of Racine? Does that period come to an end with the end of his tragedy? Does he stop writing tragedy because he has fundamentally understood something? The problem is that if, upon completing *Phèdre,* Racine comes to this understanding, if he is thus eligible to move into the third stage of Pascal's description, that of "great souls," his gesture in abandoning the theater and reaffirming his worldly identity is, paradoxically, a gesture which attempts to prolong the middle stage of his life, for what Racine wants is to keep his tenuous grip on the "science suffisante" which one needs to go on living in any social context. Continuing to write tragedy would mean finally understanding—and being unable to deny—the insufficiency of the units which are the very bases of social communication and interaction. And this is precisely what Racine shows us he has understood by refusing to understand it, by keeping silent.

Let us then read this silence of Racine which follows his tragic middle as an expression of the "disproportion" of man, his immeasurability; the impossibility of reducing him to a proportion. Let us turn once again to the Pascalian middle:

> For what is man in nature? Nothingness in relation to the infinite, everything in relation to nothingness, a middle between nothing and everything, infinitely separated from any understanding of the extremes; the end of things and their principles are for him inevitably hidden in an impenetrable secret. . . .
>
> Limited, as we are, in every way, this state which holds the middle between two extremes is perceptible in all of our powers. . . .
>
> That is our true state. It is what makes us incapable of certain knowledge and of absolute ignorance. We drift along on a vast middle, always uncertain and floating, pushed from one end toward the other; whatever is the end to which we think we can attach ourselves and anchor ourselves, it shakes free and gets away from us. ("Disproportion de l'homme"[19])

Leaving the middle means leaving humanity.[20]

The "milieu" is the "lieu" of the human condition. The extremes—God, nothingness, the infinitely large and the infinitely small—escape us, out of our mediocre reach, but what makes us conscious of these extremes is the very middle which also keeps us from them. The middle, the human condition, carries with it the unbearable awareness of its own inadequacy.

Tragedy shows us that any "milieu" of communication conceived by a creature who is half-god and half-beast cannot exclude the middle—for "leaving the middle means leaving humanity" – but that humans will never cease trying to exclude the middle so long as there is a heroic impulse which makes them wish to resolve their composite nature by reaching up toward the univalence of the gods. Understanding the artificiality of the excluded middle may mean never being able to use it again. But having used it also means never again being able to do without it. If the milieu of communication – be it ethical, social, metaphysical, or theatrical – ever succeeded in excluding the middle, it would be excluding itself as an expression of its own insufficiency. Like the Racinian "individual" fully formed – one final contradiction in terms – it would have nothing more to say. But to the extent that excluding the middle is nonetheless necessary to constitute a certain conception of meaning, recognizing the impossibility of excluding the middle forces one to understand what the medium of communication can never express, to realize that one will always be in danger of being trapped by the medium itself.

The law of excluded middle as one of the laws of thought may be our stepping stone up to the divine. But our need for it is also a proof of our insubstantiality, our fragility:

> Man is but a reed, the weakest in all of nature, but he is a thinking reed. The whole universe need not rise up to crush him; a vapor, a drop of water is enough to kill him. But even if the universe crushed him, man would be nobler still than what killed him, since he knows he is mortal; he knows the advantage that the universe holds over him. The universe knows nothing of it.
>
> Thus all of our dignity consists of thought. That is how we must lift ourselves up, not through space and time, which we have no way of filling. So let us work at thinking well: that is the principle of morality.[21]

The thinking reed is a hollow being, but it is his hollowness which makes him think. If he cannot "fill" space, he can at least think "about" (and also thanks to) the vacuum at his center; it is his awareness of his emptiness which is his greatest asset. And he may in fact think "well" even if he does not think according to the "principle of morality," for his weakness – his *hamartia*, his inability to hit the middle – is his ultimate strength.

Is there, then, any certainty that in such circumstances speech means more than silence?

> The eternal silence of these infinite spaces frightens me.[22]

It is the emptiness of space, the problem of the middle spreading into infinity in the form – or rather the formlessness – of the abyss, that forces us to speak, or not to speak. Could Racine have "said" any more by saying more about his tragic middle than by being silent? Roland Barthes begins his remarkable analysis of *Phèdre* with a paraphrase of the line from *Hamlet* which is undoubtedly the most famous excluded middle in the history of tragedy:

To speak or not to speak? That is the question.[23]

But is it?

Notes
Index

Notes

Chapter 1. Racine and the Classical Middle

1　See, for example, the organization of Geoffrey Brereton's *Jean Racine: A Critical Biography* (London: Cassel, 1951): part 1, The Varied Prospect (1639–1663); part 2, Through the Jungle (1663–1677); and part 3, The Promised Land (1677–1699).

2　Henri Peyre's formulation of Classicism as a "need for order, measure, equilibrium, and harmony" (*Le Classicisme français* [New York: Maison Française, 1942], 33, trans. mine) is fairly representative of a certain definition of Classicism.

3　*Jean Racine,* trans. Isabel McHugh and Florence McHugh (New York: Ungar, 1972), 13 and 18–19.

4　Jean Racine, *Oeuvres complètes,* ed. Raymond Picard, 2 vols., (Paris: Gallimard, Pléiade, 1950 and 1966), 2:923. All subsequent references to this edition will be given in the body of the text.

5　Racine owned a 1560 edition of the *Nicomachean Ethics,* and his marginal comments have been preserved in *Oeuvres complètes* 2:932–34.

6　Aristotle, *Nicomachean Ethics,* trans. H. Rackham (1926; rpt. London: Heinemann, 1982), 77. All translations of the *Ethics* are taken from this edition; subsequent references will be given in the body of the text.

7　Jean-François Marmontel, *Poétique française* (Paris: Lesclapart, 1763), 2:199. This and all translations from the French, unless otherwise noted, are mine.

8　Roy C. Knight, in his excellent study of Racine's Hellenic connections, makes light of these marginalia, saying that Racine "is reading as a cultured 'honnête homme' who is interested in everything involving the mind but doesn't 'lose his head' over specializing in anything outside of his trade, that of a French poet." *Racine et la Grèce* (1951; rpt. Paris: Nizet, 1974), 170. Knight, like Vossler, thus makes Racine into an "honnête homme," a practitioner of moderation. I believe Racine's relation to this material is more complex than it might appear, and probably even than he himself was aware.

9　*Poetics,* VI and XIX. Aristotle even links the two terms (*Poetics,* XI, 1452b11).

10　Blaise Pascal, *Pensées,* in *Oeuvres complètes,* ed. Louis Lafuma (Paris: Seuil, 1963), 526–27.

11　Pascal, *Oeuvres complètes,* 577.

12　Paul Bénichou, *Morales du grand siècle* (Paris: Gallimard, 1948), 144–46.

13　Ibid., 141–42.

14　This is attested to by Louis Racine in his biography of his father: "My father . . . was convinced that these words were directed against him" (Racine, *Oeuvres complètes* 1:24).

15 Pierre Nicole, *Les Visionnaires ou Seconde partie des lettres sur l'Hérésie Imaginaire* (Liège: Adolphe Beyers, 1667), 295.

16 This wordplay may seem fanciful, but Denis Diderot makes use of a similar (perhaps subconscious) wordplay in an extended metaphor comparing Racine to a tree: "He's a tree who has dried up several trees planted in his vicinity; who has stifled the plants growing at his feet; but he has lifted his top into the heavens; his branches have stretched out into the distance; he has lent his shade to those who have come, are coming, and will come looking for rest around his majestic trunk; he has produced fruits of an exquisite taste which are never depleted" (*Le Neveu de Rameau* [Paris: Garnier-Flammarion, 1967], 44).

17 *Athalie,* 140. This is the only use of the word "racine," singular or plural, in Racine's drama (Bryant C. Freeman and Alan Batson, *Concordance du théâtre et des poésies de Racine* [Ithaca, N.Y.: Cornell University Press, 1968], 2:1033), and the fact that it comes not only in his last play — as a sort of autograph, or even epitaph — but also in the plural once again evokes the problem of establishing "one" Racine, a single, noncontradictory, unified vision of the poet. Cf. "New Criticism, whose Racine, or rather Racines, are not mine" (Knight, *Racine et la Grèce,* preface).

18 George Steiner, *The Death of Tragedy* (1961; rpt. New York: Oxford University Press, 1980), 80.

19 Pierre Corneille, *Oeuvres complètes,* ed. André Stegmann (Paris: Seuil, 1963), 830.

20 Jean Racine, *Principes de la tragédie: En marge de la Poétique d'Aristote,* ed. Eugène Vinaver (Manchester: Editions de l'Université de Manchester, 1944), 48–49.

21 The word "irradicable," which Vinaver seems to have invented, is removed from the 1951 edition; the word may well have been the result of a subconscious word play on "Racine."

22 Georges Poulet, "Racine, poète des clartés sombres," in *Mesures de l'instant* (Paris: Plon, 1968), 59.

23 It would appear that Racine owned a 1629 edition of the complete works of Aristotle in Greek and Latin, or at least this work appears in the "état estimatif" of the poet's library made at the time of his death in 1699 (P. Bonnefon, "La bibliothèque de Racine," *Revue d'Histoire Littéraire de la France* 5 [1898]: 180), but we cannot say with certainty what Racine might have read in this volume. Nevertheless, as we have seen, the Jansenists are fairly obsessed with the problem of the middle. And it is perhaps not completely coincidental that the law of excluded middle attracted the attention of a philosopher who was born during Racine's lifetime: Christian Wolff (1679–1754), whose Latin translation of Aristotle's law, "Non dari medium," is considered to be the source of the phrase "excluded middle."

24 Lucien Goldmann, *Le Dieu caché* (Paris: Gallimard, 1959), 60.

25 Roland Barthes, *Sur Racine* (Paris: Seuil, 1963), 45 and 51–52.

Chapter 2. The Virtuous Middle and the Excluded Middle in Aristotle

1 Aristotle, *Nicomachean Ethics,* trans. H. Rackham (1926; rpt. London: Heinemann, 1982), 77. All subsequent quotations from the *Nicomachean Ethics* will be taken from this edition and references will be given in the body of the text.

2 W. F. R. Hardie, *Aristotle's Ethical Theory* (Oxford: Clarendon, 1980), 129. See also the commentary of René Antoine Gauthier and Jean Yves Jolif in their edition of *L'Ethique à Nicomaque* (Louvain: Publications Universitaires, 1970), II, 1, 143.

3 Aristotle's use of the metaphor of "hitting" the mean of virtue—e.g., "Virtue has the quality of hitting the mean" (tou mesou an eie stochastike [II, vi, 9, 1106b15; Rackham, p. 93])—may well be conceptually related to the image of missing the target which underlies the term "hamartia," sometimes (badly) translated as "tragic flaw." "Hamartia" is related to the verb "hamartano," the first sense of which is "to miss the target." See J. M. Bremer, *Hamartia* (Amsterdam: Hakkert, 1969), 63.

4 Kathleen V. Wilkes, "The Good Man and the Good for Man in Aristotle's *Ethics,*" in *Essays on Aristotle's Ethics,* ed. Amélie O. Rorty (Berkeley: University of California Press, 1980), 341–42.

5 E.g., Aristotle, *Metaphysics,* I, ii, 16, 983a: "But we must end with the contrary and (according to the proverb) the better view" (trans. Hugn Tredennick [1933; rpt. London: Heinemann, 1975], 17). The proverb alluded to is *deuteron ameinonon,* "second thoughts are better." All subsequent quotations from the *Metaphysics* will be taken from this edition and references will be given in the body of the text.

6 Hardie, *Aristotle's Ethical Theory,* 130.

7 Ibid., 131.

8 Gauthier and Jolif, *L'Ethique à Nicomaque,* II, 1, 145 and 150.

9 Greek text in *Physics,* trans. Philip Wicksteed and Francis Cornford (London: Heinemann, 1934), 2:180; here trans. mine. Subsequent quotation of the *Physics* will be taken from this edition and translation and will be noted in the body of the text.

10 Henri Bergson, *Introduction to Metaphysics,* trans. T. E. Hulme (New York: Putnam, 1912), 71. First published in *Revue de Métaphysique et de Morale* (January 1903).

11 Two of Zeno's four paradoxes mention halves explicitly: the paradox of the dichotomy and the paradox of the stadium. The paradox of Achilles and the tortoise is also frequently stated using halves (e.g., W. V. Metcalf, "Achilles and the Tortoise," *Mind* 51 [1942]: 89), even though any proper fraction— i.e., any fraction less than one—would do as well. This is, of course, also true of the paradox of the dichotomy: before covering a whole unit of terrain, we must first cover one-third of it, or eight-thirteenths, etc.

12 Hardie, *Aristotle's Ethical Theory,* 133.

13 See John Ferguson, *Aristotle* (New York: Twayne, 1972), 19. For discussions of Zeno's paradoxes, see Henri Bergson, *Creative Evolution,* trans. Arthur Mitchell (New York: Modern Library, 1944), 335–40; *Monist* 22 (July 1912): 179–98 (Russell on Bergson's theory of motion); and Bertrand Russell, *Our Knowledge of the External World* (New York: W. W. Norton, 1929).

14 Bergson, *Creative Evolution,* 333–35.

15 Bergson, *Introduction to Metaphysics,* 76.

16 Henri Bergson, *La Pensée et le mouvant* (1938; rpt. Paris: Presses Universitaires de France, 1975), 8.

17 John Neville Keynes, *Formal Logic* (London: Macmillan, 1894), 49.

18 Ibid., 49–50, 87.

19 The laws of excluded middle, contradiction, and identity are sometimes grouped together as the "laws of thought," one of the bases of classical logic. The Greek term for the "excluded middle," "metaxy," is not the same as the term used to describe the virtuous middle, "meson" or "mesotes," but it does clearly deal with a conceptual middle: "metaxy," literally the term "between," is usually translated "intermediate." Moreover, when Aristotle admits that the middle or intermediate can exist between contraries—as it must in fact exist in the doctrine of the middle (meson)-as-virtue—he calls this existing middle "metaxy," the same word he uses of the excluded middle only to deny its existence (*Metaphysics,* X, vii, 1–3, 1057a18–30). I am not in fact suggesting that the two theories are logically contradictory, since the difference between contraries and contradictories is certainly a crucial one. I am claiming, rather, that the two theories are based on incompatible conceptions of the middle and that the incompatibility is in itself significant as an expression of a fundamental hesitation in Aristotle's thought. Although my focus here is the law of excluded middle, much of what I say also applies to the law of contradiction.

20 Jan Lukasiewicz, "Aristotle on the Law of Contradiction," in *Articles on Aristotle 3, Metaphysics,* ed. Jonathan Barnes, Malcolm Schofield, and Richard Sorabji (London: Duckworth, 1979), 62.

21 John Stuart Mill, *Systems of Logic* (London: Parker, Son, and Bourn, 1862), 1:309; bk. 2, chap. 7, #4.

22 *Dictionary of Philosophy and Psychology,* ed. James Mark Baldwin (New York: Macmillan, 1928), 1:356.

23 Friedrich Ueberweg, *System of Logic,* trans. Thomas M. Lindsay (London: Longmans and Green, 1871), 263.

24 "Some, indeed, demand to have the law [of contradiction] proved, but this is because they lack education; for it shows lack of education not to know of what we should require proof, and of what we should not" (*Metaphysics,* IV, iv, 2, 1006a6–8; Tredennick, p. 163).

25 E. J. Lemmon, *Beginning Logic* (Indianapolis: Hacket, 1978), 53.

26 G. C. Field, "The Nature of Ethical Thinking," in *Psychical Research, Ethics and Logic,* Aristotelian Society Supplementary Volume 24 (London: Harrison and Sons, 1950), 5.

27 Ibid., 18–19.

28 Werner Jaeger, *Aristotle,* trans. Richard Robinson (Oxford: Clarendon, 1934), 221–22.

29 Ibid., 396–97.

30 Aristotle, *Poetics,* XIII, 2–5, 1452b–53a, trans. W. Hamilton Fyfe (1927; rpt. London: Heinemann, 1973), pp. 45–47. Subsequent quotations from the *Poetics* will be taken from this edition and references given in the body of the text. The word "hamartia" might better be translated "error" than "flaw."

31 It is possible that "good" and "bad," the two poles between which Aristotle places his hero, are not in fact contradictory (i.e., mutually exclusive), but rather are two ends of a continuum like black and white, between which a middle is possible. But the inconsistency of Aristotle's terms, here as in other cases, seems to me to reflect a genuine hesitation between two positions, expressed in part by the fact that he does not use the terms that most commonly denote the single opposition of good and bad in Greek, "agathos" and "kakos," and does not even repeat any of his terms for good and bad here: "epieikes," "seemly" or "fitting," yields to "arete," "excellence" or "virtue," and "mochtheros," "base," "unworthy," gives way to "poneros," "wicked" or "evil." It is as if the poles of goodness and badness were themselves destabilized by this variation.

32 For "spoudaios" opposed to "mochtheros," see Antisthenes (Plutarch, *Pericles* 1) in *Fragmenta Philosophorum graecorum,* ed. Fr. Mullach (Paris: Firmin Didot, 1867). For "spoudaios" opposed to "poneros," see Xénophon, *Helléniques,* II, iii, 19, trans. J. Hatzfeld (1936; rpt. Paris: Belles Lettres, 1973), p. 86.

33 Trans. T. M. Knox, in Georg Wilhelm Friedrich Hegel, *On Tragedy,* ed. Anne and Henry Paolucci (New York: Harper and Row, 1962), 237.

34 A. C. Bradley, "Hegel's Theory of Tragedy," in *Oxford Lectures on Poetry* (London: Macmillan, 1955), 72.

35 Cf. the description of Corrective Justice in book V of the *Nicomachean Ethics,* esp. V, iv, 1–4; Rackham, pp. 273–75.

36 René Girard, *Violence and the Sacred,* trans. Patrick Gregory (Baltimore: Johns Hopkins University Press, 1977), 14–15.

37 Ibid., 158.

38 Bradley, "Hegel's Theory of Tragedy," 72–73.

39 Girard, *Violence and the Sacred,* 149.

Chapter 3. The End Is the Beginning

1 Jean Racine, Preface to *Iphigénie, Oeuvres complètes,* ed. Raymond Picard, 2 vols. (Paris: Gallimard, Pléiade, 1950 and 1966), 1:671. The quotation is from Aristotle, *Poetics,* XIII, 1453a.

2 André Rivier, *Essai sur le tragique d'Euripide,* 2d ed. (Paris: Boccard, 1975), 161. This and all other translations from the French are mine unless otherwise noted.

3 D. J. Conacher, *Euripidean Drama* (Toronto: University of Toronto Press, 1967), 230.

4 *The Phoenician Women,* trans. with an introduction by Peter Burian and Brian Swann (New York: Oxford University Press, 1981), 4.

5 H. D. F. Kitto, *Greek Tragedy* (London: Methuen, 1939), 356.

6 Gilbert Murray, *Euripides and His Age* (1918; rpt. London: Oxford University Press, 1965), 74.

7 Burian and Swann, *Phoenician Women,* 4.

8 For a good review of the textual controversy, see Marylin B. Arthur, "Euripides' *Phoenissae* and the Politics of Justice" (Ph.D. diss., Yale University, 1975).

9 Even if Jocasta's scene of mediation, traditionally believed to have been invented by Euripides, did have a precedent in lyric poetry, as has been suggested by a recent archaeological discovery, Aeschylus, who probably knew the lyric version of the scene as well, did not include the scene of mediation in his *Seven against Thebes*. See Rachel Aélion, *Euripide héritier d'Eschyle* (Paris: Belles Lettres, 1983), 1:201.

10 René Girard, *Violence and the Sacred,* trans. Patrick Gregory (Baltimore: Johns Hopkins University Press, 1977), 155.

11 See, for example, Aristotle, *Nicomachean Ethics,* VI, vii, 5, 1142a12–17.

12 Helene P. Foley, *Ritual Irony: Poetry and Sacrifice in Euripides* (Ithaca, N.Y.: Cornell University Press, 1985), 122–23. Philip Vellacott also speaks of Jocasta's appeal as "the human aspect of the eternal law of Nature" (*Ironic Drama* [London: Cambridge University Press, 1975], 169).

13 This and all quotations from the play are taken from *Euripide V, Les Phéniciennes,* ed. Henri Grégoire, Louis Méridier, and Fernand Chapouthier (Paris: Belles Lettres, 1973). All English translations of Euripides are mine.

14 We must not forget the frequency of plowing images in the Oedipus story, starting with the metaphor of Oedipus plowing the field where he himself was sown (Sophocles, *Oedipus Tyrannus,* 1497–98).

15 A number of critics have pointed out that Jocasta's position is essentially democratic (as opposed to an oligarchic or a tyrannical one), among them Jacqueline de Romilly, "Les *Phéniciennes* d'Euripide ou l'actualité dans la tragédie grecque," *Revue de Philologie* 39 (1965): 30; Burian and Swann, *Phoenician Women,* 6; and Foley, *Ritual Irony,* 123.

16 Jean Bollack, *La réplique de Jocaste,* Cahiers de philologie 2 (Université de Lille III, 1977): 85–86.

17 Thucydides, *History of the Peloponnesian War,* trans. Charles Forster Smith (1920; rpt. London: Heinemann, 1953), III, 82.3–82.8; vol. 2, pp. 143–49.

18 Romilly, "Les *Phéniciennes* d'Euripide," 36–37, and Marylin Arthur, "The Choral Odes of the *Phoenissae*," *Harvard Studies in Classical Philology* 81 (1977): 185. Vincenzo Di Benedetto also cites this passage of Thucydides in speaking more generally of Euripides' attitude toward the middle class. *Euripide: Teatro e società* (Turin: Giulio Einaudi, 1971), 211.

19 In fact Aristotle himself uses the example of courage in his first exposition of the doctrine of the virtuous middle in the *Nicomachean Ethics,* and he defines courage [andreia] as the mean between being rash [thrasos] and being cowardly [deilos] (II, ii, 7, 1104a20–23). In the quoted passage, Thucydides uses two of these terms.

20 Six in eleven lines. Cf. the opening of Sophocles' *Antigone,* in which the heroine's first speech is riddled with negatives, as if in anticipation of the character's subsequent capacity for opposition.

21 Foley, *Ritual Irony,* 108; Burian and Swann, *Phoenician Women,* 4; Walter Ludwig, *Sapheneia: Ein Beitrag zur Formkunst im Spätwerk des Euripides* (Ph.D. diss., University of Tübingen, 1954), 130–35.

22 Aeschylus, *Seven against Thebes,* 375–685. My analysis of the shield speech scene in Euripides' play is indebted to Froma Zeitlin's study of Aeschylus' scene, *Under the Sign of the Shield* (Rome: Edizioni dell'Ateneo, 1982).

23 Emile Boisacq, *Dictionnaire étymologique de la langue grecque,* 4th ed. (Heidelberg: Winter, 1950), 629.

24 Girard points this out in *Violence and the Sacred,* 44–45.

Chapter 4. The (Still) Birth of the Racinian Individual

1 "Where the French tragedian particularly finds fault with his Greek model is the inadequacy of dramatic concentration, the lack of rigor and *necessity*" (Raymond Picard in Jean Racine, *Oeuvres complètes,* 2 vols. [Paris: Gallimard, Pléiade, 1950 and 1966], 2:1135, note to Racine's own notes to the *Phoenissae*). Future references to this edition will be given in the body of the text.

2 Jean Racine, *Théâtre complet,* ed. J. Morel and A. Viala (Paris: Garnier Frères, 1980). Future references to *La Thébaïde* will be taken from this edition, and line numbers will be given in the body of the text.

3 I disagree with J. M. Otho, according to whom "both plays plunge the audience *in medias res*" ("Euripides' *Phoenissae* and Racine's *La Thébaïde:* A Comparative Analysis," *Museum Africum* 6 [1977–78]: 82). *Dramatically* Euripides' play begins very slowly, Racine's instantly.

4 Marcel Gutwirth observes that "in Jocaste two distinct modalities of lucidity coexist without ever joining: Phèdre's prophetic lucidity and Oenone's practical lucidity" (*Jean Racine: Un itinéraire poétique* [Montréal: Presses de l'Université de Montréal, 1970], 18). The "Phèdre" in Jocaste sees the inevitable movement toward disaster which the "Oenone" in her nonetheless attempts to put off indefinitely.

5 Judd Hubert in his fine chapter on *La Thébaïde* points out the importance of the word "obstacle": "Terms like *bord, bornes, obstacle, partager, intervalle, dernier, limite* abound in *La Thébaïde:* they express man's inability to put a brake on fatality and to create a stable order in the world" (*Essai d'exégèse racinienne* [Paris: Nizet, 1956], 42). Michael Edwards also notes the para-

doxical nature of the word, in *La tragédie racinienne* (Paris: La Pensée universelle, 1972), 346, n. 85.

6 Jules Brody emphasizes the importance of the word "sang" in the play: "in no
other play, according to available statistics, is a single word used so frequently"
("Racine's *Thébaïde:* An analysis," in *Racine: Modern Judgements,* ed. R. C.
Knight [Nashville: Aurora, 1970], 179).

7 "The very last" could also mean that the entire royal family must die in order
to bring peace to Thebes (Brody, "Racine's *Thébaïde,*" 179), but to the extent
that the strength of the oracle lies in its potential as a goad to action, or at
least as an escape form the very doom which, at some level, it generally an-
nounces, this bleakest interpretation must be kept in the background, which
is in fact the case here: even those who claim to be fatalistic still act as if a
way out were possible.

8 Maurice Grévisse, *Le Bon Usage* (Gembloux, Belgium: Editions J. Duculot,
1975), 272, #298. "Sang" can be pluralized in the sense of different kinds of
blood, but in that case the unit is established (each kind of blood). A doctor
could of course speak of the last blood available, but again this works only
to the extent that a unit is understood (e.g., the last pint of blood).

9 Cf. "Il rendrait à chacun son légitime rang. / . . . il se rend" (454–56), an all
but explicit wordplay on "rang"/"rend." See also 488–91.

10 Hubert, *Essai d'exégèse racinienne,* 52, n. 3.

11 Georges Poulet, "Notes sur le temps racinien," in *Racine,* ed. Wolfgang Theile
(Darmstadt: Wissenschaftliche Buchgesellschaft, 1976), 104.

12 As Hubert puts it: "In general, in Racine's theater, the unity of time takes on
a paradoxical and antithetical character: it constitutes a luminous focal point
on which all the most evil and active influences of the past, and sometimes,
as in *Iphigénie* and *Athalie,* the determinations of the future converge" (*Essai
d'exégèse racinienne,* 52, n. 4). I would add only that if there were not *initially* a possibility of freedom of definition in the present, there would be no
"play" in the relation between past and future, and therefore no tragedy.

13 These lines came after line 1054 in the original edition of the play (*Théâtre
complet,* p. 803).

14 The impossibility in Racine's play of distinguishing between the two brothers,
even in death, is exacerbated by Racine's making them into (presumably) identical twins, thus "resolving" (or rather sidestepping) the contradiction whereby
Sophocles makes Polyneices the elder brother (*Oedipus at Colonus,* 374–76)
and Euripides makes him the younger (*Phoenissae,* 71).

15 "That minor but nonetheless threatening character found in all of Racinian
tragedy as the Destruction of Tragedy, the Individual" (Roland Barthes, *Sur
Racine* [Paris: Seuil, 1963], 67). Whether the individual is the "destruction
of tragedy" or not still remains to be seen.

16 As Brody puts it, "The Créon-Antigone-Hémon love triangle is badly out of
tune with the terrible tenor of the rest of the drama" ("Racine's *Thébaïde,*" 186).

17 See lines 660–62, 729–30, 1204–5, 1337–38, 1386–90, 1476–78.

18 The total line count for the two characters is very close, about four hundred lines each.

Chapter 5. Euripides' *Andromache*

1 For an excellent overview of the critical history of the problem, see D. J. Conacher, *Euripidean Drama* (Toronto: University of Toronto Press, 1967), 171–72.

2 Van Lennep, "Euripides, poietes sophos" (Ph.D. diss., University of Amsterdam, 1934), quoted in J. C. Kamerbeek, "L'Andromaque d'Euripide," *Mnemosyne* 11 (1943): 48.

3 E.g., G. M. A. Grube, *The Drama of Euripides* (New York: Barnes and Noble, 1941), 211, n. 2.

4 A. W. Verrall is perhaps the first to defend the theory that Neoptolemos' murder takes place before the play begins, but he bases that theory on the hypothesis that the *Andromache* is the second play of a trilogy, and thus reestablishes the play's temporal unity only at the expense of its dramatic integrity. *Essays on Four Plays of Euripides* (Cambridge: Cambridge University Press, 1905), 1 and 15–16. As far as I know Albin Lesky is the first to have fully understood the play's chronology. *Gesammelte Schrifte,* ed. Walther Kraus (Bern: Francke Verlag, 1966), 144ff.

5 As Kamerbeek points out, "He is being spoken of at every instant" ("L'Andromaque d'Euripide," 67).

6 *Andromache,* 1. All quotations of the play are taken from *Euripide II, Andromaque,* ed. Louis Méridier (Paris: Belles Lettres, 1973). Subsequent references to this edition will be indicated by line numbers given in the body of the text.

7 "A woman from 'the continent' is an Asian" (Méridier, *Andromaque,* 119, n. 2).

8 Méridier, *Andromaque,* 127, n. 3.

9 "[W]e attribute Considerateness, Understanding, Prudence [phronesin], and Intelligence [noun] to the same persons when we say of people that they 'are old enough to show consideration and intelligence [noun],' and are prudent [phronimous] and understanding persons." *Nicomachean Ethics,* VI, xi, 2, 1143a26–28; Rackham, p. 361. See also p. 328, note a: "the popular use of the word [nous] [is] 'good sense' or practical intelligence."

10 See Patricia Neils Boulter, "*Sophia* and *Sophrosyne* in Euripides' *Andromache,*" *Phoenix* 20 (1966): 56.

11 For a more explicit wordplay of the same nature, see Aeschylus, *Agamemnon,* 689–90; Helen's name is there interpreted as meaning "helenas," "helandros," and "heleptolis": destroyer of ships, men, and cities.

12 Anne Pippin Burnett, *Catastrophe Survived: Euripides' Plays of Mixed Reversal* (Oxford: Clarendon, 1971), 149–50.

13 Paul Friedländer, "Die griechische Tragödie und das Tragische," *Die Antike* 2 (1926): 101, trans. mine.

14 Once again my analysis here is influenced by Girard, but I do not see Neoptolemos as a clear-cut example of a sacrificial victim, for in this case the choice of the victim is not arbitrary, that is to say it is not a pure difference. The crowd's goal is not merely to establish a difference (in the person of the victim) and expel it in order to unify the community and reaffirm its identity; rather, the victim already stands for the principle of heroic difference, and the collectivity here aims to destroy (rather than use) the principle of difference itself. I would therefore see the struggle in terms of two opposing principles or mechanisms, and this does not, I think, completely conform to Girard's analysis of the sacrificial crisis.

15 At 1116; at least this is a more honorable title than the one Orestes confers upon himself just before making his inelegant exit from the drama, "metrophontes," "mother-murderer" (999).

16 "It is clear from 1161–5 that the narrator holds Apollo to be responsible and Eur. is not concerned to indicate his personal belief. The indefinite *tis* is used elsewhere in similar contexts either because the identity of the deity is uncertain or to add a touch of mystery" (*Andromache,* ed. P. T. Stevens [Oxford: Clarendon, 1971], 233).

17 Friedrich Nietzsche, *The Birth of Tragedy,* trans. Walter Kaufmann (New York: Vantage, 1967), 45–46.

18 Mythologically this refers to the fact that Neoptolemos was raised on the island of Skyros.

Chapter 6. *La Guerre de Troi(e)s*

1 *Mithridate* also opens with mention of fidelity ("On nous faisait, Arbate, un fidèle rapport"), once again playing on Racine's own attitude toward his material ("J'ai suivi l'histoire avec beaucoup de fidélité," preface to *Mithridate*).

2 E.g., "Particularly characteristic of *Andromaque* . . . is its marvelous unity" (Judd Hubert, *Essai d'exégèse racinienne* [Paris: Nizet, 1956], 76).

3 Peter France, *Racine: Andromaque* (London: Edward Arnold, 1977), 27.

4 The closest the play comes to allowing all three members of a love triangle to cohabit the stage is in a very brief transition between two confrontations, one between Andromaque and Hermione (III, iv) and one between Andromaque and Pyrrhus (III, vi).

5 It is quite possible that Racine plays with the homonyms "trois" and "Troie" in several places. Andromaque in speaking to Pyrrhus describes Hector, Astyanax, and herself as "tous trois, Seigneur, par vos soins réunis" (379), "tous trois" thus being a kind of de facto representation of "tout(e) Troie." Also, the word "Troie" occurs several times in context with the ordinal numbers "premier" and "second" (230, 632, 1592).

6 The patterns of the four characters are revealing. Pyrrhus is evenly divided between saying "Oui" and saying "Non," with five occurrences of each ("Oui" at 185, 365, 617, 949, 1281, "Non" or "Non, non" at 217, 229, 674, 693, 917).

Hermione begins with one "Oui" (533) in a brief attempt at good will toward Oreste but the fact that she then limits herself to "Non" (845, 1163, 1315, 1407, 1418, 1473) is in keeping with her contrary nature, which virtually defines *l'esprit de contradiction*. Andromaque, finally, reverses Hermione's pattern. After exclusively using "Non" (305, 335, 897, 1009, 1036, 1037) as a reflection of her refusal of the present, she pronounces one all-important "Oui," her promise to marry Pyrrhus (1064).

7 In this Oreste is a trendsetter, since both *Iphigénie* and *Athalie* also begin with the word "Oui."

8 "Racine's main characters . . . are often aware that they have a kind of inferiority, and their entire effort consists not of discovering or affirming their heroic individuality in the eyes of the others, but rather of cheating, either by masking this inferiority to their own eyes, or by trying to change their identity" (Hubert, *Essai d'exégèse racinienne,* 77). In Racine this masking is itself a part of the constitution of the heroic individual.

9 Eléonore M. Zimmermann calls Oreste "le plus déraciné" of the play's characters, but he is by the same token one of the most "racinien"; it is his own alienation from himself which keeps him tied to the problem of his identity. *La Liberté et le destin dans le théâtre de Jean Racine* (Saratoga, Calif.: Anma Libri, Stanford French and Italian Studies, 1982), 28.

10 Andromaque-Pyrrhus (I, iv; III, vi–vii); Pyrrhus-Hermione (IV, v); Hermione-Oreste (II, ii; III, ii; IV, iii; V, iii); Andromaque-Hermione (III, iv); and Pyrrhus-Oreste (I, ii; II, iv).

11 Georges Poulet, "Notes sur le temps racinien," in *Racine,* ed. Wolfgang Theile (Darmstadt: Wissenschaftliche Buchgesellschaft, 1976), 103.

12 The word "île," whether in the singular or the plural, occurs only here in all of Racine's theater. Bryant C. Freeman and Alan Batson, *Concordance du théâtre et des poésies de Jean Racine* (Ithaca, N.Y.: Cornell University Press, 1968), 1: 629.

13 J. Morel and A. Viala in Jean Racine, *Théâtre complet* (Paris: Garnier Frères, 1980), 842.

14 Marcel Gutwirth, *Jean Racine: Un itinéraire poétique* (Montréal: Presses de l'Université de Montréal, 1970), 50.

15 I disagree strongly with Lucien Goldmann, who claims that Andromaque loses her tragic status by choosing life over death. *Le Dieu caché* (Paris: Gallimard, 1959), 358. Goldmann grossly oversimplifies Andromaque's final action, which is rather a refusal of any simple choice.

16 In Racine's first version of the play, Andromaque actually appears in the final act and confesses her attachment to the dead Pyrrhus: "Pyrrhus de mon Hector semble avoir pris la place" (*Oeuvres complètes,* ed. Raymond Picard, 2 vols. [Paris: Gallimard, Pléiade, 1950 and 1966], 1:1089). In Euripides' play Andromache's growing attachment to Neoptolemos is suggested but remains implicit: even though she bitterly refers to him as the murderer of Hector (*Andromache,* 403), she also asks their son to give him a goodbye kiss for

her when she thinks she is about to die (416–18). Racine's genius is in making Andromaque's ambiguous feelings for Pyrrhus explicit (first version), and then in masking them (revised version).

17 "The end aimed at is the representation not of qualities of character but of some action; and while character makes men what they are, it is their actions and experiences that make them happy or the opposite. They do not therefore act to represent character, but character-study is included for the sake of action" (*Poetics,* VI, 1450a, trans. W. Hamilton Fyfe [1927; rpt. London: Heinemann, 1973], 25).

Chapter 7. The Heroic Oath

1 The prologue has been persistently attacked as inauthentic, but Bernard Knox makes a thoroughly convincing defense of it, speculating that Euripides may have been experimenting with "a new form of prologue." "Euripides' *Iphigenia in Aulis* 1–163 (in that order)," *Yale Classical Studies* 22 (1972): 259.

2 This and all quotations of the play are taken from *Euripide VIII, Iphigénie à Aulis,* ed. François Jouan (Paris: Belles Lettres, 1983). All translations of Euripides and Aeschylus are mine.

3 Helene P. Foley has noted the "metatheatrical image" of Agamemnon "as a writer or rewriter of myth," acting as "the poet's double." *Ritual Irony* (Ithaca, N.Y.: Cornell University Press, 1985), 94.

4 Bernard Knox, "Second Thoughts in Greek Tragedy," *Greek Roman and Byzantine Studies* 7, no. 3 (1966): 229.

5 Philip Vellacott, *Ironic Drama* (Cambridge: Cambridge University Press, 1975), 174.

6 E.g., D. J. Conacher, *Euripidean Drama* (Toronto: University of Toronto Press), 260; Knox, "Second Thoughts," 231.

7 At line 801 out of 1629. Even if we admit the problematic nature of calculating the middle with precision because of textual difficulties, it seems reasonable to assume that Achilles' arrival onstage was felt by the audience to be more or less the middle of the play.

8 François Jouan, *Iphigénie à Aulis,* 143, n. 2 (trans. mine).

9 As Jouan points out (151, nn. 2 and 3), the contradictions in Achilles' position have led critics to question the authenticity of a number of his lines in this scene. Although the issue of textual interpolations is beyond the scope of the present study, I might point out that it is precisely around the issue of self-contradiction, an issue crucial to Euripidean theater, that at various times critics have amended and abridged plays like the *Medea* almost out of existence.

10 It is an echo in terms of literary history, Aeschylus' play predating Euripides' by more than half a century, but an anticipation in terms of the myth.

11 Aristotle, *Nicomachean Ethics,* I, iv, 5, 1095a32–35.

12 *Poetics,* XV, 1454a, trans. W. Hamilton Fyfe (1927; rpt. London: Heinemann, 1973), 55–57.

13 H. D. F. Kitto, *Greek Tragedy* (London: Methuen, 1939), 369.

14 Albin Lesky, "Psychologie bei Euripides," in Fondation Hardt, *Euripide,* Entretiens sur l'antiquité classique 6 (Geneva: Albert Kundig, 1960), 148 (trans. mine).

15 Bruno Snell, "From Tragedy to Philosophy: *Iphigenia in Aulis,"* in *Greek Tragedy,* ed. Erich Segal (New York: Harper and Row, 1983), 403–4.

16 André Rivier, *Essai sur le tragique d'Euripide,* 2d edition (Paris: Boccard, 1975), 72 (trans. mine).

Chapter 8. Middle, Model, Muddle

1 Jean Racine, *Oeuvres complètes,* ed. Raymond Picard, 2 vols. (Paris: Gallimard, Pléiade, 1950 and 1966), 1:671. Subsequent reference to this edition will be bracketed in the body of the text.

2 Timothy J. Reiss sees debt and economic exchange as organizing principles in *Iphigénie. Tragedy and Truth: Studies in the Development of a Renaissance and Neoclassical Discourse* (New Haven: Yale University Press, 1980), chap. 10, "Classicism, the Individual, and Economic Exchange (*Iphigénie*)," 240–58.

3 On this point I am somewhat in disagreement with Gérard Defaux's analysis of *Iphigénie.* Defaux says, in discussing the meaning of Eriphile's sacrifice, "In such a [Girardian] system [of sacrifice], the identity of the victim basically has little importance." "Violence et Passion dans l'*Iphigénie* de Racine," *Papers on French Seventeenth Century Literature* 11, no. 21 (1984): 701. But I would argue that Iphigénie and Eriphile are extremely important examples of Girard's mimetic doubles, even more interesting in fact than the enemy brothers of the *Phoenissae* and *La Thébaïde,* for in *Iphigénie* the mimetic link between the two cousins remains implicit and is, I would argue, the crux of the play. Now it is true that in Girard's system even an arbitrarily chosen victim bears a relation of mimesis to his or her sacrificers, by the very mechanism of sacrifice. But in any case the identity of Eriphile in Racine's play is far from gratuitous, and it seems to me that the essential link between the two cousins is what is lacking in Defaux's analysis. He interprets Iphigénie's crucial line, "Oui, vous l'aimez, perfide!" as "serving only one purpose, which is to tell us once again that Violence is the father and king of everything" (709).

4 Charles Mauron, *L'Inconscient dans l'oeuvre et la vie de Racine* (Gap: Ophrys, 1957), 138.

5 Roland Barthes, *Sur Racine* (Paris: Seuil, 1963), 104.

6 Eriphyle is mentioned by Pausanias (*Description of Greece,* "Corinth," II, 1, 8, and II, 23, 2), whom Racine also names as his principal source for the character that he himself calls Eriphile, i.e., the daughter of Helen and Theseus, but that character remains nameless in Pausanias ("Corinth," II, 22, 6). Perhaps the idea of using the name "Eriphyle" was suggested by this juxtaposition. Eriphyle is also mentioned in a passage of Aristotle's *Poetics* which Racine translated (XIV, 1453b). Georges May speculates that in the spelling "Eriphile"

(rather than "Eriphyle"), Racine may have been influenced by Ariosto's spelling of the name ("Eriffila") (*D'Ovide à Racine* [Paris: Presses Universitaires de France, 1949], 146–47). But is the insertion of the "-iphi-" element not another possible motive?

7 Agamemnon in fact changes his mind about the sacrifice no fewer than seven times. He is first against it (67–68) and is then convinced by Ulysse to go through with it (89–90) and to send for Iphigénie and Clytemnestre (*#1*); writes the second letter forbidding them to come (129–32) (*#2*); receives the news of their arrival as a sign of the inevitable (389–90) (*#3*); weakens before Clytemnestre's fury (1318) (*#4*); reconfirms his decision because of Achille's resistance (1425–28) (*#5*); orders Clytemnestre to flee in secret with Iphigénie (1465–66) (*#6*); and finally must give in to the sacrifice when Eriphile spreads the story of the oracle's demands (1704–6) (*#7*). As Russell Pfohl puts it, "Racine is by no means immune . . . to Euripides' fundamentally ironic view of vacillations that attempt to pass for heroism and unmitigated paternal sorrow" (*Racine's Iphigénie: Literary Rehearsal and Recognition* [Geneva: Droz, 1974], 60). In fact Racine makes Agamemnon's irresolution, which in Euripides' drama is essentially played out in a single time span of hesitation at the beginning of the play, into a sort of vibrato, an endless back-and-forth movement typical of Racine's characters.

8 Lucien Goldmann, *Le Dieu caché* (Paris: Gallimard, 1959), 402–3; Barthes, *Sur Racine*, 104; Reiss, *Tragedy and Truth*, 251–52.

9 Barthes, *Sur Racine*, 107 (emphasis in the original).

10 E.g., "Iphigénie is a tragedy that ends well." R. Picard in Racine, *Oeuvres complètes* 1:1143.

11 Goldmann, *Le Dieu caché*, 405.

12 Cf. the ambiguous status of the defeated Hector at the end of the *Iliad.*

Chapter 9. "A horse! a horse! my kingdom for a horse!"

1 The *Phoenissae* and the *Iphigeneia in Aulis* are both very late plays, the latter having been produced only posthumously. Only the *Andromache* is even nearly contemporary with the *Hippolytos,* and some would put it a number of years later than the *Hippolytos.* See Louis Méridier, *Euripide II, Andromaque* (Paris: Belles Lettres, 1973), 100–106.

2 Bruno Snell, *Scenes from Greek Drama* (Berkeley: University of California Press, 1964), 59. Snell acknowledges that the link between the *Hippolytos* and Socrates was made as early as 1880, by Theodor Barthold.

3 In commenting on the *Hippolytos,* 380–81, E. R. Dodds says, "We are reminded of Aristotle's analysis of the *akrates* and the *akolastos* ("intemperate") a century later. As the Nurse puts it, you can be *sophron,* and yet desire evil" ("Euripides the Irrationalist," *Classical Review* 43, no. 3 [1929]: 99). This is of course an anti-Socratic position.

4 Aristotle, *Nicomachean Ethics*, VII, i, 6–ii, 1, 1145b13–28, trans. H. Rackham (1926; rpt. London: Heinemann, 1982), 377–379.

5 Snell, *Scenes from Greek Drama*, 65–67.

6 E. R. Dodds, *The Greeks and the Irrational* (Berkeley: University of California Press, 1959).

7 Snell, *Scenes from Greek Drama*, 69.

8 Froma Zeitlin, "The Power of Aphrodite: Eros and the Boundaries of the Self in the *Hippolytus*," in *Directions in Euripidean Criticism*, ed. P. Burian (Durham, N.C.: Duke University Press, 1985), 56.

9 This and all quotations from the play are taken from *Euripide II, Hippolyte*, ed. Louis Méridier (Paris: Belles Lettres, 1973).

10 As J. M. Bremer points out, Hippolytos' description of the meadow also goes against the poetic tradition of the erotic meadow: "The text of 73ff. and the action and attitude implied in these words were for a Greek audience a *paradoxon*" ("The Meadow of Love and Two Passages in Euripides' *Hippolytus*," *Mnemosyne* 28, no. 3 [1975]: 276).

11 J. Pigeaud sees in the description of the meadow "the refusal of the transformation, modification, and alteration of nature . . . , the absence of culture conceived as the profound modification of the soil" ("Euripide et la connaissance de soi," *Les Etudes Classiques* 44 [1976]: 7).

12 E.g., Sophocles' *Electra*, 744: "kamptontos hippou."

13 "What undoubtedly mainly emerged for the early audience [of the *Hippolytus*] was Hippolytus' immoderation, which contradicts his claim of *sophrosyne*" (Jean J. Smoot, "Hippolytus as Narcissus," *Arethusa* 9, no 1 [1976]: 40).

14 For the essential similarity of Phaedra and Hippolytos, see Bernard M. W. Knox, "The *Hippolytus* of Euripides," in *Greek Tragedy*, ed Erich Segal (New York: Harper and Row, 1983), 311–31; Charles P. Segal, "The Tragedy of the *Hippolytus*: The Waters of Ocean and the Untouched Meadow," *Harvard Studies in Classical Philology* 70 (1965): 154–59; and Bernard D. Frischer, "*Concordia Discors* and Characterization in Euripides' *Hippolytos*," *Greek Roman and Byzantine Studies* 11, no. 2 (1970): 85–100.

15 See Zeitlin, "Power of Aphrodite," 102.

16 David Claus, "Phaedra and the Socratic Paradox," *Yale Classical Studies* 22 (1972): 237.

17 Ibid., 237.

18 This is true in spite of the Nurse's confession to Hippolytos, which has infinitely less to do with Phaedra in this play than it has in Racine's.

19 There is a long critical debate on the sense of "aidos" in this passage of the *Hippolytos*. For an excellent review of the different positions, which to my knowledge all differ considerably from the one I am taking here, see Marcel Orban, "*Hippolyte*: Palinodie ou revanche," *Les Etudes Classiques* 49 (1981): 12–13, n. 26.

20 "Due measure, proportion," Liddell and Scott, *A Greek-English Lexicon* (Oxford: Clarendon, 1930), 1:859.

21 The instability of "kairos," its inadequacy as a barrier separating forward-looking from backward-looking "aidos," is, as we have seen, endemic to any virtuous middle. As J. Pigeaud puts it, "kairos" is "a virtually intemporal instant, an instant without duration" ("Euripide,"18).

22 I maintain that although the Nurse compromises Phaedra by approaching Hippolytos and revealing Phaedra's passion, Phaedra herself never ceases to resist it. As W. S. Barrett in his thorough edition of the play observes, Euripides' characterization of Phaedra demands that "she must be allowed to fight against her love to the very end, and the approach to Hippolytos must be made without her consent and indeed against her wish" (*Hippolytos* [Oxford: Clarendon, 1964], 252).

23 Méridier translates this as "il prendra . . . une leçon de mesure" (*Hippolyte*, 57).

24 At line 731 out of 1466.

25 As Méridier points out, one would expect a clearer opposition here: "Instead of 'ten d'hopos etynchanen,' one would expect 'ten d'adikon,' or 'ten phronousan tadika' " (*Hippolyte*, 65, n. 1). Barrett explains that this first voice, which is not placed in strict opposition to the just one, "might be dishonest or not" (*Hippolytos*, 340).

26 *Nicomachean Ethics*, II, ii, 7, 1104a20–23.

27 See Charles P. Segal's discussion of Hippolytos as a model of adolescence in "Pentheus and Hippolytus on the Couch and on the Grid: Psychoanalytic and Structural Readings of Greek Tragedy," *Classical World* 72 (1978): 129–48.

28 Zeitlin points this out, "Power of Aphrodite," 193, n. 32.

29 Obviously the *Hippolytos* passage could not borrow from the *Phaedrus*, since Plato was born in 427 B.C., the year after the *Hippolytos* was produced. But it is very possible that the *Phaedrus* was in fact influenced by the *Hippolytos*. As Harry C. Avery states, this was a drama that remained imprinted in Athenian minds and memories for an unusually long time (" 'My Tongue Swore, But My Mind is Unsworn,' " *Transactions of the American Philological Association* 99 [1968]: 19–35). The relation I am trying to sketch out here between Euripides and Plato is further complicated by the fact that the spokesman and central character of the Platonic dialogues, Socrates, was very nearly a contemporary of Euripides, and was indeed very active during Euripides' career as a dramatist.

30 In *Plato*, trans. Harold North Fowler (1914; rpt. London: Heinemann, 1933), 1:495–97.

31 E. R. Dodds, "Plato and the Irrational Soul," in *Plato*, ed. Gregory Vlastos (Notre Dame, Ind.: University of Notre Dame Press, 1978), 2:221.

32 T. E. Jessop, "The Metaphysics of Plato," *Journal of Philosophical Studies* 5 (1930): 42.

33 Aristotle, *Poetics*, trans. W. Hamilton Fyfe (1927; rpt. London: Heinemann, 1973), 103.

34 E. R. Dodds, "The *Aidos* of Phaedra and the Meaning of the *Hippolytus*, *Classical Review* 39 (1925): 103–4.

35 Zeitlin is perhaps correct in saying that "Hippolytus' final physical gesture at last, even if only for a moment, creates on the open stage an interior dimension for the body that by now has experienced for itself the boundary between inside and outside" ("Power of Aphrodite," 76), and a number of critics have noticed the similarity in Phaedra's and Hippolytos' gestures. Nonetheless I maintain that the distinction between "kephale" and "prosopon" is especially important here. As Zeitlin later points out (95), the "prosopon" may be necessary to play a role, and may thus suggest that Hippolytos has recognized alterity. But I would argue that in this case, since Hippolytos' face is itself his tragic mask, it also signals a refusal of depth.

36 Zeitlin, "Power of Aphrodite," 64.

37 Pigeaud, "Euripide," 23.

Chapter 10. Excluding the Excluded Middle

1 Francesco Orlando, *Toward a Freudian Theory of Literature*, trans. Charmaine Lee (Baltimore: Johns Hopkins University Press, 1978), 192 and 194. The quotations of Freud are all taken from *Introductory Lectures on Psycho-Analysis*, Standard Edition, and are, respectively, part 1, 15: 76–77; part 1, 15: 66; and part 3, 16: 301. An important progression in the four plays of Euripides that Racine used is the movement from dramas which concentrate on the relation between the individual and the collectivity (saving the city in the *Phoenissae*, Neoptolemos' heroic stand against the Delphians in the *Andromache*) toward tragedies which focus on the individual (particularly the *Hippolytos*). The articulation between the collectively oriented and the individually oriented comes in Racine's own reading of the *Iphigeneia in Aulis;* as I have suggested in my analysis, Racine's *Iphigénie* is not only about the relation between Agamemnon's daughter and the departing Greeks, as Euripides' play is, but also about the relation of resemblance between Iphigénie and Eriphile.

2 For a diametrically opposite interpretation of "l'aimable Trézène" as a place of nostalgic innocence, see Timothy J. Reiss, *Tragedy and Truth* (New Haven: Yale University Press, 1980), 265–66.

3 "*Dessein* and *dessin* are the same word. . . . In the seventeenth century *dessin* was often written *dessein*" (Emile Littré, *Dictionnaire de la langue française* [Paris: Hachette, 1963], 2:1764).

4 Liddell and Scott, *A Greek-English Lexicon* (Oxford: Clarendon, 1940), 1:76.

5 Michael Edwards notes "the almost mathematical precision of the word *moitié*" (*La Tragédie racinienne* [Paris: La Pensée Universelle, 1972], 259).

6 Hippolyte tries to leave Trézène for many different reasons: first to look for Thésée (purportedly) and to flee Aricie (really), then to consolidate his and Aricie's claims to the throne of Athens, next to investigate the rumor of Thésée's return, and finally as an exile, hoping to clear his name by killing monsters. Although the reasons for Hippolyte's attempts at getting away change, the underlying mechanism of failure to escape does not.

7 E.g., Lucien Goldmann, *Le Dieu caché* (Paris: Gallimard, 1959), 423.

8 "Dessiner," according to Littré, is nothing but a variant of "désigner" (*Dictionnaire de la langue française* 2:1764).

9 Roman Jakobson, "Linguistique et théorie de la communication," *Essais de linguistique générale,* trans. Nicolas Ruwet (Paris: Minuit, 1963), 91. In this particular essay the terms "encodeur" and "émetteur" (90) are used rather than "destinateur," which Jakobson uses elsewhere.

10 Umberto Eco, *A Theory of Semiotics* (Bloomington: Indiana University Press, 1976), 8.

11 Even the delivery of a message as straightforward as the news of Thésée's (supposed) death takes the form of an involuntary confession: "Je voudrais vous cacher une triste nouvelle, / Madame, mais il faut que je vous la révèle" (317–18).

12 Goldmann, *Le Dieu caché,* 423.

13 "To live on the pretext that one no longer needs to die: that is Phèdre's whole sin" (Marcel Gutwirth, *Jean Racine: Un itinéraire poétique* [Montréal: Presses de l'Université de Montréal, 1970], 27).

14 The prominent exception is the repeated scene between Hippolyte and Aricie (V, i, repeating II, ii). Otherwise the only repetitions are between characters and their confidants (Phèdre, Oenone; Hippolyte, Théramène). By contrast *Andromaque* repeats almost every important confrontation scene at least once.

15 Cf. "perix aphron," Euripides, *Hippolytos,* 1210. See chapter 9.

16 Jean Racine, *Théâtre complet,* ed. J. Morel and A. Viala (Paris: Garnier Frères, 1980), 601. Perhaps the reason why this error was not caught is that the error does not make the text completely nonsensical.

17 Georges Poulet, "Notes sur le temps racinien," in *Racine,* ed. Wolfgang Theile (Darmstadt: Wissenschaftliche Buchgesellschaft, 1976), 106–7.

18 Roland Barthes, *Sur Racine* (Paris: Seuil, 1963), 113.

19 Cf. Euripides, *Hippolytos,* 383–87, and Phaedra's inability to find the "kairos" or mediating moment between precriminal "aidos" and criminal "aidos." See chapter 9.

20 Cf. Martine Reid's use of the term "récits blancs" in her analysis of Oenone's account to Thésée (IV, i) and Hippolyte's report to Aricie (V, i). The "blank narrative" is "absent and present within the text, a subterranean layer which underlies the discourse of the stage, a truth which cannot manage to break the surface" ("Tout *Phèdre,* Une histoire d'enfants," *Papers on French Seventeenth Century Literature* 11, no. 21 [1984]: 660–61).

21 As Roland Barthes puts it, "the final word is stolen from Hippolyte" (*Sur Racine,* 115).

22 Clément Rosset, *La Philosophie tragique* (Paris: Presses Universitaires de France, 1960), 147 and 101.

Chapter 11. To Speak or Not to Speak

1 *La Vie de Jean Racine* (Paris: Plon, 1928), 142.

2 Jean Racine, *Oeuvres complètes,* ed. Raymond Picard, 2 vols. (Paris: Gallimard,

1950 and 1966), 1:999. Subsequent references to this edition will be given in the body of the text.

3 Eugène Vinaver, "Le pathétique retrouvé," in *Racine,* ed. Wolfgang Theile, (Darmstadt: Wissenschaftliche Buchgesellschaft, 1976), 126–27.

4 "The obsessive concern during the seventeenth century with clysters and bleedings, with assuring the efficient evacuation of peccant humors, shows plainly that the medical practices of that age were based on the principle of expulsion and purification" (René Girard, *Violence and the Sacred,* trans. Patrick Gregory [Baltimore: Johns Hopkins University Press, 1977], 289).

5 Ibid., 287.

6 Ibid., 291–92.

7 Aristotle, *Poetics,* XIII, 2–5, 1452b–1453b.

8 Michel Butor, "Racine et les dieux," in *Répertoire: Etudes et conférences, 1948–1959* (Paris: Minuit, 1960), 55.

9 Ibid., 60.

10 Francesco Orlando, *Toward a Freudian Theory of Literature,* trans. Charmaine Lee (Baltimore: Johns Hopkins University Press, 1978), 12.

11 For Racine's marginal notes on the *Phaedrus,* see Racine, *Oeuvres complètes* 2:901–2.

12 Girard, *Violence and the Sacred,* 292–93.

13 Racine owned two editions of Plato, the 1534 Basel edition and the 1578 Henri Estienne edition. The *Republic* is the only work of Plato's to which Racine left marginal notes in both editions.

14 Plato, *Republic,* trans. Paul Shorey (1935; rpt. London: Heinemann, 1970), 459–61. All quotations will be taken from this edition, and all subsequent references will be given in the body of the text.

15 "Again *meson,* 'middle,' or 'mean,' is used as a synonym for *metrion,* 'moderate' or of the right amount" (Aristotle, *Nicomachean Ethics,* ed. H. Rackham [1926; rpt. London: Heinemann, 1982], 90, note c).

16 Friedrich Ueberweg, *System of Logic,* trans. Thomas M. Lindsay (London: Longmans and Green, 1871), 270–71.

17 This is a note to *Nicomachean Ethics,* IV, i, 7, 1120a12–13.

18 Blaise Pascal, *Pensées,* #83 ("Raison des effets"), in *Oeuvres complètes,* ed. Louis Lafuma (Paris: Seuil, 1963), 509–10.

19 Ibid., #199, 526–27.

20 Ibid., #518, 577.

21 Ibid., #200, 528.

22 Ibid., #201, 528.

23 Roland Barthes, *Sur Racine* (Paris: Seuil, 1963), 109.

Index

Achilles, 82, 84–86, 88, 90, 92, 98, 112, 116–19, 122–24, 127–29, 133–35
Adrastos, 59
Aegeus, 171
Aeschylus, 3, 5–6, 11, 41–42, 58, 74, 116, 121, 194*n9*, 197*n11*, 200*n10*
Amazons, 155
Amphiaraos, 58, 130
Aphrodite, 120, 141, 145, 148, 167. *See also* Venus
Apollo, 89–92
Apostolidès, Jean-Marie, 6
Argos (person), 58
Argos (place), 49, 55, 59
Ariadne, 167–68
Aristotle, 190*n23; De Caelo,* 28; *Metaphysics,* 7, 22–24, 32–41, 181; *Nicomachean Ethics,* 6–7, 17–18, 21, 24, 25–29, 31, 41, 84, 91, 119–21, 138, 140, 144, 147, 183, 191*n3,* 193*n35,* 195*n19; Physics,* 28–29, 31–33; *Poetics,* 3–4, 16, 18, 39–40, 47, 69, 71, 78, 80, 91, 110, 122, 150, 176–80, 193*n31*
Artemis, 112–13, 116, 119, 131, 139, 148
Athena, 42, 74
Athens, 77, 148, 159, 170–72

Barthes, Roland, 4, 23, 73, 129, 131, 186
Batson, Alan, 10
Beckett, Samuel, 81, 93
Bénichou, Paul, 19
Bergson, Henri, 29–31
Bollack, Jean, 53

Bradley, A. C., 41
Butor, Michel, 177

Capaneus, 59
catharsis, 17, 176, 178, 183
city, 48–49, 53–61, 83, 171, 205*n1*
Classicism, 4, 15–17, 21, 23–24
Claus, David, 143
continuity, 28–30, 32, 35, 44, 66, 81–82, 86–87, 90–91, 93, 94, 122, 172, 183
contradictories, 32–33, 37, 41
contraries, 32–33, 37, 41
Corneille, Pierre, 3, 6, 22, 100, 105

Dante, 45
Defaux, Gérard, 201*n3*
Delphi, 37, 80–81, 86, 88–89, 92–93, 94
Diderot, Denis, 25, 190*n16*
Dodds, E. R., 138–39

Eco, Umberto, 157
Erechtheus, 171
Euripides, 3–6, 9–11, 27, 47, 136; *Andromache,* 80–93, 95, 107–8, 112; *Electra,* 11; *Hippolytos,* 137–52, 153, 155, 161, 163–65; *Iphigeneia in Aulis,* 112–24, 125–26, 146; *Medea,* 138–39; *Phoenissae,* 47–61, 62–63, 79, 80–81, 112

Faret, Nicolas, 16
fate, 87, 156–58, 168–69
Field, G. C., 37
France, Peter, 95
Freeman, Bryant C., 10
Freud, Sigmund, 150, 154–55
Friedländer, Paul, 87

209